SUBALTERN STUDIES

in Contemporary Indian English Literature

SUBALTERN STUDIES
in Contemporary Indian English Literature

Edited by

Dr. Premila Swamy D.
Dr. Sanjay N. Shende

AUTHORSPRESS

Worldwide Circulation through Authorspress Global Network

First Published in 2021

by

Authorspress

Q-2A Hauz Khas Enclave, New Delhi-110 016 (India)

Phone: (0) 9818049852

E-mail: authorspressgroup@gmail.com

Website: www.authorspressbooks.com

Subaltern Studies in

Contemporary Indian English Literature

ISBN 978-93-90891-44-3

Printed in India at Thomson Press (India) Limited

Editorial Board

Foreword

The word 'subaltern' can be traced back to Antonio Gramsci (1891-1937), an Italian Marxist scholar who used it in his Prison Notebooks. Hence in its original context, 'subaltern' referred solely to peasants who had not been integrated into Marx's conception of the industrial capitalist system. Subaltern studies seeks to fill the gap in historiography between the people's history and the perceived history of India or what Edward Said regards as Western culture's long tradition of false, romanticized images of Asia.

Subaltern Studies Group that emerged around 1982 out of the University of Sussex under the stewardship of Professors Ranajit Guha and Eric Stokes, in fact, extended and enlarged the scope of cultural studies historians in the 1960s as E. P. Thompson, Raymond Williams, and Eric Hobsbawm. The SSG had in its fold Shahid Amin, David Arnold, Gautam Bhadra, Dipesh Chakrabarty, N. K. Chandra, Partha Chatterjee, Arvind N. Das, David Hardiman Stephen Henningham, Gyanendra Pandey and Sumit Sarkar who focused on working class and particularly "peasant" historical accounts in post-colonial and post-imperial South Asia. These collaborators produced the *Subaltern Studies Journal* that focused on correcting the fallacies in South Asian history and society. Thus was born "subaltern studies" as an area of academic explorations in order to uncover the histories of marginalized/ undocumented groups within the colonial and nationalist archives, and study the interplay of dominance and subordination in colonial systems, specially India.

Subsequently, Gayatri Spivak's intervention in the form of her seminal essay, "*Can the Subaltern Speak?*" and *A Critique of Postcolonial Reason*, was an umbrage at the subaltern studies group for ignoring gender in questions of subalternity. She denounced the harm done to Women/Third World women and non-Europeans and investigates Women's Double-Colonization with regard to Dalit/Black women. Her bold stance paved the way for rethink on the discursive nature of the 'subaltern' and invited the members of the subaltern studies group to "write deconstructive histories of subjecthood." Dipesh Chakrabarty notes that subaltern studies emerged out of "anti-colonial" thought rather than "postcolonial," but cites Gayatri Spivak's work and membership with the group as integrating "postcolonial" studies into the movement. The confluence of history and literature enriched subaltern studies. As the historians gave a new thrust and direction to the art of writing history by writing the peoples' history, the litterateurs directed their focus on the faceless subalterns lost/ignored or lying buried in the socio-cultural fabric of life. Thus, the concept of the subaltern assumed a new *avatar* as it expanded in interpretation from the original configuration to apply to any population that is disenfranchised and unreachable due to hegemonic oppression. The scholars equipped with subaltern parameters began to study the subaltern in terms of class, caste, gender, race, language and culture. In brief, subaltern studies analyzes the "binary relationship" of the subaltern and ruling classes, and analyses the dominance of social groups and subordination of the subalterns in India. Consequently one could discern a sharp focus in the Postcolonial writers' narratives on decolonizing the mind, valorizing the cultural identity, demolishing the biased stereotypes and most refreshingly creating a counter-discourse to colonialism in order to deconstruct and overturn the false, biased, spurious, one-sided worn out perceptions foisted on the history by the colonial mindset and the patriarchal/caste based forces operating in Indian society..

The postulates of subaltern studies as evolved over times are fairly reflected in *Subaltern Studies in Contemporary Indian English Literature* edited by Dr. Premila Swamy D. and Dr. Sanjay N. Shende. The anthology is a commendable endeavour to interrogate the existential dilemmas, cultural prejudices, patriarchal hegemony, ethnic biases and gender discriminations that characterise the subalterns in the select contemporary Indian literary texts. The research articles critically examine various facets of subaltern life and are informed by penetrating insights into the power dynamics governing the marginalized. The articles range from traumatized tribal and Adivasi communities' existential predicament, sense of displacement/ disillusionment and quest for identity vis-a-vis the attenuating circumstances that impinge upon their sense of identity and human dignity – to Dalits' assertion for identity and space – to women's fight for equality, identity and empowerment against the unrelenting patriarchal pressures and perpetual violence – to modes of resistance

– to gender and power politics where body becomes a weapon to resist the hegemony – to mystifying silences shrouding the *Mahabharata* – to identity crisis encountered by transgender community. *Subaltern Studies in Contemporary Indian English Literature* endowed with informative and critical essays on various nuances of the 'subaltern,' will hopefully be useful addition to the ever evolving literature about subaltern studies in India.

T.S. Anand (Dr.)
formerly Professsor of English
University of Sirte (Libya)

4625 Helsinki Crescent
Windsor (Ont.) Canada
N9G 3G2

Acknowledgements

This edited volume is the result of composite efforts of many persons to whom we must express sense of gratitude.

We express our sincerest thanks to all those who were associated with this academic endeavor directly or indirectly.

First and foremost, we are thankful to all the contributors who shared their genuinely written research articles and exercised faith and cooperative spirit from the beginning till the end of publication process. Their positivity and cooperation at every stage of publication helped relieve our burden and we could accomplish this mammoth task with ease. From the bottom of our heart, we express our sincerest thanks to all the contributors.

We are highly thankful to all the reviewers from India and abroad for spending their precious time for reviewing the manuscripts and providing valuable input and comments that helped better the write ups and make them publishable. We are obliged to Dr. Albrecht Classen (USA), Mohan Singh Saud (Nepal), Omoniyi Olayinka (Nigeria) along with Indian reviewers namely Dr. M. Elangovan, Dr. C. Cadence Graceta, Dr. Nidhi Mishra, Dr. B. Spoorthi, and Ms. Josephine Sneha. T.

We would like to express our gratitude to Dr. T. S. Anand for accepting our invitation and writing foreword for this book as well as guiding us with his valuable inputs for perfection of this book.

We acknowledge the special efforts of Dr. Mallesh Reddy, Shree Shivaji College, Rajura for his unfailing cooperation in handling the technical aspects of the manuscript so as to make it uniform and publishable.

Without the support and cooperation of Authorspress, New Delhi, our publisher, this book would not have been realized. We are thankful to them in transforming our manuscript into a well-designed and readable book.

Editors

Preface

Literature has always been a powerful medium for the writers across the globe to raise the socio-political-cultural concerns that agitate their creative consciousness across the globe. Indian writers in regional and English languages have made a niche in edifying the people and forming a collective consciousness against various socio-political establishments that subjugate the *other*, the marginalized group. The term subaltern implies to someone who is assumed to be belonging to a low rank in social, political or other hierarchy. Influenced by post structuralism and post colonialism in literary theory, subaltern theory in the recent past came as an exercise to resist the dominant power structures that operate and govern in order to subjugate the other. The subaltern perspective stands for understanding the society through conditions of subordination of the people belonging to different caste, class, age, gender and race. Subaltern studies seeks to present an alternate image of society through the viewpoint of the masses usually unrepresented or misrepresented. It is an attempt to examine, rewrite or retrieve subaltern histories that may have been silenced or remained absent in elite histories written by hegemonic power structures. This emergence of collective consciousness and to voice for/against in order to establish one's identity is one of the recurring themes in contemporary Indian English literature. Radical rethinking of historical representation through literary intervention is a deliberate attempt to fight for the subaltern demographics. With the deliberations on subaltern studies by Indian historian Ranajit Guha and critical insights given by Gayatri Chakravorty Spivak's pioneering article "Can the Subaltern Speak" (1985), the concepts of subaltern gained increased prominence and attention in academic circles.

This book titled *Subaltern Studies in Contemporary Indian English Literature* presents a critical dialogue between the conceptual analytical legacies within the framework of subaltern theory and the evolving forms of hegemony and resistance in contemporary Indian literature in English. From Dalit writings to tribal musings, the essays in this volume cover a diverse range of ongoing struggle against power monopoly, marginalization and stigma that are unfolding in upcoming writers from the Indian subcontinent. The volume consisting of 20 collective essays from various researchers across academic platform analyses the diverse forms of agency to negotiate with the hegemonic power discourses that pushes one to the margins. The essays interrogate, negate and create a dialogue to foreground the various dimensions that become a part of subalternity in the contemporary Indian context. The objective of this collection of essays is to delve deep into the subaltern consciousness and voice for the underprivileged class and gender that are undermined, speechless and unnoticed in the pages of Indian history.

Critical and literary discourses of Mahasweta Devi, Amitav Ghosh, Indira Goswami, Bama, Meena Kandasamy, Temsula Ao, Anita Desai, Kamala Das and Vijay Tendulkar along with few other contemporary writers are discussed at length from a subaltern studies perspective. The collected essays range from Adivasis in literature, Subjugation of the Ho tribal community from eastern part of India to Dalit upsurge that unfurl in the Indian literary map. Critical insights established by Gayatri Spivak, Michael Foucault, Ranajit Guha are deliberated upon to rethink and re-establish the canon through literary intervention.

This edited volume of collected essays is a modest attempt of critical inquiry directed at evaluating literary texts through the lens of subaltern theories. The twenty critical essays from scholars direct our attention to the socially and economically marginalized classes that are pushed to the margins by rigid hegemonic power structures. The essays bring in literary intervention in understanding the tenets put forth by subaltern studies, the focus primarily being contemporary Indian English literature. Debates on prejudice, marginalization, manifold methods of exploitation of the tribal populace, the dynamics of subaltern consciousness, the impulse of the Dalit exuberance and identity formation in contemporary writings have been probingly interrogated. Besides, the articles critically evaluate the nuances of subaltern subjectivities, de-stigmatization of tribal ethos, the 'gaps and silences' in the epic Mahabharata and negotiate for the subaltern self through the scholarly examination of the texts.

A couple of articles on Dalit writers delve deep into examining Dalit upsurge, their fight for identity and space in the historical canon. The article on Amitav Ghosh's *The Hungry Tide* brings to forefront how the Dalit psyche gets represented in the novel and examines the question of identity and space of Dalit *refugees in Marichjhapi.* In doing so, the article also explores how Ghosh brings to the center the *forgotten* history of Marichjhapi. Dalit narratives voice the agonies of the community and is representative of their class, caste and identity. This makes their narrative different from mainstream writers which are largely individualistic. These narratives not only voice their subjugation but also aim at concretizing Dalit masses to assert, protest and mobilize against the act of monopoly imposed by the power structures. Dibyajit Mukherjee's article on select poems of Dalit writers probes into the despair and anguish of this marginalized group and determines how the Dalits have created a language of violence as a form of resistance. Aneeshya's article on Bama's *Sangati,* underpins the fact that Dalit writings are anguish of the whole community against

Brahmanic patriarchy. The article also reveals the powerful female solidarity which brings individual women experiences and articulations together to a collective whole and thereby celebrate Dalithood as well as womanhood. Another article studies the character of Karna in the Mahabharata from a Dalit and subaltern context. This article weaves together the condition of Dalits in India with the mythical character of Karna, who faced marginalization at different cross sections.

The book also generates some interesting and thought provoking scholarly articles on tribal communities, their quest for identity and recognition with the main stream literature and culture. The article on Tribal identity in Mamang Dai's *The Legends of Pensam* is an excellent study on Dai's critical outlook to de-exoticize the tribal identity and represent the brutal realities that continuously changes the face of their 'home'land. It also seeks to highlight the relevance of the construction of 'mnemocultures' and authentic documentation to safeguard the existence of the tribal population. Manoj Madavi's article traces the unexplored subaltern and marginal tendencies inflicted on the Adivasi community in two novels namely, *The Coffer Dam* and *The Strange Case of Billy Biswas.* The research article explains the triple colonization of the Adivasi's community in India in the hands of the white power of British, stereotype caste structure and gender superiority of other races over the Adivasi community, particularly over Adivasi women. This article contests that although the novels have great aesthetic literary value but has failed to represent the disparity, disillusionment and disorientation of Adivasi in true sense. Another poignant feature of this book is that it consists an interesting article on the identity crisis of the Ho tribal community of the eastern India. This article traces how the identity of this community is at threat because of misrecognition and misinterpretation of the main stream people and media and surfaces the authentic and distinct identity of the Ho tribe. An exemplary attempt done in this direction is another article by Rimpa Pal who explores the lives of the Santhal Adivasi community in Hansda Sowvendra Sekhar's collection of short stories titled *The Adivasi Will Not Dance*. The paper introspects the migration of Santhal, one of the aboriginal communities in India, their agony and their painful reality. The article seeks to explore the traumatic and physical hardship experienced by this marginalized 'other' in their native land. The article titled "Subalternity in Amitav Ghosh's '*The Hungry Tide*'" examines the traumatic and miserable condition of the homeless subalterns who take shelter in Sundarban forest in West Bengal. Belonging to the marginalized section, they face oppression in varied forms.

In any discussion on subalternity, women form a major chunk of the marginalized subaltern group because of their gender. The gender binary of man and woman relegates one as supreme and the other to a lower status. This imposition governed by patriarchal hegemony silences women and pushes them to the margins. Feminist writings fused with subaltern undercurrents object and re-interrogate various forms of oppression faced by women. Numerous articles in this collection have pointed out women's fight for equality, identity and empowerment. The article on Shashi Deshpande's *The Intrusion and Other Stories* examines how women become the marginalized section in a patriarchal Indian social structure. The article takes into consideration, three stories of Deshpande and reveals the gendered subaltern status of women who constantly face oppression in familial and social systems. Ashmita Bora's article looks at Indira Goswami's fictional works from a subaltern perspective. The article attempts to probe into the causes, the unquestioned beliefs, the practices and the rituals that perpetuate violence on women, especially the trauma faced by widowed women. The article justifies that Goswami's female protagonists struggle and protest against male dominance and break patriarchal order and reclaim their individualistic identities. Again, another article on Anita Desai's women by Sangeetha L talks about the subaltern status inflicted on women throughout ages in a male-centric ideological framework. The article exposes Anita Desai's vision on women's emancipation and reflects the confrontation of women against oppression and injustice. Prachi Bhongale's article titled Representation of subalterns in *The Dark Holds No Terrors* by Shashi Deshpande again explores the complexities of man-woman relationship in marital life and narrates the evidence of subaltern demonstration against the male-chauvinist society. Another researcher, Prafulla Panda examines Kamala Das's poems from a subaltern perspective and contends that women in Das's poetry voice for liberation, identity, marginalization and exploitation from the clutches of tradition and patriarchal hegemony. Manik Mandal makes a comparative analysis of works by Meena Kandasamy and Temsula Ao through the discourse on resistance and formation of identities. Their writings sow the seeds for women empowerment and fight against women's oppression. The article on Vijay Tendulkar's famous play *Silence! The Court is in Session* locates the various proverbs used in its disposal which points that the proverbs used about and for women both glorify and dishonour women. Subjugation of women along with the usage of proverbs becomes the central focus of this article. Manisha Patil's article explores the spatial dynamics of caste, gender and colonization in Tagore's short stories. Pawel Veliventi's article investigates Arundhati Roy's *The God of Small Things* and Kiran Desai's *The Inheritance of Loss* contends that family becomes a regulatory source for patriarchal ideals and oppression of women.

Mythological characters and mythologies are grand narratives that become mechanisms of regulating and deciphering the ideals set by the dominant group. Rajdeep Guha's article on Mahasweta Devi's *Draupadi* attempts to study the novella through the prism of the mythical character of Draupadi, in the Mahabharata. The article examines how Draupadi is a critique of the biased policies of the state and how the agencies of the state serve the vested interests of those in power. It also brings to the limelight gender and power politics where body becomes a weapon to resist this hegemony.

One significant aspect under subaltern studies is voicing for the gender minorities; the third gender. Literature becomes a major tool for articulating the need for acceptance of the LGBT community. Queer sexuality is an emerging area in gender discourses. The article on Jeet Thayil's *Narcopolis* is an attempt to examine the nexus between queer sexuality and gender and the formation of identity. The article examines the crucial identity crisis encountered by transgender community at large through the character of Dimple.

Thus, the book comprises scholarly articles on the various cross sections of the subaltern life based on caste, gender and sexuality. All the articles are well researched and give critical insights and inquiry into the various facets of subaltern studies in contemporary Indian English literature. By bringing together power dynamics, interventions in the study of subaltern politics and resistance to dominant discourses, this volume will be beneficial to all scholars with academic zeal who constantly engage themselves in the ongoing struggle and battle against all atrocities inflicted upon the marginalized. We hope this collection of articles will add new avenues to the critical discussions on Subaltern studies and benefit researchers and academicians keen on taking these arguments further.

Dear Readers, we strive to take care of your varied scholarly interests but honestly look forward to being enriched with your feedback at snpremila@gmail.com

Dr. Premila Swamy D.
Dr. Sanjay N. Shende

Contents

1

Identity and Space for Dalit Refugees with Reference to Amitav Ghosh's *The Hungry Tide*

Aishwarya Banerjee

Abstract

The Partition of India in 1947 forms a part of the most harrowing experience of human displacement in history that has left its bloody trails long after it was actually executed. The refugee crisis, even many years beyond 1947 has never failed to state how human beings, a veritable part of the State, often end up becoming pawns in the hands of the State itself. The saga of violence reaches the brink of cruelty when it comes to the people belonging to the lower rung of the hypocritical social hierarchy. The word subaltern, in this paper, represents the oppressed or the marginalized sections of the society who are always denied identity, agency and even an unhomely spatial territory. The 1979 Marichjhapi Massacre is a part of that public history where Dalit refugees were treated worse than animals, let alone citizens by the then State government of West Bengal. The massive exodus of the Hindu Bangladeshi refugees who were 'namasudras' by caste, from the inhospitable island of Marichjhapi on the grounds of it being a part of reserved forest stripped the poor of the only refuge they could incur. This paper examines how there was hardly any country, space or identity for the Dalit refugees in Marichjhapi with special reference to Amitav Ghosh's *The Hungry Tide*. It further highlights how Ghosh's portrayal brings to the forefront the forgotten history of Marichjhapi, recuperating the silenced shrieks of the Dalit refugees.

Keywords: Subaltern; identity; space; refugee; massacre; hierarchy.

Introduction

India with its colonial past and ghastly memories of partition created a vast number of displaced and dispossessed, as Arundhati Roy rightly describes, "the millions of displaced people in India are nothing but refugees in an unacknowledged war" (65). After the brutal, unplanned and disorganized refugee rehabilitation of 1947, Bengal witnessed yet another massacre in 1979. The spatial injustice that Marichjhapi incident of 1979 testifies to, raises serious questions about the State's credibility in providing a safe home to those belonging to the lower strata of the hypocritical social hierarchy. Marichjhapi massacre escaped public eye for a long time. Little is said and written about the huge blot of blood in the history of Bengal. However, Amitav Ghosh, through his *The Hungry Tide* provides a critique of the displacement and the atrocities following the deracination in Marichjhapi. Ghosh's portrayal of the incident comes as an endeavour to provide spatial justice and identity to the voices that are obliterated from the historical record.

Methodology and Theoretical Framework

In order to recuperate the massacre of Marichjhapi from the curse of oblivion, my paper shall incorporate a qualitative methodology. The theory of post-colonialism and the trauma that post-colonial India underwent through partition will be talked about to understand the research problem and investigate the question of identity and space for the Dalit refugees. To justify the aim of my research, I shall try to connect Antonio Gramsci's concept of hegemony and Louis Althusser's concept of ideology to the massacre of Marichjhapi. I shall further probe into memory studies taking the help of oral narratives assorted by Deep Halder in his book *Blood Island: An Oral History of the Marichjhapi Massacre.* Nirmal's journal also forms a part of the memory studies as it is used as a tool to recreate the bloody memories of Marichjhapi massacre.

Discussion

The influx of the huge number of people from the newly created East and West Pakistan to the truncated India continued long after 1947. The partition is marked with quick exchange of homes and countries where nearly fourteen million people were displaced (Butalia 3). The migrants who came with healthy financial support and belonged to upper castes, were easily accommodated whereas the lower caste refugees, who migrated much later found themselves homeless in their new home (3). Immediately after the partition, the lower caste agriculturalists, artisans and small scale traders of East Pakistan, who mainly belonged to the 'namasudra' caste refused to uproot themselves from their ancestral homes. Moreover, Jogendranath Mandal, a minister of the East Pakistan cabinet, provided them with assurance of security (Sengupta). However, communal riots in Khulna and Jessore made it very difficult for the Hindus to survive peacefully in East Pakistan. After the introduction of passport system between India and Pakistan in 1952, the situations proceeded towards a more difficult turn. Thus, the namasudras started migrating from East Pakistan to West Bengal in surging numbers. West Bengal, with its lack of enough resources and land, was unable to receive so many refugees, therefore the Congress government mooted out the plan of resettling the refugees in some other parts of India. This led to the introduction of Dandakaranya rehabilitation plan. Dandakaranya Project Area or DPA of 1958 was spread across the districts of Koratpur and Kalahandi of Orissa and the district of Bastar in Madhya Pradesh. Dandakaranya was an extremely inhospitable land where the infrastructure promised by the government had bare minimum existence (Mukhopadhyay 150). Refugees had no provisions for electricity, health care, education or employment. The added disadvantage of perennial conflicts with the tribals of Dandakaranya worsened the situation.

The Left Front in West Bengal started voicing the plight of the refugees by strongly opposing the refugee policies of the Congress government. Jyoti Basu, even came up with the promise that once in power, the Left Front government would rehabilitate the Dandakaranya refugees in West Bengal. The promise came as a ray of hope as the Left Front government had taken up the refugee problem as one of the top most priority during their election campaigns. Ram Chatterjee, the Left Front minister took pains to visit the refugee camps in Dandakaranya to invite people to settle in Sundarbans. The families flushed with the desire of a proper settlement sold their land and belongings in Dandakaranya to afford the movement. In 1978, when refugees from Dandakaranya started arriving in West Bengal to settle in Marichjhapi, Sundarbans, the rising population of the refugees made the Left government in power, change their refugee policies. Under the new conditions settlers were required to go back to Dandakaranya to resettle. Many were restricted entry to Marichjhapi; some were sent back but approximately ten thousand namasudra families under the guidance of the President of Udbastu Unnayanshil Samiti, settled in Marichjhapi Island (Sengupta).

Marichjhapi was made habitable by the settlers. Instead of waiting for government aids, the settlers built shanties, roads, embankments, schools and made proper provisions for health care and hygiene. In fact, Marichjhapi was the realization of the dream that Horen Mian dreamt of creating at Moynadeep in *Padma Nadir Majhi* by Manik Bandopadhyay. However, their rehabilitation was way too short-lived. The government soon declared Marichjhapi to be a part of the Reserve Forest where settlement could not be allowed. The settlement of the refugees was seen as a violation of the Forest Act and an unauthorized occupation of the forest land that supposedly encroached upon the ecological balance of the Nature. The notice for their eviction soon arrived. On January 26, 1979, Jyoti Basu ordered an economic blockade of the island of Marichjhapi. Marichjhapi was surrounded by police launches and the islanders were faced with recurrent police atrocities. Their huts, wells, fisheries were destroyed; they were tear-gassed; those who tried to escape by makeshift boats were shot at. Due to the economic blockade, there was a scarcity of food supplies which led the islanders towards death by starvation. The refugees were poor people with no weapons except makeshift bows and arrows and some of their agricultural tools. Their measures were no match for the armed police force of the State. The police force and the hired goons of the government carried on a rampage on the island by arresting men, raping their women, setting fire to their huts, poisoning their wells, and taking up every measure possible to oust the refugees of the island. Men, women, children were slaughtered and dumped into the river. The survivors were sent back to the dismal situations of Dandakaranya.

The massacre escaped public attention for nearly two decades. Even during the siege of the island in 1979, journalists, opposition parties or any kind of relief aids were debarred from entering the island. In 1980-81, Shaktipada Rajguru's Bengali novel *Dandak Theke Marichjhapi,* tried to break the silence around the incident but the novel remained out of print for several years. It was clearly visible that not only the subalterns could not speak but also who spoke on behalf of them were silenced. Amitav Ghosh's *The Hungry Tide* is one of those instances of Indian Writing in English in which he tries to recuperate the occluded tales of the Marichjhapi refugees. Along with the histories of his characters, he builds the public history of Marichjhapi where the Dalit refugees sobbed for territory and identity. The refugees who were formerly residents of East Pakistan travelled to India in search of a habitable space and an identity acknowledged by the nation but all they received was a continuous shift among several inhospitable places of India. Their final hope of rehabilitation in Bengal was also thwarted by the government but this too did not end their quest for identity and space. The refugees created their own home in the island of Marichjhapi only to be evicted from there too. The government and the nation used these poor people as mere pawns who could be oscillated from here to there at their sweet will and convenience. The condition of the Dalit refugees haunts our minds in the form of four lines by Matthew Arnold:

> Wandering between two worlds, one dead
> The other powerless to be born
> With nowhere yet to rest my head
> Like these, on earth I wait forlorn (lines 85-88).

It is quite ironical that a government, whose foundation relies heavily on egalitarianism, denigrates down to take such fatal measures against Dalit refugees. Ideology plays a significant role as the Left government clearly had an agenda of treating everyone on equal footing refuting all sorts of class discrimination. Louis Althusser's definition of ideology heavily counts here as he asserts, "Ideology is an imaginary construction that represents the real world and that this representation is so realistic that nobody challenges it" (Kulkarni and Chaskar 134). The government certainly moulds its ideology according to its political benefits in such a way that nobody tends to challenge it. Althusser talks about two apparatuses that the State uses to dominate its subjects – Representative State Apparatus (RSA) and Ideological State apparatus (ISA). In case of Marichjhapi massacre, the government uses both these apparatuses to suppress the resistance of the poor refugees. The government ruthlessly uses the RSA through institutions like police and army that ravage the island and drive the people out of their home and craftily uses the ISA through the politics of environment. The issue of the environment is pitched in a way that people feel that they are ostensibly independent in making their choice between the State and the refugees but actually their choice is unconsciously influenced by the ruling class, in this case, the government.

In *The Hungry Tide*, Amitav Ghosh weaves the incident of Marichjhapi largely through Kusum who has died in the incident. The incident is unfolded through Nirmal's journal that he has left for Kanai before death. Kusum alone stands as a representative of those innumerable Dalit refugees who underwent the gruesome experience of Marichjhapi. Kusum, as a young girl, had witnessed her father falling prey to a tiger and her mother being taken away to Dhanbad on a job offer. She, in order to meet her mother, travelled to Dhanbad where she later met her husband. It was after her husband's accidental death that she heard of people marching "to the east." She joined the march and came back to her home. Through Kusum's eyes, readers clearly perceive a proper picture of displaced people carrying bundles and children and marching in huge numbers from one world to another of the torn apart country. One of those people gave an account of their eradication from their former home and the uncertainty associated with their new home:

> Once we lived in Bangladesh, in Khulna jila, we are tide country people, from the Sundarbans's edge. When the war broke out, our village was burned to ash; we crossed the border, there was nowhere else to go. We were met by the police and taken away: in buses they drove us to a settlement camp. We'd never seen such a place, such a dry emptiness; the earth was so red that it seemed to be stained with blood. For those who lived there, that dust was as good as gold, they loved it as we loved our tide country mud. But no matter how we tried, we couldn't settle there (Ghosh 174).

When the people cross this imaginary border, drawn haphazardly across the nation, they are designated as refugees. Their status becomes more vulnerable if they belong to a social class that has already been categorized as outcasts. The namasudras, who settled in their self-created home of Marichjhapi, had neither money nor they belonged to the higher ranks of the status quo and thus they were rendered as veritable castaways with little or no identities at all.

When the Marichjhapi massacre took place, Kusum came to the front as a very prominent participant of the resistance against the State. Kusum and her five years old son, Fokir lived with the refugees at the time of the massacre. She saw people dying out of starvation because food supplies were running out in spite of careful rationing. The situation became so abysmal that the dwellers were reduced to eating grass. Many tried to survive by eating a wild grass called 'jadu-palong' which was palatable initially but later it proved to be fatal causing severe dysentery. The police atrocities reached the brink of exhaustion when, "the police had destroyed the tube wells, there was no portable water left; the settlers were drinking from puddles and ponds and an epidemic of cholera had broken out" (Ghosh 282). Despite the lathi charges, economic blockade, hunger and all other stringent measures by the government, the settlers stood their ground, as Kusum articulated her anger to Nirmal and Horen, "The worst part was not the hunger or the thirst. It was to sit here, helpless and listen to the policemen making their announcements, hearing them say that our lives, our existence was worth less than dirt or dust…" (284). Kusum's words clearly defined the value of a triply-marginalized powerless subaltern voice that had been recurrently shrouded by the powerful. The denial of Nilima's help towards Kusum and the other settlers, further underlined how the poor are always pushed against the wall by the so-called civil society and the ones who are designated as the protector of the realms. The promise of supporting the cause of the subaltern is always made but seldom executed. Nilima who was quite enthusiastic in creating a better settlement in Lusibari failed to support the Marichjhapi cause. Nilima too branded the settlers as encroachers and claimed their settlement as a hindrance towards maintaining the ecological balance. Antonio Gramsci's theory of hegemony sits fit in this situation in which ruling class plays a dominant role in the society. Political society builds force and civil society extends consent to it. The discourse of environment created by the government meets with the consent of the intellectual society thereby producing a hegemonic setup where this consent is used as a weapon to maintain policies that favour the ruling class.

Nirmal who was steeped in the fervor of revolution was a Marxist in his political affiliation but he seemed to be more influenced by the romanticism associated with it. Nirmal was indeed politically marginalized as he conspicuously lost his importance among his comrades and severed all his ties with the urban Marxists but that does not bring him in equal footing with the marginalized stateless subalterns of Marichjhapi. Despite his attack on the government for acting like a bourgeoisie and refusing to identify him as one of the Bengali "bhadraloks", he could not deny that after all, he was not a subaltern. Thus, he was just a spectator who could sympathize with the cause but not experience it first handedly. His visit to Marichjhapi, therefore, seems to be fueled by his zeal of revolution and to an extent his unarticulated love for Kusum. Nirmal's concern for the poor was restricted to his teaching the poor children and instilling in them ideas of revolution and egalitarianism. In the entire novel, Nirmal is never seen doing anything concrete to amend the situation of the poor until he records the saga of violence of Marichjhapi in his journal. Kusum's story, being narrated by Nirmal's journal highlights the fact that not only she is a subaltern but also a gendered subaltern and as Gayatri Chakravorty Spivak says:

> Between patriarchy and imperialism, subject constitution and object formation, the figure of the woman disappears, not into a pristine nothingness, but a violent shuttling which is the displaced figuration of the third world woman caught between tradition and modernization. There is no space from where the sexed subaltern can speak. The subaltern as [woman] cannot speak (306).

So, Kusum is the micro-cosmic figure for all those women who are triply marginalized over the ages and are timelessly silenced by the society to hide the naked truth of exploitation. Moreover, Ghosh's employment of a bengali "bhadralok's voice and not subalterns to speak about Marichjhapi shows that they still do not have an agency to voice their plight and even if they do, when the subaltern speaks, does the world really hear?

Human habitation in place of flora and fauna has been traced as one of the main reasons for the ecological imbalance and catastrophes. Therefore, the preservation of endangered nature has always taken priority over protection of the human population. Ghosh highlights the conflict between the demands of conservation and the needs of the local population. He is extremely critical of the environmentalists who have constantly enumerated the symptoms and not the root cause behind the environmental crisis. Social hierarchy counts heavily over here where the subaltern refugees are deliberately pitted against the nature. Ghosh, through his character Kanai, asks a very legitimate question that looms largely around the area of Sundarbans even today, "It happens every week that people are killed by tigers. How about the horror of that? If there were killings on that scale anywhere else on earth it would be called genocide, and yet here it goes almost unremarked: these killings are never reported, never written about in the papers" (Ghosh 325). The concept of the omnipotence of Nature and its domination of mankind has the very origin in the domination of a human by another human. The settlers in Marichjhapi were evicted on the grounds that the area was under reserve forest belonging to the Project Tiger. The government has justified their actions citing the importance of preserving the endangered species whereas in reality international funds were available for the protection of tigers and not refugees. The Dalit refugees of Marichjhapi were unable to incur international funds unlike tigers for "Project Tiger", so the former suffered from exclusion by the environmentalists who were trying to protect the environment at the expense of its inhabitants.

While we get a unified voice of the subaltern through Amitav Ghosh's *The Hungry Tide*, journalist Deep Halder provides us with the micro narratives of individuals who suffered the trauma of Marichjhapi through his *Blood Island: An Oral History of the Marichjhapi Massacre*. Halder's document had its source in the childhood conversations that he had with his friend who had lived in Marichjhapi and survived with a tangible memory of the incident. Halder's book contains nine narratives of people who are related to the incident in some way or the other. One of the narratives is of Safal Halder, a victim and survivor of the massacre, who says that one night someone poisoned their tube-wells that caused thirteen deaths the next day. Children were dying like vermin and women lived in the fear of rape by police personnel. He says that on 14th June, 1979, everything was over for them when police, setting fire to the huts ousted the remaining islanders from there.

Phonibala Mandal's son Suryakant Mandal who had experienced the massacre, recounts how he rescued his mother when their huts were burnt. His mother was sleeping in a corner when the hut was set afire and he had to carry her out. Though she was alive, her hand and a portion of her breast had suffered severe burns. Another victim of Marichjhapi, Bashmoni Mandal had lost her husband Durgapada and her daughter Bishakha who went missing during the siege. Activist Jyotirmoy Mandal in his interview with Deep Halder, states that 14 and 16 May of 1979, records one of the most gruesome human rights violations in India. There are several similar stories of people who have scars from the incident. While the physical wounds have healed over the years, the mental scars refuse to go away.

Present day continues to give us glimpses of Partition and Marichjhapi massacre underlining the theory of postcolonialism, where it suggests disparate representations and the past being mingled with the present, through several contemporary issues like the complete communication blackout and lockdown in Jammu and Kashmir following the scrapping of Article 370 on 5th August, 2019. The state for several months suffered from curfews, total media and communication shutdown and enhanced military actions just like the siege of Marichjhapi. Such a blockade in Kashmir is still ongoing with some relaxations. The protests following the implication of the CAA and NRC, reopened the gashes of partition and reaffirmed how State atrocities go beyond timeline. The police atrocities towards the protestors in AMU, JNU or Shaheen Bagh were no way different from the atrocities done towards Marichjhapi settlers. A student of Jamia Millia Islamia University, Aamir Aziz wrote a fiery poem *Sab Yaad Rakha Jayega,* which accurately describes the scenario that the protestors faced during the anti-CAA movement but the plight that he describes is universal. The lines by Aziz actually relates to the fact that while the Constitution proclaims Fundamental rights for its citizens, the ones in power never fail to accompany it with exploitation which has eventually become a "fundamental truth" for our nation. Some of the lines goes like this:

> *Aur din mein meethi meethi baatein karna samne se*
> *Sab kuch theek hai har zubaan mein tutlana*
> *Raat hote hi haq maang rahe logo pe laathiyaan chalana, goliyaan chalana*
> *Humi pe hamla karke, humi ko humlavar batana*
> *Sab yaad rakha Jayega, sab kuch yaad rakha Jayega* (Aziz, lines 31-35).
>
> (You talk sweet during the day
> And then assuring in public that everything is at the place and under control with a stuttering tone
> Oppressing and attacking the people at night, who are asking for their rights
> Attacking us and blaming us for being the attackers,
> It will be remembered.)

Conclusion

It is extremely imperative to have a critical thought about Marichjhapi's forgotten history and bring it under considerable light because the vicious working of casteism has always taken a toll on people's lives and consciousness. Thus, Sumallya Mukhopadhyay in his article (*Reading and Reconstructing Marichjhapi Massacre in Post Partition Historiography: Dispossession and Refugeeism in Amitav Ghosh's The Hungry Tide*) rightly suggests that "by rereading and restructuring the atrocities, it is possible to negate this casteist hierarchy and foreground the marginalized history of the minority untouchables of Marichjhapi in critical discussion" (Mukhopadhyay 155). Though we can never compensate for the immeasurable loss incurred by the refugees, we can certainly take a step forward to demand justice for the deprived people of Marichjhapi, still searching for territory and identity.

Works Cited

Arnold, Matthew. "Stanzas from the Grande Chartreuse." *Poetry Foundation,* www.poetryfoundation.org.

Aziz, Aamir. "Sab Yaad Rakha Jayega." *YouTube,* uploaded by Aamir Aziz, 11 Jan. 2020, youtu.be/PHk_5gEXDY0.

Bandopadhyay, Manik. *Padma Nadir Majhi.* Ashokh Book Agency, 2017.

Butalia, Urvashi. *The Other Side of Silence.* Penguin Random House India, 2017.

Ghosh, Amitav. *The Hungry Tide.* Penguin Random House India, 2019.

Halder, Deep. *Blood Island: An Oral History of the Marichjhapi Massacre.* Harper Collins India, 2019.

Kulkarni, Anand B., and Ashok G. Chaskar. *An Introduction to Literary Theory and Criticism.* Orient Black Swan, 2015.

Mukhopadhyay, Sumallya. "Reading and Reconstructing Marichjhapi Massacre in Post Partition Historiography: Dispossession and Refugeeism in Amitav Ghosh's The Hungry Tide." *The Criterion: An International Journal in English,* vol. 8, issue 3, 2017, pp. 148-157.

Rajguru, Shaktipada. *Dandak Theke Marichjhapi.* All Indian Digital Book, 2020.

Roy, Arundhati. "The Greater Common Good." *The Algebra of Infinite Justice.* Viking, 2001.

Sengupta, Debjani. "The Forgotten Massacre of Dalit Refugees in West Bengal's Marichjhapi." *The Wire,* 03Oct. 2018,thewire.in/history/west-bengal-violence-marichjhapi-dandakaranya.

Spivak, Gayatri Chakravorty. "Can the Subaltern Speak?" *Marxism and the Interpretation of Culture,* edited by Cary Nelson, University of Illinois, 1988, pp. 271-313.

Author's Bio-Note

Aishwarya Banerjee is an M.A. in English from University of Calcutta. She has cracked the UGC NET in 2020. She is a literature enthusiast and pursues a teaching career.

2

Re-writing Myth: A Study of Mahasweta Devi's *Draupadi*

Rajdeep Guha

Abstract

The paper explores Mahasweta Devi's novella Draupadi from the prism of the mythical character of Draupadi from the epic Mahabharata. Mahasweta Devi's protagonist fights against social injustices and unlike her namesake from the epic, Dopdi Mejhen single-handedly challenges the people who are in power. The reference to the mythical character Draupadi by Mahasweta Devi underscores the heroic stature of the tribal woman Dopdi in her work Draupadi. The paper further examines how Draupadi is a critique of the biased policies of the state and how the agencies of the state serve the vested interests of those in power. Lastly, the paper draws attention to gender politics and examines how the female body is violated by dominant powers in order to strike fear and terror in the hearts of the marginalised people. Mahasweta Devi successfully defines the various forms of resistance that people living on the periphery take recourse to while fighting against oppressive powers.

Keywords: Myth; injustice; subaltern; culture; domination

The objective of any literary work is to portray the reality. While doing this, the novelist or the author often takes recourse to imagination. Having said that, the author aspires to solve a problem that exists within the space of human life in general. Human experiences are often intermingled with myths because myths effectively explain the social order of a nation or a race. Myths can also reflect the aspirations of a society because by nature, myths are collective. Myths give wings to people's hopes, values and dreams.

Myths are the by-products of different cultures. In fact, myths transmit a universal meaning. The messages conveyed through myths, the leitmotifs contained in them transcend regions, time and space. Myths also give rise to archetypes. An archetype can be defined as the symbol or an image that gets repeated time and again in different genres and works of literature. It is said that Northrop Frye believed that archetypes are representations of conventional myths. He further said that literature is a pivotal extension of mythology and scholars must take note of it (Frye 6). This paper explores the use of the mythical character Draupadi from the epic *Mahabharata* by the noted Bengali writer of fiction Mahasweta Devi in her novella by the same name.

Mahasweta Devi was primarily an activist writer. She took an ardent interest in various social causes and is considered to be a seminal figure in the field of cultural studies. For her contribution to literature, she received the Ramon Magsaysay award, Jnanpith, Padma Shri, Padma Vibhushan, Sahitya Akademi, etc. Her other fortes include mythologies, sociological and anthropological studies, etc. Her main purpose of writing has always been to fight injustices, both social and political. No wonder, she participated, even when was quite old, in the Singur and Nandigram land agitations that took place in West Bengal in the first decade of the present century against the forcible land acquisition executed by the then West Bengal government. She often said that she aspired to lend a voice to the otherwise voiceless tribal communities. She also felt that mainstream literatures and criticism often ignored the subaltern communities and did not cater to their aspirations and concerns. She protested vehemently against the class and caste exploitations. The brutal feudal structure also finds mention in many of her writings. In an interview given to Gayatri Chakravorty Spivak, Mahasweta Devi says, "The tribal and the mainstream have always been parallel.... The mainstream simply doesn't understand the parallel... They can't keep their land, there is no education for them, no health facilities...they are denied everything... That is why I started writing about the tribal movements and the tribal world... I repay them their honour" (Devi x). Thus, to carry forward her mission of advocating for the rights of the marginalised, Mahasweta Devi adopts the revisionist narrative technique and recasts mythological figures in her own ways. The purpose of this exercise is to expose the brutality of social realities. Furthermore, the mythological characters act as the foil characters to her own protagonists. Therefore, the message that is ingrained in her texts is successfully conveyed to the targeted audience. The use of the Draupadi myth by Mahasweta Devi was primarily meant to highlight the subjugation of women over the ages and how sexual humiliation was considered a potent weapon to silence the voice of women who did not toe the line of the grand narrative. Mahasweta Devi always felt that the female body has been the site of exploitation by those in power.

Like other texts of Mahasweta Devi, *Draupadi* is a scathing attack on the exploitation perpetrated by the state machinery on the hapless tribal people. *Draupadi* is compiled in the collection *Breast Stories* and is narrated from the point of view of DopdiMejhen, a poor tribal woman. The narration brings to the fore the politics of domination and the social inequalities that are at play. The present discussion uses the theoretical framework of gender studies and investigates with the help of the prism through which the author juxtaposes the mythical character of Draupadi to highlight the power politics that takes place in postcolonial India.

The *Mahabharata* is an epic that is believed to embody the essence of Indian culture. In fact, scholars have opined that the epic offers multiple perspectives of study ranging from the mythological, philosophical, literary and to some extent, religious as well. The epic is divided into 18 volumes and is believed to have been written between 300 BCE and 500 BCE. Some scholars observe that the epic was most likely written when the Aryans migrated to India and settled in the Indo-Gangetic plains. Readers have always found the *Mahabharata* a treasure trove of different customs that embody multifarious cultural traits.

Recent studies conducted by scholars of gender studies have often pointed out the Brahminic patriarchy that is unmistakably present in the *Mahabharata*. Therefore, we find instances where there are cultural hegemonic influences designed to oppress the lower caste people and women. Even when looked at from a philosophical perspective, the epic showcases the eternal themes of greed and the quest for power. While this quest for power takes place between the Pandavas and the Kauravas, it is characters like Draupadi who face humiliation and neglect by the other characters. Draupadi, by dint of her marriage to the five Pandavas, was considered to have committed a very reprehensible act and so, she ought to be punished. Thus, it is significant to note that even in the epic, the character of Draupadi is considered to be rebellious and had the courage to challenge the social customs of the age. Draupadi breaks the gender barriers and remains resistant towards the prevalent social customs. However, it is also to be noted that Draupadi in the *Mahabharata* is looked upon as a victim who is rescued by Lord Krishna from a state of abject misery and humiliation. The focal point on her character is more on her victimhood rather than her courage to take on the patriarchy prevalent during the time. She is an image of constant suffering and repression that actually satiated much of the popular consciousness of the time. The fact that Lord Krishna rescues Draupadi from imminent humiliation and Arjuna's resolution to fight the Kauravas in order to avenge the humiliation also asserts the prowess of the male supremacy and once again, relegates the character of Draupadi into a state of suffering and pittance. Thus, Draupadi becomes the archetypal female who suffers perennially.

However, contrary to the portrayal of Draupadi in the epic, Mahasweta Devi paints her protagonist in a completely different light. The fiery author considers her Draupadi to be capable of challenging the male hegemony. Her Draupadi is the embodiment of strength and power who, instead of suffering, throws a challenge to the establishment that shakes the latter by its roots. Unlike Draupadi of the *Mahabharata*, who is infinitely clothed by Lord Krishna to save her from dishonour, the tribal woman DopdiMejhen attains a hero's stature because she fights all alone against the malevolent society, without any help. After her arrest, her body is violated and mutilated.

It is an irony that myths are often created to assert social justice and fair play. However, Mahasweta Devi's borrowing of the character from *Mahabharata* actually highlights how Dopdi is a victim of the unjust society. Hence, in her case, the mythical connection does not ensure fairness. However, Dopdi, by using her nakedness as a weapon establishes her courage in the face of utmost adversity.

Draupadi, written and published in 2010 by Mahasweta Devi is a critique of the contemporary times. Time and again, Mahasweta Devi has been an advocate of tribal rights and the subaltern. She has never shied away from protesting against the corporate greed and the hegemonic influences of various agencies. In *Draupadi*, Mahasweta Devi projects the realities of existence of women who are constantly subjected to oppression. In fact, it appears as if the systematic restraints that are imposed upon women actually inspire Mahasweta Devi and encourage her to write and expose the anomalies.

Mahasweta Devi's *Draupadi* begins with the introduction of the character DopdiMejhen. The name Dopdi is a tribalised form of the name Draupadi. Mahasweta Devi wants us to take note that Dopdi is an adivasi women and this makes her more vulnerable to the agencies of repression. Furthermore, it is to be noted that the adivasis have always been removed from their habitats. Their lands have been usurped since time immemorial. Right from the days of the *Mahabharata* when the Aryans invaded India and occupied the lands to more recent instances when the tribal people were at the receiving end and their lands were forcibly taken away by the so called civilised people of our society. Thus, by referring to the *Mahabharata*, Mahasweta Devi wants us to take note of the fact that hegemony existed even during the times of the *Mahabharata*. Even during that time, patriarchy existed and women liberty was a far cry. The trend continues to this day when social constructs aim at subjugating the women and the marginalised members of the community.

Scholars believe that the Aryans introduced the Sanskrit language; the Vedas, certain deities, laws of Manu, literature, etc. that perhaps played a role in the obliteration of the indigenous tribal cultures. Other social structures such as the caste system or the extended family were also the products of the Aryan culture. Therefore, much like the Dopdi Mejhens, the indigenous people during the times of *Mahabharata* also suffered the anguish of losing their own cultures and practices. Later, when the British came to India, the same story was repeated. The colonisation of India affected the indigenous cultures because the British had imposed their culture, language and rituals and the adivasis had to fight against this new invasion.

We come to know that Dopdi and her husband Dulna are wanted by the police because they had participated in a revolt against the atrocities committed by the landowners. The state machinery also accused the duo of subversion. In order to arrest and apprehend Dopdi and her husband, a character named Senanayak comes to the fore. Mahasweta Devi's story highlights how power is abused by those in power. She also emphasises on the forces of resistance that were born to fight the hegemonic agencies represented by the landlords, the state and the law enforcers. In fact, in many of her stories, we find instances of adivasi resistance against the colonisers, the police, etc. Within the narrative of *Draupadi*, we find Mahasweta Devi commenting about Senanayak, "He is Prospero as well" (Devi 23). This comment brings our attention to *The Tempest* by Shakespeare where Prospero, the coloniser conquers Caliban's island and makes him a slave. The reference to Shakespeare's play is significant because we find the same power politics mentioned in *Draupadi* as well. The naming of the character Senanayak is also significant. The literal meaning is chief of the army. The significance is that the character's identity is self-explanatory. It needs no further introduction. Senanayak is the proverbial character who obeys and carries out the orders given by the capitalist class. Senanayak also turns a blind eye when the village landlord uses nefarious means to torment the farmers and make the land unfavourable for tilling.

Senanayak chases Dopdi but the latter flees and hides in the forest. The police kill Dopdi's husband Dulna and uses the dead body as a bait but Dopdi does not fall into the trap. Therefore, the narration amply reflects the tyrannical machinery that is at work to apprehend the tribals who fight for their rights and legitimate dues. The way Mahasweta Devi narrates the description of Dopdi is significant. Dopdi wears a wretched look "with some rice knotted into her belt... as she walked, she picked out and killed the lice in her hair" (Devi 27). The description highlights how the tribal characters live constantly in a state of penury and fear. Mahasweta Devi also describes the circumstances that led to the peasants revolting against the landlord who was later killed by the tribals. It so happened that the landlord had constructed several wells in his property that caused severe drought in the region. The strategy was to fleece the poor tribal people because a drought would ensure impoverishment in the region that would, in turn, give rise to farmers coming to the private money lenders for bailing them out. The vicious cycle actually involved money lenders, unscrupulous landlords and corrupt policemen who were in close collusion with one another. The state turned a blind eye when Surja Sahu, the landlord refused to share the water of his tube wells with the tribals. When he is killed by the desperate villagers, a manhunt is launched by the government to nab the killers. Dopdi and her husband Dulna are forced to flee and live like fugitives. The miserable condition of the peasants can be gauged from the statement by Dulna, "My great-grandfather took a bit of paddy from him, and I still give him free labour to repay that debt" (Devi 30). Thus, there was absolutely no way through which the peasants would make themselves free. They were indentured labourers who had to remain committed to the unholy landlords throughout their lives.

When Dopdi is arrested by the police after a long pursuit, the former puts up a fight. She protests the injustices meted out to her community and demands justice. She does not submit easily to the wrongful restraint by the police. Her arrest is followed by a spell of torture and pain perpetrated by the law enforcers. Senanayak orders his men to "do the needful" (Devi 35) to Dopdi. The order translates into rape of Dopdi. The imageries used by Mahasweta Devi are grotesque and unnerving.

They reflect the inhuman torture that was inflicted upon the poor tribal Dopdi. "Her breasts are bitten raw, the nipples torn. How many? Four-five-six seven – then Draupadi had passed out" (Devi 35). It is pretty evident that Mahasweta Devi chooses the name Draupadi for her protagonist in order to intensify the impact of the repression that Dopdi experiences. The naming of the protagonist is not a mere coincidence.

Contrary to her namesake in the *Mahabharata*, DopdiMejhen does not have Lord Krishna coming to her rescue. She fights back on her own and endures the pain all by herself. Furthermore, the reference to *Mahabharata* does not end here. It appears that the aspiration to control land, a region was present during the times of the epic as well. The same urge happens in Mahasweta Devi's *Draupadi* as well thereby connecting the two works of art thematically. It is characters like Dopdi who fight against the corrupt multinationals who are hell bent in extracting and exploiting resources from the forest lands that have been the habitats of the tribal people for ages. Therefore, it can also be said that the struggle and fight of Dopdi actually transcends ages and also time and space. The struggle attains a universal entity that is not restricted to the village of Dopdi alone. This struggle can be found in other parts of India as well. In fact, the fight of the marginalised communities and the subaltern is ubiquitous throughout the world and not restricted to a nation space alone.

The resistance offered by Dopdi is significant. The subtle, yet powerful form of resistance put up by Dopdi when Senanayak's men rape her speaks volumes about the resilience offered by the tribal people against the capitalists and the bourgeoisie. When Senanayak orders his troops to "do the needful" (Devi 35), it is characters like Dopdi who fight back with endurance and courage. The rape becomes a tool of oppression for the police. "Draupadi is all covered in blood and has lost all hope: "Perhaps they have abandoned her. For the foxes to devour. But she hears the scrape of feet... Draupadi closes her eyes. She doesn't have to wait long. Again the process of making her begins. Goes on" (Devi 35).

Dopdi does not ask for heavenly intervention when she is raped unlike her namesake in the epic *Mahabharata*. She suffers, yet she survives and dares the police chief to humiliate her more. She resists the authority and refuses to acknowledge the claim of supremacy made by the capitalists and their agents. She tears her last piece of cloth and exposes her nakedness to the police officer.

> "You asked them to make me up, don't you want to see how they made me? Where are her clothes? Won't put them on, Sir. Tearing them.... What's the use of clothes?... There isn't a man here that I should be ashamed... What more can you do? Come on, counter me – come on-, counter me –?" (Devi 36-37).

Senanayak does not know how to respond in such a situation. "Draupadi pushes Senanayak with her two mangled breasts, and for the first time Senanayak is afraid to stand before an unarmed target, terribly afraid." (Devi 37). Senanayak could never estimate the power of an adivasi woman who could put such a formidable amount of resistance. Shankar Narayan Gaura feels that Senanayak's lack of understanding "is symptomatic of a larger incomprehension and a more extensive exclusion from the world of patriarchal protections and controls" (Gaura 250). Using her body as a weapon, Dopdi challenges those in power. Thus, unlike Draupadi in *Mahabharata,* DopdiMejhen refuses to yield and ask for heavenly assistance. Dopdi tears her piece of cloth with her teeth and walks towards Senanayak saying, "You can strip me, but can you clothe me again? Are you a man?" (Devi 37). Mahasweta Devi successfully interweaves the mythical strains with the contemporary patriarchal and capitalist hegemonies and the result is a powerful text that lends a voice to voiceless people like Dopdi Mejhen.

Mahasweta Devi's portrayal of Dopdi aligns with the demands of India's realities. Her manner of portrayal challenges the traditional modes of representation with respect to the colonised subject. The challenge posed by the author is all the more intense because the protagonist is a female. Hence, the resistance against the hegemonic forces acts on multiple fronts. Urmimala Sarkar Munsi observes that Dopdi, "was a political character, created specifically to critique the state and its oppressive machinery, where the plight of the marginalised and exploited people was highlighted alongside the additional vulnerability of the women in those communities" (Munsi Sarkar 1). It also happens at times that the marginalised individual cannot speak because s/he has not been given the power to speak. Still, we find pockets of resistance thriving and the characters raising their voices against injustice by the dominant power that has happened over the years. The rewriting of Draupadi successfully projects the inanity of the patriarchal discourse and the folly of the capitalists who never shy away from exploiting the tribal people who have traditionally considered the forest their home.

The foreword of *Draupadi* was written by Gayatri Chakravorty Spivak. Spivak writes:

> "Draupadi is the name of central character. She is introduced to the reader into two uniforms and between two versions of her name Dopdi and Draupadi. It is that as tribal she cannot pronounce her own name (Draupadi), or the tribalised form, Dopdi, is the proper name of ancient Draupadi. She is on the list of wanted persons, yet her name is not on the list of appropriate names for the tribal women" (Devi 7).

The connection between the two characters, one from the *Mahabharata* and the other from Mahasweta Devi's work cannot be missed. Mahasweta Devi re-creates the character in her own way and re-writes an episode from the epic in order to show how the protagonist DopdiMejhen fights against injustice. The deconstruction and reconstruction of the mythical character Draupadi appeals to every social space and therefore, attains a universal tone. In this context, Githa Hariharan comments:

> "When a woman's naked body speaks, its language can turn the victimized body into a speaking, fighting one. Her body is no longer only for the powerful male to inscribe upon; her body turns her into an inscriber. Surely we have heard this language before,

in homes or on the streets? It should be familiar, but something, its challenge to acceptable language, perhaps, makes it bold, even shocking. Draupadi's story travelled from Bengal in the East to Manipur in the Northeast" (Hariharan 18).

As mentioned before, Mahasweta Devi has always championed the rights of the subalterns and the marginalised. Many of her protagonists take recourse to violence when they see that the state machinery is overwhelmingly oppressive and unjust. Her protagonists believe that violence is one of the effective ways to ensure the expected social transformation. Thus, we find that in Mahasweta Devi's *Draupadi*, the protagonist creates her own identity. Her forceful assertion to Senanayak, "What more can you do? (Devi 37) is a direct challenge to the men in power. She defeats the people who had raped her. She ultimately overcomes the shame and instead, confronts the criminal state machinery in an open of defiance.

Arup Kumar Sen believes that Mahasweta Devi's *Draupadi* was "written in the context of police repression against the Naxalites, tells a tale of brutal state violence suffered by a tribal woman and her unique signature of resistance. The story reminds us of contemporary violence against the tribal community in Chhattisgarh and other tribal regions" (Sen 1). Her act terrifies a merciless police officer like Senanayak "and for the first time Senanayak is afraid of to stand before an unarmed target, terribly afraid" (Devi 37).

To sum up, it can be said that Mahasweta Devi's writings have always challenged the traditional and expected notions that have been formed by the society over the ages. Thus, we find many a rebellious character like Sujata of *Mother of 1084* or Dopdi of *Draupadi* challenging the so called value systems and constructs of certain social spaces. Her belief that a woman is equal to man finds mention in many of her writings. Furthermore, Mahasweta Devi's urge to expose the hypocrisy and ignorance of mainstream discourses with regard to the tribal and rural communities makes her one of the formidable writers of subaltern literature. The use of myths in her writings imparts power and strength that have the capacity to shake the pillars of dominance. Her forceful writings compel us to take a hard look at the existing social constructs. In today's age, when social injustice is rampant, Mahasweta Devi's writings have become all the more relevant because they envision an egalitarian society where everyone has a voice. Mahasweta Devi becomes a crusader for the people, living on the social periphery, and tirelessly champions their causes who otherwise, are forgotten by the mainstream society.

Works Cited

Devi, Mahasweta. *Draupadi*. Seagull Publishers, 2010.

.... *Imaginary Maps: Three Stories*. Routledge, 1995.

Frye, Northrop. *The Anatomy of Criticism: Four Essays*. Princeton UP, 1957.

Gaura, Shankar Narayan. "Phoolan Devi: Gendered Subaltern; Caste Warrior." *Feminist Formations*, vol. 30, no. 2, Johns Hopkins University Press, Summer 2018, pp. 231-253.

ProQuest,search-proquestcom.library.britishcouncil.org.in:4443/docview/2156098366?accountid=145163, doi: http://dx.doi.org/10.1353/ff.2018.0025.

Hariharan, Githa. "When Bodies Speak." *World Literature Today*, vol. 91, no. 2, 2017, pp. 16-20. *Pro Quest*, search proquest.com.library.britishcouncil.org.in:4443/docview/1955977330?accountid=145163.

Munsi Sarkar, Urmimala. "Draupadi's Travels and Travails." *Economic and Political Weekly*, Dec 10, 2016. *Pro Quest*, search-proquest-com.library.britishcouncil.org.in:4443/docview/2153696978?accountid=145163.

Sen, Arup Kumar. "Mahasweta Devi (1926-2016)." *Economic and Political Weekly*, Aug 06, 2016. *Pro Quest*, search-proquest-com.library.britishcouncil.org.in:4443/docview/2153696899?accountid=145163.

Author Bio-note

Rajdeep Guha is a PhD scholar at the Dept. of English, Lovely Professional University, Punjab. He completed his MA in English from the Universities of Calcutta, India and Otago, New Zealand. Presently, he works as a Content Manager in Delhi. He has published articles in journals and presented papers in several international conferences.

3

Home in Conflict: The Ambivalent Existence of Tribal Identity in Mamang Dai's *The Legends of Pensam*

Meghalee Mitra

Abstract

For centuries, the Adis have been caught in a constant battle against the threats of assimilation and north east erasure. The dominant cultural narrative often attributes stigma and shame with their history, wholly misrepresenting the Adivasi. Their language, tribal folklore, and their homeland, are key aspects of their identity formation – aspects which are perpetually in flux. A poet, journalist, and ex civil servant, Mamang Dai's *The Legends of Pensam* seeks to create a repository of collective memory, using it to resist the far reaching destruction of cultural hegemony. Exploring both mythology and reality, colonialism and war, Dai seeks to de-exoticize the tribal identity. The 'home' among the Adis is a perpetually shifting paradigm, being reinvented with each onslaught of globalisation. Dai looks to memory and cultural roots in order to stabilise this 'home' and prevent cultural amnesia. This article traces the effects of the 'sahib' and mainlanders on the North East forest ecology, and the brutality that continuously changes the face of their 'home'land. It analyses tribal folklore, and its distinctive nature separate from the dominant ideology. Lastly, the article seeks to highlight the importance of the construction of 'mnemocultures' and authentic documentation to safeguard the existence of the tribal population.

Keywords: collective memory; cultural amnesia; mythology and reality; north east erasure; tribal folklore; tribal identity

The oral narratives and tribal folklore of the North East provide an extensive understanding of tribal identity, and their relationship with their homeland. With years of political tussle chasing the existence of the Adis and other tribes, their cultural repository – indigenous writing, folklore, myths, and other authentic documentation – is of supreme importance to prevent north east erasure.

> "...the oral discourses always tried to subvert the hegemonic colonial design to penetrate and map certain inaccessible areas of the tribal society where the spokenword continued to reign supreme" (Misra 24).

In her book, Dai lays local tribal lives as testimony to the wounds of cultural hegemony. She traces a perpetually losing struggle between the Adis and the mainland-ers, or colonisers. She brings to life the 'other' side of the discourse, erstwhile dominated by the majority. Kallol Bhattacharjee, in his review of the book, mentions what a "colossal loss" it is to have the North East be completely excluded from the national historiography of India. Such bias and ignorance inevitably paves the path to opposing narratives, Rashomon-esque 'truth's. Be it the torturous expeditions of the sahibs, the poaching of village youth into unrelenting labour, the animistic mythology, or simply the tales of ordinary tribal existence, Dai chronicles the contrasting stories of the oppressor versus the oppressed.

> "The truth, after all, exists only in portions, and the rest is a matter of words changed by each person's perception" (32).

'Pensam', meaning 'in-between' hints at the Adis existing in a constant state of ambivalence, caught between two opposing forces. Some say it is that of progress versus primitivism. Some assert that it is one of mythology versus reality. But at the base of this all is a struggle between home and homelessness. With the landscape of 'home' constantly shifting with invasions, the threat of tribal assimilation looming large, their identity is in a perpetual tug-of-war. The mainland lies with all its promise of progress, of modernity, and globalisation, but so too does it signal tribal erasure. Struggling against the British, the politics of the mainland, and the global culture that labels them as savages, the Adis cling to their collective memory, zealously protecting their identity, their 'home'. Chronicles such as this is a crucial necessity of subaltern Literature.

The Sahib at Home: The Postcolonial Image of Tribal Identity

Arunachal Pradesh, where Dai originates from, houses twenty six tribes and more than a hundred sub-clans. All of them speak a different language or dialect, co-existing in a land cushioned by rivers, mountains, and nature through and through. The animistic faith practised by the Adis is centred around the lush forests' ecology. There being few roads, land criss-crossed by flowing rivers, the journey to distant places is beyond toiling. "But the old villagers who walk miles every day say: 'When you look at the land you forget your aches and pains.'" (Author's Note) This sentiment lies at the heart of the North East's fervent struggle to protect its home. Speaking of secessionist movements, of clinging dearly to one's own tongue, of navigating the politics of language and minority culture – the concept of 'home' is continuously in flux.

Homi K. Bhaba says the term home itself is an ambivalent terminology. On the one hand it has "something to do with the normalized...the original." It is associated primarily with the "thereness" and "hereness" of our hearts, and identities. It is a sense of 'our'-ness – our people, our land, our home. On the other hand, Bhaba posits a second facet of 'home', "the kind of Conradian idea that home is what you return to." Home, says Bhaba, is placed in-between the concept of "emergence" and "return" (Kläger and Stierstorfer 11-20).

The home of the Adis, has been tampered with for hundreds of years. Some have coaxed it towards becoming a nameless limb of the mainland, others have roughly plundered the forests, and mutilated their land beyond recognition. In "small histories recalled in the season of rain" (36), Mamang Dai recounts the nature of the early 1800s. Change was afoot, and the villagers could feel it in their bones, in the way the land shook, in the spirals of the dust settling. This was when the 'white', the "migluns", had begun arriving with their stocks. There were priests rooting for the conversion of uncivilised tribals and their animistic beliefs. There were soldiers setting up camp, studying, preparing to use the undisturbed North East as a weapon in their war. "Since then, people from other worlds had come and gone, though the only records of their journeys are the stories that the older men and women remember" (Author's Note).

In the section "songs of the rhapsodist" (45), Dai traces the origin of the Abor Expedition from the tribe's resistance to assimilation. When Assistant Political Officer in the districts of Sadiya and Lakhimpur, Mr Noel Williamson was murdered, the Abor Expeditionary Field Force was deployed to avenge the death of him and his entourage. Dai writes about the ambivalence of the story behind the attack. "No one is quite sure what provoked the attack" (48). Some say it was a miscommunication where the approaching white man's troop inspired fear in the local tribes who did not want to give up their homes. Some say he had insulted a tribal man who, with wounded honour, killed him. The government however, held it as an act of uncivilised brutality which prompted the need for tribal 'purification'. They let loose troops of armed soldiers who were "trampling the sad, disquieted hills and hunting the killer with all the might of the universe" (51). The villagers alleged that the sahib's soldiers had insulted a local man, poking fun at his complexion, language, and culture. "Why should anybody look at a man with disgust when he was a man of the land and the other was a visitor trying of conquer the villages with lies and bags of gifts?" (51). Dai asks. Yet they were the ones punished.

It is ironic that the Expedition was preceded by the term 'Abor'. To outsiders, it meant the location of Abor Hills, or the erstwhile moniker of the Adi people. In Assamese, 'Abor' means 'independent' or 'living freely', closely associated with tribal identity. It was this essence of freedom that the Adis sought to protect by resisting colonial invasion, by resisting even the benefits that the British were extending in exchange for their compliance.

The first mention of north east erasure in Dai's book, comes in the form of a cultural metaphor, a tussle connecting mythology and reality. In the lap of an animistic culture, the "Breetees" attacked nature. Under heavy workload and maltreatment, the elephants "strained and quivered to the shouts of their mahouts...lost their footing and hurtled off the mountainside bellowing like mythical beasts..." (39). It was a direct attack on the spirits from the tribal folklore, and, in extension, Adi lives. The local labourers they recruited "died like flies" (39). Under the garb of 'progress', the white man's expeditions were a direct attempt to facilitate north east erasure. When they were done, the small village was "permanently awash in debris" (164).

Throughout *The Legends of Pensam*, there is mention of the "road" that is perpetually in a state of construction. "The village had moved to its own quiet rhythm for centuries, with old certainties and beliefs, but the road was changing all that" (148). As the construction of the road required the digging up of iron ore, the locals referred to events around it as the "story of the red pool" (149). It was considered cursed, doused in the colour of blood, perhaps the same blood of the villagers who resisted the sahib. It stands as a metaphor for the failures of colonialism and dominant bias cutting its way into the heartland of the North East. The road requires local men to enlist in labour, young men who are lost to the inhuman working conditions, yet the construction seems never-ending. It is the underlying vine of colonialism that pervades the tribal village imagery from the first page to the last. The town of Pigo was mysterious, secure in their sense of belonging, of tribal identity. "They were beyond time. Till the road came" (147).

The "kebang" is another institution gradually lost under the coloniser's footsteps. It is similar to the panchayat system in India. A group of village elders with "well-worn sticks" (159), chosen for their experience, knowledge, and honesty, would preside over important matters and issues of transgression in the village. Soon the kebangs disappeared, replaced by the rigid, and often faulty mechanism of the modern judiciary. Dai laments that the loss of the personal took the human touch away from village lives.

"The bridge is broken,' the boys would say metaphorically" (163). The passage signified the cross over to the 'other' side, to the side of the colonisers, where men from the village were recruited as government officials. Everything was changing rapidly, moving steadily towards north east erasure. No longer were there groups of elders sitting with deviant boys, explaining the rights and the wrongs or sitting with protesting youth, helping them vent for hours. The Adis were caught in a whirlwind of forced modernity. "When they returned, Rakut's father was wearing hunting boots and a camouflage outfit" (39). It was as though the familiar had been painted over with colours of another place, another people, another culture.

Tribal Folklore and Mythology: Radical Exoticisation of Adi Culture

Joseph Campbell in his *Primitive Mythology: The Masks of God* asserts the need for myths. "Man, apparently, cannot maintain himself in the universe without belief in some arrangement of the general inheritance of myth" (11). It structures the cultural ethos of a group. Especially among a minority, the collective memory of a shared culture encourages healthy identity formation.

The incoming of the "migluns" marked a potential end to the olden days, to the sanctity of tribal existence, but, most importantly, to the preservation of their home. Mythology and reality, never so different before then, were pitted against each other. Dai's book talks about it extensively.

> "In the old days life was very hard,' he would say. 'We crept out of the rocks and called to each other because we were afraid to be alone in the wilderness. Now the ayings are taking our land and we have to creep back into the boulders and stones. Waah!" (97).

'Home' did not only mean the land that they occupied, the land of their ancestors. It also encompassed their deep-rooted cultural learnings, their language, and, most importantly, their mythology. The Adis practise an animistic faith, reflected in their tribal folklore. The Oxford Dictionary defines this as "The attribution of a living soul to plants, inanimate objects, and natural phenomena." The tribes have, for centuries, gleaned their ways of life and learning from nature. Even though the stories originated from one place or another, and not everybody had seen the 'spirits' they obeyed, the legends were embedded into the collective memory of the lot.

In Dai's book, we learn of tribal folklore from village elders in Sirum, Pigo, Duyang, Yelen, and Gurdum in the Siang Valley. In "the boy who fell from the sky" (7), we read about the "Biribik, the water serpent" (9). Interestingly, it is a vengeful spirit. One who sees it, has disaster befall them soon after. The myth can be traced back to a fisherman who saw a serpent with horns, and died the following year. In "the silence of adela and kepi" (17), Togum shoots a king cobra who had wrapped itself around logs, scaring the elephants. Soon after, his child, Kepi, loses his speech and movement. Kepi's "stiff" and "twisted" torso made it seem as though a giant serpent had wrapped itself around him. Both these myths embody spirits which avenge the destruction of Nature. In the collective conscience of the Adis is the silent knowledge that nothing good ever comes out of harming Nature. This grounds for their strong, long-standing relationship with the forest ecology, and why all of their spirit gods are embodiments of Nature itself.

Often, the Adi mythology is dismissed as unreasonable, as 'exotic' and mystic. It shames the believers into cultural amnesia – a deliberate forgetting of heritage. But what need we of reason in faith when there is no reason to existence or suffering, Dai asks:

> "'Reason! Reason! What reason?' she yelled. 'By what reason are we here with the rain and the mud and the fungus, can you tell me that?'" (75).

In fact, Barthes supports the unreal, the unreasonable-ness as a basis of myth making in *Mythologies*. "The function of myth is to empty reality: it is, literally, a ceaseless flowing out, a haemorrhage, or perhaps an evaporation, in short a perceptible absence" (142).

Assimilation poses threat of obliteration for this knowledge system and tribal identity as a whole. The dominant ideology of the Indian mainland is saturated with images from the Hindu mythology. "Cultural hegemony creates binary oppositions such as the distinction between folk and classic, where folk is looked down upon while the 'classical' is preserved," says Dr. Usham Rojio, academic counselor at IGNOU. (Anu) There are the "tiger spirit" (28) who sets houses on fire, banishing inhabitants to the forest; the influence of "si-ye" (29) that made men like Kamur go mad and kill his children; the "village of widows" (12), and much more – inextricably a part of the Adi tribal identity.

The "miri" is an essential part of the village fabric. The term refers to a shaman who holds in-depth knowledge of the spirits, their workings, and is called upon often to ward off evil. He offers a "body of tradition" (Dai, *Tribal Religion* 88) which is inherited, expanding with time, providing a repository of tribal knowledge. "In the beginning, there was only Keyum. Nothingness" (56). The story of the Adi's creation is of the "cosmological myths of ex nihilo nature" (Biju, 3). This has no reference to the Indian Vedic mythology, positing a completely different, alternate view of life and living. To them, "Donyi-Polo", the sun and the moon, are representatives of ultimate beauty, and eternal truth (Ering 36).

In the quiet villages of the Adis, mythology and reality are not contradictory forces. Lessons are learnt from stories passed down through generations. They are content with their reason, or the lack thereof. They don't need the false riches of the coloniser, or the glamour of converting to a dominant ideology. They are just "peripheral people, thinking out (their) thoughts" (Dai, *Pensam* 190).

Authentic Documentation: An Antidote to Forced Cultural Amnesia

> "What happens to the people and the places we forget? Where do they go?" (Dai, *Pensam* 177).

In *The Book of Laughter and Forgetting* Milan Kundera writes, "The first step in liquidating a people is to erase its memory." He refers to comrade Clementis, who had offered Communist leader Klement Gottwald his hat, while the latter was delivering a speech in Prague, in 1948. A few years later, Clementis was accused of seditious practices and executed. The pictures of that day in 1948 show a lonely Gottwald, and bare wall where Clementis used to be. He was erased out of the photographs, out of collective memory, the hat on Gottwald's head being the only remaining mention of him. "It is 1971, and Mirek says: The struggle of man against power is the struggle of memory against forgetting." (Kundera 2)

This is precisely Dai's initiative, to create a 'mnemoculture'. The term 'mnemonic', derived from Ancient Greek, signifies "in relation to memory". Using myths laden with historical context as a memory device, Dai fights a lonely fight against mass cultural amnesia and north east erasure. She incites the locals to take up their "mnemopraxial responsibility" (Goswami 469) to prevent their heritage from slipping through the cracks of globalisation. We see here the practise of postcolonial 'anamnesis', the reinvention or re-discovery of the past, of "whatever was forgotten conveniently – forgotten, with a design" (Goswami 472).

> "...we believed in the 'word' as composed in our myths and legends. It is here that we may find that peculiar, indefinable something by which we recognise each other, and make others see us as a group, a society, a people of a particular community" (Dai, *Oral Narratives* 2).

The rise in technology, in science, in the need for a rational basis to life, threatens the erasure of indigenous cultures. These memories are not widespread, or familiar to the dominant ideology. They are exclusive to lived experiences and the cultural memory of the tribes. The North East's distance from the mainland is precisely this fear of erasure, this loss of a sense of identity. The exoticisation of the Adi culture, by mainland and coloniser alike, is also a recurrent means to force their integration into dominant culture. They have, over time, been painted as the uncivilised, the barbaric, the primitive entities clinging to a long forgotten past. This progress of dehumanisation made them easier to exploit. In The Hindu's 'A History of Conversions', Pralay Kanungo draws an example from Orissa:

> "...in order to rationalise the exploitation, it built up certain stereotypes. For instance, Kandhas were stigmatised as a heinous criminal tribe as they practised meriah (human sacrifice) – completely overlooking the role of some of the princes and zamindars who actually encouraged this practice."

In an interview with *Livemint*, Easterine Kire, celebrated Naga author, asserts that the use of terms such as "insurgency" and "secession" have unnecessarily sensationalised a very primal and universal struggle of identity protection. She says that if only mainland journalists would explore the North East on a regular basis, reporting life as it is lived everyday, then the "exotic" label to North East existence, would begin to fade over time. This is primarily what Mamang Dia seeks to do. She writes not only of myth, but of war, of love, loss, death, and the changing landscape of a place called home.

The retention of this knowledge system can root out the threats of cultural amnesia. In "the golden chance" (Dai, *Pensam* 169), Mona and the film crew offer to document the lives of the Adis. The villagers wonder "Who wants to see us?" (171). The protagonist, on the one hand, is concerned about the "dying breed" of rhapsodists, the gradual loss of a cultural repository. On the other hand, there is a perpetual fear of being misrepresented by the outsider. If they tell the film crew about the caves where children feasted on bats, then is that all they will be remembered by?

Will 'they' remember Komsing? Or the memorial stone for the sahib which the tribals still take care of, just like the coloniser had instructed? Will they remember the lives lost, the trees felled, the ecology disrupted in the name of vengeance? Will anybody remember the other side of the story?"...We are not a village of shame" (56).

Conclusion

The white man's burden, carried forward by the dominant narrative of the mainland, has always sought to 'purify' the Adivasi, leading to north east erasure and cultural amnesia. Dai's 'Pensam' seeks to show that harm of such forced interference. The Adi lives, their tribal identity, is secure in their cultural practises, and collective memory. They exist in an 'ecotopia' "where living and the non-living elements...live and communicate with peaceful cohabitation" (Malik 132). With mythology and reality in harmony, the Adis are gradually constructing their sense of agency, rebuilding their individual history. Tribal folklore remains an indispensable component of maintaining indigenous freedom. Their recollection is gradually enabling them to extricate themselves from the colonial aftermath. Dai's work of constructing such memory devices is a unique act of resistance against the allegedly modern world that seeks to humiliate 'different' lifestyles. It seeks to situate the beloved 'home' of a minority, in an ever-changing world.

Works Cited

Anu, Toko. "Death of the 'Indigenous': Views From the North East of India." *News Click*, 16 Nov. 2019, www.newsclick.in/death-indigenous-views-north-east-india.

Barthes, Roland. *Mythologies*. Hill and Wang, 2013.

Bhattacherjee, Kallol. "Flight of the Hornbill." *Rev. of The Legends of Pensam,* Biblio: A Review of Books, 2006.

Campbell, Joseph. *The Masks of God: Primitive Mythology,* Arkana, 2001.

Dai, Mamang. "Oral Narratives and Myth", *Glimpses from the North-East*, National Knowledge Commission, 2009, pp. 1-8.

Dai, Mamang. "The Nature of Faith and Worship Among the Adis", *Understanding Tribal Religion*, edited by Tamo Mibang and Sarit K. Chaudhuri, First ed., Mittal Publications, 2004.

Dai, Mamang. *The Legends of Pensam,* Penguin Random House India, 2006.

Ering, Oshong. "Philosophy of Donyi Polo", *Understanding Tribal Religion*, edited by Mibang, Tamoand Chaudhuri K. Sarit, First ed., Mittal Publications, 2004.

Goswami, Harajit. "Postcolonialism and the Retrieval of the Past: A Critical Study of Mamang Dai's Legends of Pensam." *International Journal Of English Language Literature and Humanities*, IV, 2016.

Kanungo, Pralay. “A History of Conversions”, *Frontline,* Frontline, 26 Feb. 2004, frontline.thehindu.com/other/article30221163.ece.

Kläger, Florian, and Klaus Stierstorfer, editors. “Homi K. Bhabha in Interview with Klaus Stierstorfer on ‘Diaspora and Home”, *Diasporic Constructions of Home and Belonging,* DE GRUYTER, 2015, pp. 11–20.

Kundera, Milan. *The Book of Laughter and Forgetting,* translated by Heim H. Michael, 1979.

M.A, Biju. “Myths and Legends from Netherworld in Mamang Dai’s Novel The Legends of Pensam, Ruminations: The Andrean Journal of Literature 2013”,*St. Andrew’s College of Arts, Science and Commerce | Education for All*, 2018, standrewscollege.ac.in/ruminations-2013-2/.

Malik, Santosh Kumar. “Retrieving the Ethnic World of the Adis: An Ecocritical Reading of Mamang Dai’s The Legends of Pensam”, *Vidyasagar University Hosted Services,*2020, inet.vidyasagar.ac.in:8080/jspui/bitstream/123456789/5421/1/14_Santosh%20Kumar %20Malik.pdf.

Misra, Tilottoma, editor. *The Oxford Anthology of Writings from North-East India.* OUP India, 2010.

Sharma, Sanjukta. “Political Animals: Nagaland’s Voice.” *LiveMint,* 27 Nov. 2013, www.livemint.com/Opinion/ju1TBgOUrpK5Bv88QmFNAN/POLITICAL-ANIMALS-Nagalands-voice.html.

Author’s Bio Note

Meghalee Mitra has a Master’s degree in English Literature, from the University of Calcutta. Her favourite areas of work are Gender Studies, Media, Dalit and Subaltern Literature. She freelances as a Culture and Politics writer, a developmental editor, and researcher.

4

Despair and Anguish in Select Poems of Dalit Writers

Dibyajit Mukherjee

Abstract

The caste system of India has exemplified itself to be a pernicious impediment to the realization of the resolution of equality, liberty and fraternity as enshrined in the Indian constitution for majority of the Dalit people. It is in an environment of such marginalization that poets have created a language of resistance through their poems by depicting the real situation about the plight of these people who were previously labelled as untouchables. Along with the problem of caste, it also needs to be mentioned that the capitalist mode of production will not be able to ameliorate or annihilate the problem of the structurally inequal caste system as the capitalist system also creates systematic inequality which continuously needs to depend on a massive group of people who own almost nothing apart from their own labor power which they need to sell to an employer in return for wages. In this paper I have discussed the aspects of social margination which I have termed otherization and concluded that the reasons behind despair and anger of Dalits have created a language of violence as a form resistance which is used to counter the structural violence of the varnashrama.

Keywords: otherization; inequality; caste socialization; hegemony; despair; social marginalization.

The Indian Social structure is still tarred with the viciousness of the caste or varna system. The Khairlanji murders, the Unnao lynching along with the Hathras rape incident and the murder of Vikas Kumar Jatav by four upper caste men in 2020 can be exemplified as just few of the many incidents of atrocities and humiliation that take place in an almost everyday basis. It was reported in the newspaper "The Hindu" that crimes against Dalits increased by 6% between 2009 and 2018. Without a radical annihilation of the caste system, the pillars of equality, liberty and fraternity enshrined in the Indian Constitution which the Preamble adopts as its resolution will remain a hollow phrase as the caste system promotes systematic division not only of labor but also of laborers and hence erases the "demos" (people) of democracy which essentially refers to people's rule. Bhikhu Parekh in his *Logic of Humiliation* notes:

> For centuries the untouchables in India were confined to segregated areas and prevented from coming into physical contact with upper caste Hindus. Even an accidental contact with them was considered polluting and required a ritual bath. In parts of south India, they were required to make loud noises when passing through upper caste areas, so that the upper caste residents could quickly retreat into their houses and avoid even their shadows. Untouchable women were not allowed to wear certain kinds of dress or even cover their breasts, this being an exclusively high caste privilege (Guru 24).

Along with the problem of caste it needs to be mentioned that the capitalist mode of production will not be able to ameliorate or annihilate the problem of the structurally inequal caste system as the capitalist system also creates systematic incquality which continuously needs to depend on a massive group of people who own almost nothing apart from their own labor power which they need to sell to an employer in return for wages. This too has to be done by competing against other people who are ready to sell their labor and hence unemployment is a perpetual disease if one may use the word metaphorically. The capitalist system might create a handful of Dalit bourgeois who might be subservient to the capitalist method of producing and reproducing the conditions for the extraction of surplus value through the surplus labor of the workers but it has not been able to ameliorate the lives of majority of the Dalits who are "khet mazdoors" or poor peasants selling their labor by toiling and tilling the land of people who own those plots of land as their privatized property. In a very recent article published by "The Wire" this source of information can be traced. According to the report the Dalits in the state of Punjab constitute 32% of the population but own a minimal 2.3% of the land. Hence, an inequal structure existing in the shape of the ancient and vestigial varna system along with the capitalist modus operandi of inequal land distribution and the concept of allotting land to people who are not related to any form of labor on that land can have a tendency to exacerbate the polarity observed in the Indian social structure. It is from the soil of this discrepancy that Dalit literature arises. In this paper I shall proceed to highlight the themes of otherization, despair and anger which forms the nexus of the selected poetry of poets like Waman Nimbalkar, Hira Bansode and Keshav Meshram.

Eleanor Zelliot in the book *An Anthology of Dalit Literature* writes:

> The meaning of Dalit in Hindi and Marathi "ground down, depressed" and is now used by politicized Untouchables in preference to any other designation. The term is one of pride – Untouchables have been oppressed by others; there is nothing inherently wrong with them. Their insistence on the use of Dalit has been recognized officially, and the state governments of Maharashtra, Madhya Pradesh and Uttar Pradesh have issued orders that Dalit be the term used rather than the Harijan, Scheduled Caste or Untouchable (Anand and Zelliot 2).

It would be obvious that if some people are denounced and tagged as untouchable or unclean from the moment of their birth, otherization will be an inherent condition of their existence. Otherization must not be confused with alienation. Marx used the word alienation or Entfremdung to signify the condition of the proletariat who are involved in the production of goods and services but cannot own even half of what they produce due to very low wages. On the other hand, even though this was exploitation and very brutal, they formed an important part of the industry and factory and were not considered as untouchables. The varna system had reduced these people who were outside the four-fold structure commonly known as chaturvarna as untouchables. A brilliant description of this otherized human condition is located in the poem named "Caste" penned by Waman Nimbalkar. The poem starts by saying:

When I knew nothing, I knew
My caste was low (Anand & Zelliot 123)

On the surface it seems to be a contradiction as how can someone know something before knowing anything. But poetry according to Cleanth Brooks often speaks in a language of paradox. This paradox is used by the poet to strengthen the point of inequality existing in the structure of the caste system as from the moment a baby is born in this society, he/she is allotted to a caste and as this child starts growing, the way he/she is looked at or spoken to will be on the basis of his/her caste. The poem then goes on to elaborate this process of being looked at and being treated through violent gestures of people belonging to the upper caste:

The Patil had kicked my father,
Cursed my mother.
They did not even raise their heads.
But I felt this 'caste' in my heart (Ibid).

This is a classic case of caste socialization. But what do I mean by caste socialization? Socialization is the process by which a child socializes or acquaints himself or herself to the society within which he/she is born into. This socialization can also be internal and external. Internal in the sense how society looks at home and external in the sense that how society is structured outside the home. So, when this child observes according to this poem "Caste" by Waman Nimbalkar that his mother is being verbally abused while his father is being physically abused and both of them are tolerating this with their heads bowed down, the child then internalizes this process of violence being meted down onto Dalit people from the upper caste who have been portrayed with the help of the signifier "Patil" in the poem. The process of caste socialization continues when the child experiences the institutional space of the school which according to Louis Althusser forms the ideological state apparatus. Waman Nimbalkar writes:

When I climbed the steps to school
Then too I knew my caste was low.

I used to sit outside, the others inside.
My skin would suddenly shiver with little thorns,
My eyes could not hold back the tears (*Ibid*).

A school is thought to be a space of learning and teaching children the methods to create a harmonious society. On the contrary we see that Brahmanical hegemony exists rampantly in schools as the poet narrates that because of his lower status he was often marginalized from the spaces of learning and he used to sit outside with melancholic emotions accompanying him. The poet uses the word thorns very dexterously as it seems to operate literally as goosebumps and figuratively as thorns of the caste system which act as impediments to a democratic space even in school. In the last stanza of the poem, Waman Nimbalkar talks about caste as a social construction which creates vilifying levels of otherization in Indian society. According to him caste is like an invisible virus which is contagiously threatening to a humane society. It is expected from the Dalits that they will not respond to humiliation but will rather tolerate this harassment with a smile on their faces – "Our Lips must smile when they cursed" (Ibid).

The next poem brings to light the theme of despair when the poet shares her state of hopelessness when caste discrimination is meted on to her from her bosom friend. The poem is named "Bosom Friend" composed by Hira Bansode. She starts the poem by saying that she was very happy that her bosom friend had come to dine at her house. She was not only happy that her friend came to dine but also because she thought that her friend had come by erasing the traditions of the inequal caste system by forgetting her caste identity:

Today you came over to dinner for the first time
You not only came, you forgot your caste and came
Usually women don't forget that tradition of inequality
But you came with a mind large as the sky to my pocket size house
(Anand & Zelliot 27)

The poet at first seems to be very happy because her friend has "ripped out all those caste things" (Ibid) and she thought that finally the bridge of equality could be created. Unfortunately, things take a different turn and her desire of equality even in her friend's attitude meets with the sharp thrust of the caste system. Here we see a structural difference in food habits. Upper caste people are habituated to serving food in a particular way which is very different from most of the poverty-stricken Dalits who are content only in having food. The poet initially compared herself to Shabari and arranged the food on the plate until it met with revocation from the guest. Hence the poet locates this in the lines:

But the moment you looked at the plate, your face changed

With a little smirk you said Oh My – Do you serve chutney – koshimbir this way?
You still don't know how to serve food Truly, you folk will never improve (Ibid)

By just the "little smirk", the friend creates a sense of otherness on the basis of difference in the way she serves food. But democracy means plurality and a sense of inclusion. By these gestures we will see that a casteist democracy would be an oxymoron as exclusion of people can never be the mantra of a democratic society. This poem is precisely a narration of this exclusion through gestures and speeches. The despair in the poetic voice can be noted when she writes – "I was ashamed, really ashamed/ My hand which had just touched the sky was knocked down" (Ibid). The tirade of humiliation doesn't stop there as her friend is flummoxed because she was not served buttermilk or yogurt with the last course of rice. The poet lets us know about the sharp contrast of the upper caste's lifestyle and Dalit lifestyle by harping on this point. Whereas the upper caste people are acclimatized to eating healthy and living lavishly the poet remarks that:

> You know, in my childhood we didn't even have milk for tea
> Much less yogurt or buttermilk
> My mother cooked on sawdust she brought from the
> Lumberyard wiping away the smoke from her eyes
> Every once in a while we might get garlic chutney or coarse bread
> Otherwise we just ate bread crumbled in water (Ibid 28).

So, on one hand we see the upper caste woman demand yogurt as a necessity whereas the same yogurt or buttermilk for a Dalit would mean a dream or luxury. The poet ends the poem by saying that her tongue had never tasted the "halva" or "basundi" and hence highlighting the caste inequality existing within the essence of Indian social structure. We also note the tone of despair, loss of hope for an inclusivist friendship and a development of anger when she vehemently asks her friend:

> Today the arrangement of food on your plate was not properly ordered
> Are you going to tell me what mistakes I made?
> Are you going to tell me my mistakes? (Ibid 29).

Apparently, it would seem that the poet is humbly asking the upper caste friend, if one may call her that, what her mistakes were and how that can be rectified. But if we concentrate on the words "you" and "me" we will notice that the reiteration of these words in consecutive lines is rather like a development of anger that comes from despair. With this anger in mind, I would like to highlight an aggressive expression of anger which can be observed in the poem by Keshav Meshram with the notorious title "One day I cursed that Mother-Fucker God". Before understanding the reason of such a disparaging title, one must comprehend the history behind abusive language. Interestingly, Leon Trotsky in his essay "The Struggle for Cultured Speech" contained in his book *Problems of Everyday Life* had noted that "abusive language and swearing are a legacy of slavery, humiliation and disrespect for human dignity – one's own and that of other people" (Trotsky 65). He further wrote that "swearing in the lower depths was the result of despair, embitterment and above all, slavery without hope, without escape. The swearing of the upper classes, on the other hand, the swearing that came out of the throats of the gentry, the authorities, was the outcome of class rule, slaveowner's pride, unshakable power" (Ibid 66). This theory as propounded by Trotsky can be relevantly applicable to the deplorable condition of Dalits. In this poem the swearing is directed to the concept of a benevolent God who is believed to be the creator. Since the realistic conditions of the Dalit do not match the fictional narrative of God, the Dalit speaker in this poem curses the object of the belief system which was a result (if one uses Trotsky's theory) of despair and embitterment with the caste system. In this poem, the poet Keshav Meshram also indicts the University system where scholars attend many conferences on Dalit emancipation but majority participate in those conferences and seminars for the advancement of their personal careers rather than organize struggles which would pave the way for annihilating caste. He writes:

> The University Buildings shuddered and sank waist-deep.
> All at once, scholars began doing research
> Into what makes people angry.
> They sat in their big rooms fragrant with incense,
> Their bellies full of food,
> and debated (Anand & Zelliot 117).

This is a scathing criticism on careerist scholars who dwell more in air-conditioned seminar halls and debate about the plight of Dalits rather than fight for the annihilation of the caste system from the grassroot level. The phrase "rooms fragrant with incense" is a stark opposition to slum houses where many Dalits live and "bellies full of food" are also a marked opposition to the malnutritional reality of Dalits. A data produced by National Family Health Survey analyzes that 53.6% Dalit children are malnourished. The anger of the poet keeps mounting and he writes:

> I cursed him, I cursed him again.
> Whipping him with words, I said
> "Bastard!
> Would you chop a whole cart of wood
> for a single piece of bread?
> Would you wipe the sweat from your bony body
> With your mother's ragged sari?
> Would you wear out your brothers and sisters
> for your father's fix?
> Would you work as a pimp
> to keep him in booze? (Ibid 118).

Throughout the entire length of these lines, the poet expresses economic sufferings when he narrates the hard physical tasks he needs to do just for a piece of bread and then goes on to talk about his family problems thus indicating that both at home and in the world the Dalit is socially and psychologically oppressed. The curse that he hurls at God must be analyzed as a tremendously oppressed person venting his anger at society and directing this horrifying realism to a fictional entity.

Conclusion

Hence, it is evident that the Dalit problem in India is a huge sore in the scope of democracy in India. The systematic exclusion of a huge population of people and their humiliation and harassment almost on a daily basis can create social marginalization along with psychological despair and project itself as anger. The poems from the selected texts of the aforementioned writers prove this point vehemently. The violence that we see for example in above poems can be identified as what Slavoj Zizek, the Slovenian philosopher locates as subjective violence. He notes:

> Subjective violence is just the most visible portion of a triumvirate that also includes two objective kinds of violence. First there is a 'symbolic' violence embodied in language and its forms, what Heidegger would call 'our house of being'. As we shall see later this violence is not only at work in the obvious – and extensively studied – cases of incitement and of the relations of social domination reproduced in our habitual speech forms: there is a more fundamental form of violence still that pertains to language as such, to its imposition of a certain universe of a meaning. Second, there is what I call 'systemic' violence, or the often-catastrophic consequences of the smooth functioning of our economic and political systems (Zizek 1).

There is nothing called natural language but there exists naturalized or normalized language. Language of the upper castes are tainted with social distancing towards the people who are outside the caste system, the Dalits. This is what Hira Bansode underlines in her poem. They are known to be bosom friends, their language isn't independent from the caste structure and although it might seem that the person is only trying to suggest some ameliorations in their food habits, even food becomes a cog in the wheel of the economic structure as Dalits are not accustomed to the lavish yogurt which the people stratified in the higher layer are habituated with. Universities also perform a similar effect in Keshav Mesram's poem where scholars interpret reasons of anger and stop there rather than trying to annihilate the conditions of political economy which give rise to and maintain in a very organized way "systemic" violence as seen by Zizek, in this case which is the preservation of the caste hierarchy.

Works Cited

Anand, Mulk Raj and Eleanor Zelliot. *An Anthology of Dalit Literature*. Gyan Publishing House, 2018.

Mukherjee, Dibyajit. *Amiri Baraka: Art and Struggle*. Power Publishers, 2015.

Guru, Gopal. *Humiliation: Claims and Context*. Oxford University Press 2011.

Trotsky, Leon. *Problems of Everyday Life*. Pathfinder Press, 2020.

Zizek, Slavoj. *Violence*. Profile Books Ltd, 2009.

Author's Bio note

Mr. Dibyajit Mukherjee is currently teaching as an Assistant Professor in English at Prabhat Kumar College in West Bengal and is also a doctoral research scholar at Rabindra Bharati University. He is a gold medalist graduate from Calcutta University and is the author of three books.

5

The Gendered Subaltern: Exploration of Women's Psyche in Shashi Deshpande's *The Intrusion and Other Stories*

Beulah E.

Abstract

Shashi Deshpande is among the most important voices in Indian Writing in English. In her career spanning four decades, she has written novels, short stories, children's books, essay collections and more. Her writings have the force and vigor that opened up closed worlds. She shows great sensitivity to women's feelings and her place in society and lays bare bitter truths through her uncompromising writings. She realistically portrays how women are treated as subalterns in the Indian patriarchal social structure. As a subaltern they are subjugated and forced to stay in the margins in the social and familial domains. The male-dominated women in India at the margins of a patriarchal society are the centre of her writings. This article examines three stories from Deshpande's *The Intrusion and Other Stories* from a subaltern perspective. It focuses on the psyche of Indian women, who are constantly faced with gender oppression and inequality in their marital life, yet striving to sustain and articulate resistance.

Keywords: Dominance; subaltern; subservient; suppressed; monotonous; assertive; injustice

Introduction

Women assume multiple roles as a mother, daughter, sister and wife and all their relationships seem inevitable without men. Indian society being largely male dominated and conservative, women are bound to live up to the expectations of men. An Indian woman is often marginalized, repressed and silenced and hence remains a subaltern. Decisions are primarily taken by the male and women have to stay resigned to their subordinate roles. Among many writers who have raised their voice in support of women, Shashi Deshpande stands tall and prominent. *The Intrusion and Other Stories* was first published in 1993. It shows both women who are subservient and women who are assertive. Shashi Deshpande makes a deep probe into the psyche of her female characters. In each of the stories, the women characters are emotionally marginalized and oppressed by their husbands and other family members. Deshpande voices the struggles and frustrations of the Indian middle class women. She attempts to delve deep into the inner psyche of the modern women who are subjugated and suppressed by the male. The women in her stories are unable to express their thoughts and feelings freely as they are muted by the rules and restrictions of the male hegemony. An endeavor has been made in the present chapter to examine the feelings and emotions of three of the women protagonists in the story collection.

The First Lady

A woman in India is not treated equal to man in any sphere of social life. For ages, she has been pushed to the margins, suppressed and denied a space of her own. She has always been expected to act according to the male authority. Deshpande is grimly mindful of the predicament and the pain of the Indian women. A careful investigation of her stories manifests that her women protagonists despite being blameless, have been subject to male domination and yielding to their desires. A woman becomes a doll in the hands of a man who is indifferent to her emotions and desires. Educated or illiterate, employed or a homemaker, her status and position have remained practically unaltered. She is ruled by her father, spouse and children in turns, and she is expected to dance to their tune.

The First Lady is the first story in the collection depicting the plight of a woman who had married a political leader. Her marriage to him was her own choice in admiration of his Gandhian ideals but shockingly her hopes of a joyful life are shattered. Her wedded life becomes mechanical and meaningless. She had to comply with her husband's wish and be present at public events and too soon she is reduced to a puppet. Her comfort zone at her parent's home remains a thing of the past about which she can never ever dream of. She becomes weary and frustrated of the boring routine but eventually resigns herself to her lot. Her life is one of pretence and artificiality and she is never her own self. Shashi Deshpande in a talk states: "The good woman – whether she is the wife, mother, sister or daughter-in-law doesn't matter – is always so selfless that she negates herself to the point of extinction" (Deshpande 1997). She endures the compulsion to be in public glare and learns to respond mechanically to the smiles around. She exclaims in exasperation, "What is it after all, but a performance that we go through? All that we need are the correct gestures…a smile, a faint inclination of the head, folded hands, the right word for the right person" (TFL 2).

The woman protagonist learns the art of public conduct from her husband, a seasoned politician. Whenever he declared that he was ready to serve the people as long as he lived, she found his statement false and hollow, nevertheless, "she had some compunction about destroying his illusions about himself especially the one that he was indispensable and powerful. She had said nothing" (TFL 3). Her presence in public occasions turns out to be dull and formal that she becomes unaware of the event for which she was called for. The magazines called her "The First Lady" which makes little sense to her as she earns it at the expense of smothering her innermost desires and by sacrificing herself. Indeed, her title merely serves as a constant reminder that she exists at the margins of society and in the shadow of her husband. To her, keeping up appearance is quite an ordeal, yet she had to, for the sake of her husband. She heaves a sigh of relief whenever her role as a guest of honor is over. "Thank God that's over. Another boring function done with" (TFL 8).

The biggest injustice is inflicted on her when her husband announces his wish to follow celibacy. As for him giving birth is the prime objective of marrying and since they have had three children already, there is no need for a bodily relationship. He states, "The purpose of sex is procreation. And since we don't intend to have any more children…" (TFL 7). She realizes that "the passionate and dedicated face she had fallen in love with was incapable of loving another human being" (TFL 6). Yet, she agrees, since self-denial is something that she had learnt to accept and had a long time back succumbed to his whims and fancies without regret. To quote Ruth Sherry, "There has been a general tendency to assume that 'important' activities are those, which occur in the public sphere while private feelings are less important, of concern only to the individuals involved" (Sherry 6). The wife easily compromises her individuality and readily grants her husband 'a kind of perverse satisfaction in denying oneself pleasure, a kind of hysterical urge for self-denial...' (TFL 7) Her husband's decision to abstain from sexual relationship deprives her of marital bliss and makes her long for physical touch by her husband's most devoted disciple. The husband treats his wife as a static, inanimate thing and not as a fellow human made of flesh and blood. He limits her femininity to the level of a reproductive machine. The woman sacrifices her identity to be a part of her husband's active social life. Her willful subjectivity drives her to accept the subaltern status. The story thus narrates the painful loss of self and sense of disorientation experienced by a woman after becoming a wife of an unfeeling celebrity.

Why a Robin?

Mother-daughter relationship takes up a significant place in Deshpande's fiction. Deshpande doesn't equate mother with a goddess, rather she renders her with human qualities, longing for love and affection from her own family members. When a mother is denied the recognition and acceptance that is due to her and given a subordinate position, she develops a feeling of insecurity. Sometimes it so happens that even the daughter takes side with the father and ignores the mother. The father is considered 'the know all' person and the mother, a dim-wit. This bias and lovelessness pushes her to the periphery playing havoc on her psyche. Though her psyche is tormented on account of the unfavorable domestic milieu, she nevertheless perseveres and stays strong and stable.

The story *Why a Robin* portrays the strained relationship between a mother and a daughter. The daughter has poor regard for the mother. She considers her as ignorant and incompetent. When she has to write a composition on the small red breasted Robin, she feels her mother incapable to help and therefore seeks the assistance of her father. According to her, it is her father who knows everything and her mother knows nothing beyond the household chores. When her mother offers to help her to write about a peacock with which she is familiar, she retorts angrily, "We can't choose the subject ourselves. You don't understand. You don't know anything" (WAR 10). Sadly, even a daughter discredits a mother as a father does. The father being the bread-winner is assumed to be superior and the stay-at-home mother pales into insignificance. She is totally neglected and made to feel like a stranger in her own house. Whenever she wanted to ask anything to her husband, she anticipates the response that she would get from him, "But I know he would walk out on me the way the child has, irritated, impatient, but not angry. He is rarely moved to anger. But his silences, more eloquent than any anger, freeze me" (WAR 10). Both the husband and daughter treat her with indifference but she endures it all with an admirable composure.

It is a pity to see the mother yearning to connect with her daughter in vain. She longs to be loved, valued and needed. She longs to fondle her daughter but she is scared of being rebuffed. She confesses sadly, "I know she won't respond. I don't have the key to open up this beautiful child, though she is mine. I don't have the key to her father, either. It is as if I am, in my own house, confronted with two closed rooms. I am condemned to sit outside and gaze helplessly at the closed doors" (WAR 11). The two closed rooms serve as metaphors of her husband and her daughter, representing the poor relationship between her and her family.

The mother recollects how as a child she used to go to the temple with her grandmother in delightful anticipation of seeing peacocks. She had collected peacock feathers which she now wishes to show her daughter but fears that she would not share in her excitement. Her inability to connect with her daughter is unbearable to her. Her place at home is one of an outsider. She is treated with indifference by her husband's family too who think she is beneath their status. Yet she learns to resign to her lot and persevere. She balances multiple roles in the family.

> Sometimes I think we are all chameleons. We change colour, become different beings with different people. With my servants I am authoritative, with my parents, irresponsible, happy-go-lucky, but with my husband and child I am foolish, stupid, inarticulate. When I am with them, I become dull and brown – no not even that. I lose colour completely. And with his family too. They cannot never forget that he married beneath him. Neither can I. Before they visit us, I take endless trouble to tidy the house. But it remains dull, dead. Till he, or the child does something. A small touch and the house looks different. I slog in the kitchen for his family: I must

> impress them showing them he is well looked after. They sit at the table carelessly eating the food I have prepared and talk of many things ignoring me. The talk flows above and around me, leaving me untouched. An outsider in my own home (WAR 11-12).

The mother wonders if she is responsible for locking herself in. She feels guilty of being a failure as a wife and a mother. She thinks that she has nothing in common with her brilliant and beautiful daughter. She is filled with grief when she sees her daughter eagerly listening to her father as he explains about a robin. Her desperation being an outsider and her anguish about her ignorance is deeply felt when she says, "The reading lamp casts a halo of light around their glowing faces but the light does not reach the corner where I am sitting" (WAR 12). She is confused as to what use she was to the family other than taking care of the routine tasks. She wonders how long she has to live a life of drudgery and self-abnegation just to keep on going. Tong rightly points out that, "sometimes women play their roles not so much because they want to, as because they have to survive economically and psychologically. Virtually all women engage in the feminine role playing" (Tong 208).

Eventually things change for the better. It is the daughter's attaining puberty that finally connects the mother and the daughter. As a muffled cry is heard from the daughter's room on a cold night, the mother for a moment hesitates to intrude as the child may want her father. But the mother realizes that it was her turn now to reach out to her daughter and a strong conviction grows in her that a bond is after all possible and that it is for her to create something out of nothing. A sudden positivity and hope fills her and she takes the first step forward to break the ice. "Bridges have to be built. They do not come out of nothing, they have to be created" (WAR 14). The daughter, on the brink of womanhood responds to her mother's love and a tender understanding and intimacy develops. The mother finds herself gaining ground by sharing a secret of her daughter, a secret that her knowledgeable husband did not know much about. They talk about how the mother felt about her first period when she was young, about the peacock, and about the beautiful grandmother of the mother. After a night of whispering, the mother is filled with warmth and contentment as she puts her daughter to bed. "I talk to her gently, trying to make her feel it is natural, a part of growing up, something to be welcomed, accepted" (WAR 15). The daughter feels reassured and the mother could see that the look of bewilderment is gone from her eyes.

Deshpande makes it clear that no matter how much a daughter loves and adores a father, it is the mother who can touch the intimate chord of her daughter's heart and women are capable of rising from insignificance if they stay determined. Her subaltern position is likely to change if she refuses to obliterate her role in the family. Though seemingly weak and helpless, she reaches out and connects to the daughter instead of letting herself wallow in self-pity. She transforms from a 'submissive' to a 'smart' woman. Therein lies her greatness.

The Intrusion

Shashi Deshpande shows how women in the name of tradition are grievously taken for granted. Her protagonists enter into marriage with the fond hopes of friendship, mutual love and sharing. Contrary to their expectations, soon after marriage they become their husband's lawful property and victims of lust. They are denied right over their own body and fall prey to forceful sex. Marriage turns out to be a mortifying and crude experience when a husband gives no consideration for his wife's feelings. There is no golden hour to let the wife develop an emotional bond and intimacy with him. Her body is forcibly invaded without taking her consent which is an act of violence. Her initial revolt ends up in accepting the inevitable.

In the story *The Intrusion*, the emotional discomfort of a woman after her marriage is explored. The woman comes with her husband for a honey moon to a sea facing resort. Although wedded, her husband is a total stranger and hence she feels apprehensive about connecting with him physically. She feels no excitement or pleasurable tinge within her typical of a newlywed. Unaware of her discomfiture and in anticipation of a sexual union, the husband tries to strike up a conversation.

> He suddenly burst into speech, telling me how fortunate he was to get this place for our honeymoon. What luck, he said, that one of the top executives, who was to have come here, had cancelled his visit at the last minute, so that we were here all by ourselves. 'Complete privacy', he smiled, emphasizing the words and I felt suddenly, completely sickened. He went on, unaware of my feelings, telling me it was only the lucky few who could get this place to stay (IT 36).

The woman desperately wishes that she was back to the comfort of her home. She now looks back at her memories before she got married. The marriage had been an arranged one and her parents had been joyous over their daughter being accepted by the groom's family. She recalls the conversation between the two families. No one asked her for her opinion for it had been taken for granted. She remembers how a few days prior to the wedding she had gone to her father stricken with doubts about adapting to a new environment. He had answered in shock, "What will you do then? What will I do? (TI 37). It is obvious that in the traditional Hindu family, the husband is the protector, master and hence the superior figure and the wife's duty by all means is to serve him faithfully. Such subordination is what is expected of a woman and the notion of a modern woman is a taboo. Her father's words, "I have two more daughters to be married" (TI 37) silence her. Deshpande brings to light the fact that a woman has to marry just to ease her family of a burden and her innermost desires are never taken into account.

The woman finds herself helpless and uneasy in her husband's presence. The sexual advances of her wedded partner sicken her. She feels frigid and incapable of responding to his lustful urges. Being alone with him frightens her and she finds the situation tense and awkward. "And at present we were not friends, not acquaintances even, but only a husband and a wife" (TI 38). Like a child, she longs to go out to wet her toes in the sand, pick up shells and sit on the rocks and let the waves touch her bare legs. His secret glances embarrass her and she feels sick from within. Further, the sight of the beds made for their first night together to make them truly husband and wife makes her home sick.

> I thought with a wistful pang of my own narrow bed at home and of how I would lie on it, curled into a comfortable ball, reading into the late hours of the night. I felt a constriction in my throat, a longing for all the things I had left behind me forever: a melancholy that always assails one when away from home at this time, neither day nor night (IT 38).

The intrusion into her privacy had been too forceful, sudden and insulting. Her feelings were disregarded. She wished to become well acquainted and know all about him. She wanted to tell him her fears and the way she felt about marriage. She wished to sit the whole night and talk to him enjoying the beautiful environment.

> I want to know all about you, I wanted to say. What you think, what you feel and why you agreed to marry me? And what did you think of as we went through all those ceremonies together, and do you like the things I do and will we laugh together at the same jokes, enjoy the same books? And there were all those fears crouching in me – would his breath smell, and were his feet huge and dirty with uncut toenails, and did he chew his food noisily and belch after meals? I wanted to tell him how shy and frightened I was about exposing the mysteries of my body to him and how homesick I was for my mother's face, my father's laughter and my sisters' chatter (TI 40).

However, everything happens contrary to her expectations. As she refuses to respond to his desires, she is forcibly molested while at sleep. On waking up she feels hurt and humiliated at the violation into her privacy, yet she could do nothing. Deshpande criticizes the tradition that gives the husband the right to satisfy his sexual urge irrespective of his wife's willingness. This is the cause of crimes like marital rape. As Indrani Jaisingh opines: "It is assumed that by marrying a man, a woman has given her consent to sexual intercourse with her husband at any time. Thus, even if he forces himself on her, he is not committing an offence as her consent is assumed" (qtd. in Trivedi 147).

Though Indian tradition doesn't recognize marital rape, rape within marriage becomes the ultimate means by which a husband asserts ownership over his wife. Deshpande shows how sexual liberties are not granted but taken. Marriage gives the husband the license to make the wife his possession which he can rightfully manipulate. The uneasiness of women in the traditional role, which expects her to be patience personified, subservient and always in earnest to make sacrifices for the happiness of her family is well brought out by the author.

Conclusion

Through her short stories, Shashi Deshpande endeavors to represent the multi-dimensional facets of the female psyche trapped within domestic space. She drives home the fact that women play a subaltern role in the Indian household. They know that there can be no running away from familial responsibilities. The unnamed women protagonists in the three stories are forced to endure 'a not so pleasant' world. They grapple with the challenges of having to negate their selves for the sake of their families. Their marriage had driven them to a subaltern position, one of surrender and self-abnegation. They are compelled to make readjustments to keep their identity intact. Tolerance and lack of protest are the typical traits in them. Deshpande had brilliantly explored the female psyche and the suppressed feelings and frustration of women within the family set up. At the same time, the protagonists of the stories have the ability to compromise, accept their lot with poise. She makes it clear that a 'house' becomes a "home' only in the hands of a woman. Despite her subaltern status, her role in the family is significant and commendable.

Works Cited

Deshpande, Shashi. *The Intrusion and Other Stories.* Penguin Books, 1993.

Deshpande, Shashi. a talk on *The Indian Woman – Stereotypes, Images and Realities*, 30 Oct.1997, Zurich, under the auspices of The Swiss Indian Society Zurich and The Volker Kundemuseum der Universitat, Zurich.

Tong, Rosemarie. *Feminist Thought.* Routledge, 1993.

Trivedi, Nisha. "Treatment of Love, Marriage and Sex in *The Binding Vine.*". *The Fiction of Shashi Deshpande.* Ed. R.S. Pathak. Prestige Books, 1998. 144-49.

Sherry, Ruth. *Studying Women's Writing: An Introduction.* Edward Arnold, 1988, 6.

Author's Bio-note

Beulah E works as an Assistant Professor at the PG and Research Department of English, Government Arts College (Autonomous), Kumbakonam, Tamil Nadu. She has 13 years of experience teaching English at UG & PG level. Indian Writing in English and Environmental Literature are her areas of interest.

6

The Unexplored Cultural Displacement of Subaltern Adivasis in *The Coffer Dam* and in *The Strange Case of Billy Biswas*

Manoj S. Madavi

Abstract

The fifth world of Indigenous Literary writing is now becoming an unavoidable discourse in the contemporary world of creative writing. The main responsibility of mainstream Indian English writers is to establish these new voices of subaltern and marginality of Indigenous people's crave for identity and existence in the mainstream literary canon. Postcolonial literature in India has given voices to the marginal world of women and Dalit writings but it kept on a purposeful silence on Adivasi lives and their struggle for existence both in colonial and postcolonial Indian mainstream society. This research paper aims to represent the unexplored subaltern and marginal aspect of Indigenous Adivasi world as reflected in the novel *The Coffer Dam* and in *The Strange Case of Billy Biswas*.The research paper explains the triple colonization of the Adivasis community in India through the hands of the White power of British, stereotype caste structure and gender superiority of other races over the Adivasis community, particularly over Adivasis women. Though we find a great aesthetic literary value in both novels this article makes clear that the disparity, disillusionment and disorientation of Adivasi has been marginalized and proper representation of Adivasi as subaltern does not take real appearance through these novels.

Keywords: Imperialism, Hegemony, Postcolonialism, Post-truth, Subjugation, Subaltern.

An Introduction to Postcolonial Indian English Novel Writing

Postcolonial literature across the globe shows the freedom of expression of the native countries from the clutches of white power imperialism. Creative literature writing which blooms and produces after emancipation from the corporate British power came to be known as Commonwealth literature or the literature of the third world. The fifth world of Indigenous Literary writing is now becoming an unavoidable discourse in the contemporary world of creative writing. The main responsibility of mainstream Indian English writers is to establish these new voices of subaltern and marginality of Indigenous people's crave for identity and existence in the mainstream literary canon.

Postcolonial literature in India has given voices to the marginal world of women and Dalit writings but it kept on a purposeful silence on Adivasi lives and their struggle for existence both in colonial and postcolonial Indian mainstream society. This research paper aims to represent the unexplored subaltern and marginal aspect of Indigenous Adivasi world as reflected in the novel *The Coffer Dam* and in *The Strange Case of Billy Biswas*. Though we find a great aesthetic literary value in both novels this article makes clear that the disparity, disillusionment and disorientation of Adivasi have marginalized and proper representation of Adivasi as subaltern does not take real appearance through these novels. Postcolonial literature which was written in India deals with the east-west encounter, the struggle for freedom, and the subjugation of women in patriarchy and gender discrimination.

Postcolonial literature across the globe shows the subaltern aspect of identities of native groups which was once smothered by British imperialism and now tried to dominate by the Americanization of the world. During and after Indian Independence postcolonial marginal sensibilities of the Indian English creative writing was spread over the European literary world. Bhabhani Bhattacharya, Mulkraj Anand, R.K.Narayan and Manohar Malgonkar dealt with partition trauma, the theme of poverty, draughting situation in India also represented through many novelists in postcolonial writing of India. After the nineteen seventies, Manju Kapur, Anita Desai, Nayantara Sehgal dealt with the subjugation of women, patriarchy and gender dominance of women in Indian social stratification. Indian English women writing particularly fiction became prime focus in subaltern literature and studies. Women novelists in India were particular about the female marginalization in a male-dominated society and they exposed this through free expression of womanhood by introducing rebellious characters with their quest for self and identity. The originality of the expression in the Indian English writing can be noticed through the following positive notes:

> "Indian English Literature began as an interesting byproduct of an eventful encounter in the late eighteenth century between a vigorous and enterprising Britain and a stagnant and chaotic India and now nearly two hundred years old. It is no part of English, American, or Australian Literature. It is legitimately a part of Indian Literature since its difference is the expression in it of an Indian ethos" (Naik 1).

Adivasis as Subaltern and Voiceless in *The Coffer Dam*

The magnificent novel *The Coffer Dam* of Kamala Markandeya was published in 1969 and the literature readers for the first time noticed the issue of displacement and disparity of Adivasi life in mainstream literature writing. The novel deals with the ethnic and racial superiority feeling of the white man over indigenous Adivasi culture. The novel *The Coffer Dam* also dealt with external as well as internal colonialism of the Adivasi people in India. Does this novel put a big question before the literature readers of what to choose between development or justice? Bashiam is an educated Adivasi engineer, having his marvelous remarkable engineering skill; he gets ugly racial comments and hateful casteistbehavior. Regarding racial discrimination and white supremacy over indigenous people in this novel, A.K.Chaturvedi points out; "To Clinton, Bashiam despite being an educated and skilled technician is a junglywallah having a low status because of his roots in anAdivasi community to which he is now a stranger because of his growing affinity with the British staff" (Chaturvedi 64).

The novelist has revived romanticism in the novel through the characters like Helen and Clinton. A sophisticated feudal way of living life is explained by the novelist but she could give much focus on the issue of displacement of Adivasis people which is the reality of Indian territory for the last many decades. The Adivasi community in India is a much distorted and displaced community since pre-independence to the globalization of India. The issues and basic problems of food, shelter, forest, natural resources, identity and existence are much older but still, they are a subaltern and marginalized community in the history of the literature of India. Internal disorientation of subjugated communities is the dark phase of Indian social reality. Adivasis-Dalits have experienced the horror and injustice of this caste-race discrimination in the past but the contemporary situation is not the positive one in this regard. These communities still look upon as inferior to mainstream hegemonic society. The novelist does not speak about the external hegemony and internal casteistbehavior of mainstream characters. Mr. Das and Mr. Krishan seem slaves of orthodox social stratification where Adivasis seems touched between the eastern theory of untouchability including gender bias and western racial-and-ethnic superiority theory. The native indigenous souls in this novel seem broken with identities that are twice and thrice colonized. A.K.Chaturvedi aptly remarks:

> "Bashiam is called, as junglywalah only he belongs to tribes that symbolize the severe retardation of its civilization. The poor Adivasis laborer who rattled around like peas in a tin is seduced by our own Indian Mr. Krishan and Mr.Das" (Chaturvedi 64).

Internal Disorientation of Subaltern Adivasis in *The Strange Case of Billy Biswas*

The Strange Case of Billy Biswas is the utopia of the modern world. The aesthetic values in this novel are much appreciating. The novel was written by Arun Joshi in 1971. When one reads the novel with a subaltern point of view it can be noticed that the Adivasis are shown as stereotype as they are in films and cartoons. An irresponsible picture of the Adivasi culture is circulated throughout the novel. It seems that novelist has nothing to do with the Adivasis history of revolt and the long list of the Adivasis warriors who got to martyrdom. The Adivasi community in India was the first to oppose the land encroachments and tax revenue of the British East India Company. Adivasi in every part of India whether they were from Odisha, Maharashtra, Bengal, Rajasthan, Telangana, or Kerala, everywhere they have fought against the mighty British empire of Colonialism with barefooted and with their bow-arrows. Such gigantic history must be the part of literature writing but the revolt of Adivasi warrior Tilka Manzi, Birsa Munda, Gundadhur Dhurva and Kumral Bhimu from Telangana is still subaltern and barely exist in the mainstream literature of India. There is nothing like this revolutionary content in the novel written by Arun Joshi about the Adivasi community of Satpuda hills of Madhya Pradesh. Santhal Hool was registered as the massive revolt against the British power including the local landlords in India which was discussed by Carl Marx in his notes on Indian history. He considered it as the people's revolt against the economic disparity and poverty maintain by corporate imperialism. During the colonial period of 1855. *"Santhal Hool" took* place for Adivasi rights on forests and natural resources. Thousands of Santhal were slaughtered during this Hool. This seems very surprising that Arun Joshi doesn't show any acquaintance with this great bravery of 'Adivasidom', their fights against imperialism. Only romanticism, self-indulgence comes from his narration. About the bravery of Santhal Adivasi, famous critic Peter Anderson comments;

> "The Santhal, a major Adivasis group of India is known for their Hool, an important rebellion led by charismatic heroes in 1855 and analyzed by subaltern historians as conveying political and intellectual concerns, such as peasant's consciousness, pertinent to postcolonial India. The Santhal – the marginalized people experienced colonial modernity but succeeded in negotiating for themselves the potential of national decolonization" (Anderson 1).

Billy Biswas the main character in the novel is shown as subaltern but the fact is, the novelist has missed the outlook to give voice to express the subaltern consciousness of poor Dhuniya and Bilasia who represented the Adivasis community with all their misfortune. Arun Joshi has taken much effort to present the introspective life of Billy. Throughout the novel, his character runs with the same quality of self-indulgence. Finally, he becomes the victim of the bullet of police while combing operation through the jungle. Billy wins the hearts of the readers and critics but Adivasis life, their pangs of suffering, emotional turmoil of Adivasis lady Bilasia, Old Dhunia and his craving for a Adivasis identity all remain in darkness. *The Strange Case of Billy Biswas* presents only one side of materialistic, sophisticated, hegemonic and westernized elite values but does not touch the nativity, broken identity, distorted history and indigenous values of first nation people. Observation of Billy about Adivasis life during the seventies seems full of romanticization and much irrelevant. His perceptions about Adivasis history and livelihood seem unauthentic when he opines:

> "Nobody is interested here in the prize of food, grain or new seeds, roads or elections and the stuff like that. We talk of the supernatural, violent death, trees, earth, rain, storms, river, forests, dance, singing, and we talk a lot about women and sex" (83).
> What kept us happy, suppose were the same things that have kept all primitive happy through the ages: the forest the rainbow, the liquor from mahua, an occasional feast,

a lot of dancing and lovemaking and more than anything else, no ambition, none at all" (Joshi 86).

As stated earlier, Indian English Novel writing was very rebellious to give free expression to the marginal world of Indian women in postcolonial literature but this vigor and enthusiasm have not shown by the celebrated women novelist of India regarding the representation and the characterization of the Adivasis lady Bilasia her longings of the single life. Her divorced life and struggle for livelihood have not taken a serious appearance in the novel. This shows the hegemonic approach of the mainstream women as well as male writers towards the grave issues of the women in the Adivasis community. Billy's erotic thought and daydreaming about Bilasia is enough to claim him as a 'lustful' still novel adores him as the tortured soul on earth. It seems strange how can this novel be considered as 'Universal Myth of Primitivism'. Billy's derogative thought process about Adivasis Bilasia can be noticed through the following statements;

> "I started to knot and all the time I was thinking of Bilasia, the fever rising within me once and my chest beginning to chock. Finally stopped clutching the ball in my hands as though it were a limb of Bilasia, her head, her breast. (07).What do you think going to happen to you? Are you going to run away with Bilasia? May all you want is to get her into bed? Anyway, do you think you have survived more than a day in this wilderness even with the help of ten Bilasia" (Joshi 95).

Adivasis social exclusion, their wait and watch situation for assimilation in the mainstream, their double subjugation and triple disposition, cultural disorientation, struggle for existence find no proper upliftment and representation in both the novel though both the novel were written when Adivasis came to know very well, the advantages and disadvantages of politics of power and communal pedagogy. Social, economic issues of Adivasis were checked during this period but the novelist claims them as superstitious because they watched Billy speaking with the man-eater of that jungle. Mainstream society has tried with their great efforts to demean the existential issues of the Adivasi community and tried to present them as the strange objects in the museum. This seems hilarious when Adivasi leader Dhunia praised Billy and finds godlike qualities in him when he comments; "A tiger has been roaming in the jungle for a week, killing our cattle. Billy Bhai went into the jungle and spoke to the tiger and the tiger went away. That was when we first came to know of his powers" (Joshi 114).

Exploring Cultural displacement of subaltern Adivasi Voices in selective Indian Regional Novel Writing

Adivasis novels dealing with the indigenous ethos and harsh realities written originally in the regional language of India like Marathi, Malayalam, Oriya and Hindi. Translated and transcreated novels from regional to English novels became widely popular because of their ground realities about imperial racial, casteist and hegemonic treatment towards Adivasis by the feudal lords and Corporates. The pang of disposition of Adivasis from their forest, land, resources and ancient heritage in the period of new globalization and neoliberal age, is so real in this translated novel that no Indian English novel matches the style, presentation, characterization and content of it. Gopinath Mohanty's novel *Ancestor* (1944), *Paraja* (1997), Narayan wrote *Kocharethi* (2011), Pratibha Roy wrote *The Primal Land* (2001), C.K. Janu wrote, *Mother Forest* (2004), Mahaswata Devi wrote, *Chotti Munda And His Arrow* (2002), Hariram Meena wrote, *When the Arrows were Heated Up* (2016) deals with Adivasis disillusionment, deculturization, deprivation from economic and forest rights and a wide gap between capitalistic-hegemonic mentality and marginal-misery of native son's of the soil. We find much difference between the understanding and observation of mainstream Indian English Novelist and writer writing in Regional languages with the factual observation about Adivasis reality in Adivasis land. Therefore famous critic Anand Mahanand, comments on the one-sided representation of Adivasis by Indian English writers from whose creative writing, alienation of Adivasis is missing. Noticed his statement:

> "Joshi fails to notice social alienation, bare existence of Adivasis in mainstream, subjugation and disposition of Adivasis and more of internal colonialism upon indigenous Adivasis life and provides an only partial view of indigenous life which is convenient and easy for the writer" (Mahanand 67).

Conclusion

Both the novels *The Coffer Dam* and *The Strange Case of Billy Biswas* could be good enough only for those who merely believe in the ideology of 'Art for Art Sake', who possibly seeks imaginative flights of romanticization and glorification. This general notion must be admitted by everyone that literary discourse about gender, caste, Adivasis, minority, Dalit will never reach their goal of strengthening community until *Established Literary Canon* will strengthen their mainstream voices for those smothered, chocked identities which stood on the threshold of *Fifth World Literature*. We must study the serious message of Gordon Brotherston to mainstream writers of the mainstream literary canon of the world and India:

> "Redefining of native myths, culture, and customs through their available oral literature is an important source of understanding and listening to the ancestral voice that instructs to find their connection with their prehistoric cultures. The consciousness of the fourth world is the result of the constant effort of aboriginal representation. The evolution of the Fourth World is in reflection with the socio-economic, literary and cultural circumstances that affected the lives of aboriginals which is needed to be explored by mainstream writers" (Brotherston 37).

Social, economic and cultural alienation of the Adivasis does not find proper presentations through these novel writings of Indian English. The voices of the subaltern Adivasis have moved from the periphery towards the center in the last five decades. Both the novels lack sympathy and authenticity while depicting Adivasis marginalization, therefore, a revisionary critical approach in literary criticism and literary discourse is necessary for the aestheticism of Indian English Fiction writings. The intensity of racial dominancy of the elite classes over the Adivasi community seems weaker in these selected Indian English Novels. Dalit and minority literature has raised the question from a Dalit – minority-centric point of view just as feminism has been studying literature through a gendered lens, in the same manner, Adivasi history, culture, problems should be observed through the spectacle of adivasidom.

Novels are cultural documents and have written on the socio-historical background of a particular discourse whether it is Tribal-Dalit or Feminist discourse. That is an expression of a writer with a particular vision to bring some positive change in the rigid norms of the society but in *Strange Case of Billy Biswas*. Billy's erotic thoughts are the sign of the demeaning to the tribal womanhood. Indian English Fiction writers still seem the byproduct of the British and American value system therefore they seem very close to corporate values denying livelihood issues and social separation of the Adivasi community in Indian society. While depicting Adivasis characterization and the socio-cultural background of Adivasis, Indian English fiction writers have exaggerated the Adivasis life, culture and traditions. The original aboriginal community with its several hardships did not figure predominantly in the novel *The Strange Case of Billy Biswas.*

Novel writing is not a mere task of storytelling but an earnest attempt to explore the subjugated culture which was unexplored earlier. This task is spontaneous as well as challenging too because for the reasons you have to break the stereotype norms of the mainstream literary canon. Disillusionment Displacement and disorientation of the Adivasi have not presented appropriately in the light of postcolonial Indian English Novels. The struggle of the Adivasis for their rights on their forest and natural resources has not been shown or even slightly discussed in the mainstream Indian English novels like *The Coffer Dam* and *The Strange Case of Billy Biswas.* Regional Adivasi novel writings are more convincing and informative about the ground realities of the Adivasis. The Adivasis life seems ethnic others in the presentation of the literature which endorses the notion of nation-narration in Indian English fiction and other literary cannons.

Both the novels *The Coffer Dam* and *The Strange Case of Billy Biswas* are slightly unresponsive in strengthening the voices of the subaltern communities and characters. Postcolonial Indian English fiction writers have neglected the threatening results of Imperialism, Neocolonization and Neoliberalism on Adivasi culture, identities and existential issues. Indian English Fiction is promoting Neoglobal, Westernize values of Imperialism leaving behind the existential issues of the common population of India. Multiculturalism and Cosmopolitanism have damaged the Indian way of humanitarian and compassionate writings about native – indigenous communities and massive marginal classes but both the novels *The Coffer*

Dam and *The Strange Case of Billy Biswas* hardly speak about this unspeakable community and their subaltern subjugated voice throughout the centuries.

Indian English fiction writing must confess this reality that ideological discourses should be the platform of creative writing for the representation of the Adivasi community in India because Adivasis are the indigenous international communities by their race, clan, language and ancient culture. They are not barbaric, junglee or history less as mainstream novels tried to depict them usually in their creative writing. Novels that are written in a particular era are the voices of cultural upbringing in that particular period. Such novel writing delineates the displaced culture and the violation of human rights therefore novel is the most popular genre in the literature to acquaint ourselves with the different cultures from different continents.

Adivasis in India and Indian literature are systematically made marginal and subaltern on having all the claim of Indigeneity on natural resources of tribal territory. The present novels are far away from this unexplored cultural displacement of the Indigenous community. The mainstream writing world in English shows the romanticization, glorification, body celebration and brutal hegemonic racial indifference towards the Adivasi community. Subjugated and the displaced world is still to explore and the voices of the subalterns for cultural justice are still waiting for the mainstream Indian English writing world to give tongue to unspeakable. Mainstream Indian English novel writers should wash out the stigma given to the Adivasi community as *Dishonors by Literary History*.

Work Cited

Anderson, Peter. *From Fire Rain to Rebellion.* New Delhi, Manohar Pub. 2011. Print.

Brotherston, Gorden. *Book of the Fourth World: Reading Native America through Their Literature.* London. Cambridge Uni. Press. 1993. Print.

Chaturvedi, A.K. *Tribals in Indian English Novel,* New Delhi. Atlantic Pub. 2008. Print.

Gavit, Najubai. Ador. *Vadodara.* Purva Prakashan. 2013. Print.

Joshi, Arun. *The Strange Case of Billy Biswas.* Delhi. Hind Pocket Book. 1971. Print.

Mahanand, Anand. *Representation of Tribal India in Fiction.* Germany. Lambert Pub. 2011. Print.

Markandeya, Kamala. *The Coffer Dam.* Delhi. Hind Pocket. 1969. Print.

Naik, M.K. *History of Indian Writing in English Literature.* New Delhi, Sahitya. Academy. 2007. Print.

7

Identity Crisis of the Ho Tribe: Misrecognition and Misinterpretation of the Community and their Culture in the Era of Globalization

Santi Ranjan Sing

Abstract

Most of the Indian tribal communities are still in the unexplored stages in terms of their culture, nature, language and scripts which are the pillars of their identity. On the other hand, the identity of some particular tribes is on the verge of extinction due to hybridity and misinterpretations of those communities. This paper seeks to examine how the Ho tribal community of eastern part of India is facing the problem regarding their identity because of the misrecognition and misinterpretations of the tribe by the outsiders as well as the census authority of India in this globalized rather glocalized era. Often these Hos are confused with the Santals and Mundas, and unfortunately, most of the time; they are mistakenly regarded as the integral part of Hinduism. This paper has an aim to clarify these confusions and simultaneously this paper attempts to explore the authentic and distinct identity of the Ho tribe and its present situation in modern India.

Keywords: Identity, hybridity, tribe, culture, Ho, Kol, subaltern

Introduction

In recent years, several researchers, writers and even administrators have expressed various views regarding the identity of the cognate branches of the Indian tribes. Naturally, there are views also about the Ho tribe of India. Some researchers argue that the Santal, Kol, Munda, Kora, and Ho are the common names of the same tribal group. While few others argue that Kol and Ho is not the same tribe and they are entirely different tribes originated from Kolarian genus or group. It is worth mentioning that the previously mentioned views about Ho tribe are not completely correct. This is how the identity of the community is being misinterpreted. This confusion can be sorted out by investigating the origin and facts regarding the further development of the Ho tribe.

Who are Hos or Kols? To find out the answer to this question, one has to go deep into the origin and meaning of the word 'Kol' and 'Ho'. The Ho people are an ethnic group of India. This group is concentrated in the state of Jharkhand, Odisha and West Bengal where they constitute around 10.5% of the Scheduled Tribes. According to *Kol Bhasar Utsa Charit* (2013) by Kartik Chandra Bawanda,

> The word 'Kol' is the distorted form of the word 'Kal' which, according to the language of this community, means 'formation' or 'collective position'. Earlier, the people of this community lived collectively in large number. And thus, the name 'Kol' is gradually been associated to this tribal community (Bawanda 22, translaton).

The word 'Ho' means 'man' i.e. the 'man' of the Kol tribe. It is mentioned in the *Ethnographic Notes on the Scheduled Tribes of West Bengal* (2003) that "the Ho is also known as Kol or LarkaKol. The name Ho is merely a contracted form of the word Hor or Man." (43). The word 'Larka' is another name of this tribe. Grierson in the chapter called 'Ho or LarkaKol' of his *Linguistic Survey of India* (1906), stated that "in Singbhum they are usually known as LarkaKol i.e. fighting Kols" (116).

The 'Ho' community has their own culture, rituals and language which are not to be confused with the culture and languages of Santals and Mundas. Though the religious views of Santals, Mundas and Hos are same, the language of Ho tribe is different from that of Santals and Mundas. They possess the "Sarna" religion. In the 2001 national census, 91% of the Hos declared that they professed "other religions and persuasions", meaning they do not consider themselves to belong to any of the major religious groups and follow their indigenous religious system called "Sarna" or "Sarnaism". Though "Sarnaism" is the religion of both Santals and Hos, there are certain differences between these two tribes. The Santals worship Marang Buru, while the Hos are the worshipers of Singbonga, the sun or the creator. The Singbonga is often called as 'Sim-bonga', as the deity is supposed to be given 'Sim' or hen as a tribute. They celebrate four major festivals which are 'MarangBonga' [Great Ritual], 'Mage Parab' in the month of Magha, 'Baa Parab', the festival of flowers and the 'HerohBonga', the sowing festival. During these festivals they enjoy the dances of various forms. Dance is important to tribal culture in general and for Ho, it is more than simply a means of entertainment. Sir John Houlton in his *Bihar: The Heart of India* (1949), has said that the songs of Ho people are generally accompanied by dances which change with the seasons. Songs and distinctly choreographed dance are integral parts of Ho culture and art.

Traditional Ho music incorporates native instruments including 'dumeng' (mandar), 'rutu' (flute), 'dama' (drum) and 'banam' (see Fig.1), a folk fiddle, symbolic of pride and culture amongst the Hos. 'Diyeng', a sort of rice-beer is brewed during the festivals. Apart from this, a traditional game called 'Sekkor' is played by the Ho tribe that identifies alertness and spirit of the tribe. The 'Sekkor' game is said to prevent drought and bring rain. Made of wood, the 'Sekkor' is shaped like a big top with an oval plane cap. Being pointed at the base, a string closely wound on it, enables the 'Sekkor' to topple on the ground during the game. The objective of the game is to hit the Sekkors of the opponent team, which are placed at the centre of the field. Played between nine or eleven people, this game identifies the spirit and swiftness of the Ho tribals. With the passage of time, this game of deftness is no longer recognized as a popular game; hence, the Tribal Cultural Society of Jharkhand has taken initiatives to bring national recognition to this forgotten game. The use of bows, arrows and axe in traditional hunting process reduced and now it is quite abolished.

Figure 1. Men of Ho Tribe Dancing Accompanied by Musical Instruments (Sing)

Though the food habits and dress code are not that distinct from the Santals and Mundas, the language and the script of their language deserve a special mention. The script of Santali language is called "OlChiki", while the script of the Ho language, Austro-Asiatic language, is known as "Warangkshiti" or "Warang Citi" (see Fig. 2). Interestingly, a few percent of Ho speakers are literate in the language of "Warang Citi", while the language is spoken by over one million people in Eastern India. "Warang Citi" is the Ho script that is scientific as well as spiritual. The script is believed to be invented by DeowanTuri in 13th century. Guru Kol Lako Bodra rediscovered it and devised it in 1939 with the intention of creating a visually distinctive script for Ho language. The script was re-invented by LakoBodra to develop the Ho language. Witten from left to right in horizontal lines, the script begins with the letter 'Ong' – the sacred syllable, the first sound of the universe. Each consonant in the script has an inherent vowel, which is usually an 'a' but sometimes it could be an 'o' or 'e'. Only a handful of natives know how to speak and write in the Ho language. Therefore, various tribal organizations have taken upon the task to guard the spectrum of Ho literature through language classes. An important addition to the Austro-Asiatic family of languages, the "Warang Citi" script is slowly being restored.

Figure 2. "Warang Citi alphabet for Ho" (Murmu)

The Ho people occupy several 'Killis' or surnames or last names which are again the marks of their identity. There are more than one hundred and seventy 'Killis' existent in the Ho community like – 'Purty', 'Birua', 'Alda', 'Tubid', 'Kuldi', 'Bandra', 'Bawanda', 'Hemrom', etc.

Misrecognition

Ho or Kol tribe is still almost unknown and neglected in India. The main reasons of this problem are the ignorance of the outsiders about the tribes, the lack of awareness among the Ho tribe of their own identity and interestingly the misinterpretation of their identity by the census authority of India since the census of 1871. Sometimes, they are confused with Santals and Mundas and often they are categorized as Hindus. The source of this confusion is the naming disorder. The Hos themselves don't know that they are called as 'Ho'. From the very beginning, they are known by the name of Kol. The Ho people of Odisha are aware of their Kol identity. It is to be mentioned here that Ho and Kol are the different names of the same tribe in different places. In Chota Nagpur plateau or more specifically in Jharkhand, this tribe is known as both Ho and Kol; while in Odisha, they are known as Kol and in West Bengal they are known as Ho. Needless to say, this tribe of Jharkhand, Odisha and West Bengal occupy the same language, rituals and culture. On the contrary, the Santals and Mundas, though they belong to the Austro-Asiatic tribal group, are different from Hos or Kols in terms of language, rituals and scripts. Walter G. Grffiths, in his book, *The Kol Tribe of Central India* (1946), has said that "this is just as true of the Munda group to which the Kols belong" (4). Again in the beginning of this book he argues:

> The tribe itself should be carefully distinguished from the Munda tribes of Chota Nagpur which are frequently called Kols in the generic sense. There is no specific kol tribe in that area, although there is a group called the LarkaKols, or Hos, famous for an insurrection in the year 1832, and a part of the district of Singhbhum is called the

> Kalhan after then mention of the specific Kol Tribe is made only in the Census Reports of the Central India Agency and that for the Central Provinces. In the united provinces the Kols are classed as an exterior caste (1).

This kind of documentation about Ho tribals is a major threat to the identity of this community. Again, an application (Ref No – AIHDA/10/10/Date-08.09.2001) to General Secretary of ICITP (New Delhi) by K. C. Naik, the secretary of All India Ho Development Association, (Rourkela, Odisha) stated:

> Sir, we would like to state that, although the government has recognized these people as 'Ho' in Bihar (Now Jharkhand), as 'Kol', 'Ho' and 'Munda' in Orissa and as 'Ho' in West Bengal, they belong to one community. There is no difference at all among Kol, Kolho, Ho and Munda people.

Explication

A clarification is needed here about the Mundas because the Mundas have their separate identity as a distinct tribal community. These statements, claiming Hos and Mundas are the same tribe, are completely false as the Kols or Hos do not belong to the Munda group. In this respect, the statements of H. H. Risley can be quoted. In his book *The Tribes and Castes of Bengal* (1891), Risley argues:

> In summing up the characters of the people have been describing, it is necessary to separate the Hos from their cognates. The circumstances under which the character of the former has been developed are different and they are, in the opinion physically and morally superior to the Mundas, Bhumij and Santals (334).

The source of fundamental meaning of the word 'Ho' is related to other Austro-Asiatic languages. The meaning of word 'Ho' is man. In Santali language (OlChiki), the meaning of the word 'Hor' is 'man'. According to P. K. Bhowmick's *Tribal Situation in West Bengal*, "The Santals call themselves as 'Hor' meaning man" (4). And in Munda language the word 'Horo' also means 'man'. Hos are known as Kols in several places. So the word 'Ho' refers to the men or members of Kol tribe. And thus, Kol and Ho are the different names of the same tribal community. But still the Hos and the Kols are treated and misinterpreted as separate groups of tribal ethnicity. In this context, the views of contemporary director of West Bengal Cultural Research Institute should be mentioned. In a letter (Ref No-522TW/Date-15/04/96) to the project officer-cum-District Welfare officer of Midnapur, he says:

> Kol& Ho are separately enlisted as they have separate ethnical identity. Both the group Kol and Ho have originated from one same Kolarian groups long ago but at present they are entirely two different groups.

Apart from the confusions regarding naming disorder, the Hos are becoming the victims of religious hypocrisy and politics of religion. The adivasis or the tribes are the worshiper of nature and natural elements like hills, trees, water, etc. Even they possess a distinct religion called 'Sarna' or 'Sarnaism'. And so it is with the Ho community. They too are the believers of Sarnaism as they worship nature. But in recent times, they are mistakenly rather politically being victimized as they are facing a cunning attempt of proselytism by the religious leaders of other religions. There lies an attempt to convert the tribal people into another religion for several religious gains. The religious leaders of other religions refuse to admit the existence of Sarna Dharma or Sarnaism. In an interview taken by Times of India, Krishna Gopal, sahsarkaryavah of R.S.S. argues, "There is no denial of the fact that tribals are Hindus..."

These types of filthy political attempts were started just after the independence of India. The records of Census of India since 1871 clarify this confusion too. It clearly brings out the fact that the tribes of India, like Ho, do not belong to Hinduism rather they possess distinct religious customs. In the year 1871, the adivasi community is referred and enlisted as 'Aborigines' by the census authority of India. In the census of 1881 and 1891, they are addressed as 'Aboriginals'. But in the census of 1901, 1911 and 1921, they are enlisted as 'Animists'. The meaning of the word 'Animist' has also been clarified in the *Census of British India* – 1901 in table No.VI entitled "The Population by Religion". It says, "The term Animistic denotes the primitive forms of belief which are found among the jungle tribes, Mundas, Santals, Bhils etc" (57). Again in the census of 1911, the identity of the tribes has been clarified in the records of *Census of British India* saying "the Animist class, so called for want of better name, include all persons who, when asked to state their religion, replied that they were not Hindus, Musalmans, etc" (44).

In the census of 1931, the 'Animist' communities are enlisted under the title of 'Tribal Religion'. And thus they are considered as tribes not belonging to any particular religion like Hinduism, Islam or Christianity. From the very beginning, Hos, like other tribes, are practicing their religion as Sarna and their worship place is Masana and not a temple or mosque. The Ho tribe worships nature and its supreme power called 'Singbonga' or the sun, whereas, Hinduism believes in idolatry. Hence, Sarna religion is not Hindu religion.

Current Situation

While assessing the present situation of the Ho tribes, one should clearly mention their present habitation or dwelling, their growth or development as well as the rate of literacy amongst them. The Hos or the Kols are now scattered in various places of eastern India in search of livelihood. This is an agricultural tribe whose almost 95% population depends mainly on paddy cultivation. Beside agriculture, they also domesticate cattles like cows, pigs, goats and buffaloes. They always try to live together in groups like many other tribes in India and therefore their cottages are built close to each other. Previously they were concentrated in the Chota Nagpur plateau i.e. the southern part of Bihar (now Jharkhand) and north-eastern part of Odisha. But, now they are strewn into several other states of India like Madhya Pradesh, Chhattisgarh, West Bengal and Assam. According to the census of India 2001, with a population of approximately 700,000 in the state in 2001, the Hos were the fourth most numerous scheduled tribes in Jharkhand after the Santals, Kurukhs and Mundas. The census of India 2001 shows that Hos had an overall literacy rate of 39.2% and a female literacy rate of 23.9%. Among the Hos, 19.7% have completed schooling and 3.1% are graduates. The percentage of school going children in the age group 5-14 years was 37.6. However, the recent census data is quite opaque and misleading. There is no specified mention of the literacy rate of this tribe in the latest published census data.

About the status of women, Sir John Houlton, in his book called *Bihar: The Heart of India* (1949), writes:

> I do not want to give the impression, by mentioning occasional divergences from the straight and narrow path, that aboriginals are immoral. On the contrary, their standard of post-marital morality and fidelity are probably a good deal higher than in some races that claim to be more civilized. The status of women is high. Wives are partners and companions to their husbands (139).

Contamination

Changes are also taking place along with the deprivations in the customs and lifestyle of the Hotribes. Needless to say, the food habit and the dress-code are not remaining the same as before. In daily life, they do not wear the conventional dresses. Males, in their daily life, are not dressed in the traditional costumes like 'panchi' or dhotis. Females are now dressed in various modern sarees leaving behind their traditional 'laanga' two pieces of saree-like cloths (see Fig. 3). In search of progress, touched by the sparks of colonization and urbanization, they are abandoning their food habits, dressing identity and traditional ancient customs.

We have seen how colonialism is constructed by the Europeans as a civilizing mission in which a 'superior culture' of the metropolitan West comes in contact with the 'inferior culture' of the colonized periphery. The status of Ho tribe is here subjected to 'double colonization'. Firstly, they are colonized under the western influences. Secondly, they are captured under the cultural impact of the 'dikus', the non-tribals or the outsiders. Thus, they are gradually losing their cultural identity. Their once distinct and unique culture and rituals are paving their way towards extinction through the mixing of two or more distinct cultures.

Figure 3. Women Dancing in their Traditional Sarees (Sing)

Homi Bhabha argues that the concept of pure and uncontaminated culture is a myth. All culture is characterized by a mixedness which he refers to with the word "hybridity". For Bhabha, culture is not a static entity. For him, it is not an essence that can be fixed in time and space. Rather, culture is something which is perpetually in motion. And this concept of "hybridity" is applicable also to the Ho tribes of India. A sort of cultural transformation is taking place between Ho culture and non-tribal 'diku' culture as well as between Ho culture and the western culture. And needless to say, through this process of hybridization of cultures, the 'inferior' Ho culture is being abolished by the influential, 'superior' non-tribal cultures.

A clear binary between the 'inferior' Ho culture and 'superior' non-tribal cultures has been created. This is how the politics of domination works. This is how the identity is suppressed by the dominating cultures of the outsiders. The process of portraying the culture of the non-tribals as 'superior' becomes effective by showing the other cultural entities as opposite, contradictory and minor. In this context, while discussing Bhabha, P. K. Nayar, in his *Contemporary Literary and Cultural Theory*, he says:

> The colonizer establishes his identity by positioning himself against and in opposition to the native. This means, effectively, the colonizer can never possess a self-identical identity, because it requires the colonized to validate it. Identity, therefore, is constantly shifting, luminal and displaced (168).

Thus, the shift of the cultural uniqueness of the Ho people is taking place because of the influence of several other culture, religion and language. Ho tribe is forgetting their own food habit, dress code, rituals and language. As for example, a large number of Ho people of Odisha, Jharkhand and southern part of West Bengal have been converted into Christianity. They are now celebrating Christian rituals forgetting their own culture. Of course, there are reasons behind these conversions. The poor, penniless Ho people hardly manage to make their family run. They face hunger, famine, draught and epidemic frequently in their lives. The natural resources from the surrounding forests are not enough to fulfil their basic demands for running their livelihoods. Hunger means a lot to them than the rituals or traditional culture. As a result, they travelled far from their native land in search of food and livelihood. They worked as the coolies and labourers in various states of India. After the reservation policy is implemented in India in 1950, these tribal people are paving their way towards progression but very slowly and minimum in numbers. They now work in various governmental service sectors. But in this process, again, they are forgetting and abandoning their customs, food habits and language.

One of the agenda of postcolonial studies is to foreground the voice of the oppressed and to create conditions so that the people subjugated by colonialism can be heard. This effort, the ethical interventions are already prominently displayed in the works of Edward Said, the founding father in the field of colonial studies. And, in Gayatri Chakravorty Spivak too, we find a continuation of ethical imperative that underlines post colonialism. Spivak, in her seminal essay "Can the Subaltern Speak?" argues that the core problem for the poorest and most marginalized in society (the subaltern) is that they have no platform to express their concerns. The women among them are doubly oppressed. So is the case of the Hotribals. The entire community is doubly colonized; while the women are doubly oppressed and exploited. Their voice, the voice of both male and female of the community is not regarded as important. The source of this problem is the complexity of language. The language of the tribes is not being treated with due importance. For years, their voice is thus being cancelled as their language is considered as low by the so-called 'superior' non-tribals. The voice of the tribals is rejected and neglected while the voice of the others is taken for granted. This depends on the power relations between these two languages, rather between two societies of Hos and non-tribals. Discourse, as Foucault argues, is a way of constituting knowledge. So we can say, the importance will be given to the language with more knowledge. Hence, the language of the Ho tribe is neglected just because it is considered as inferior to the non-tribal languages.

Often the problem centres in perceiving the language known to both sides. Now the people of Ho tribal community have learnt the local non-tribal languages like Bengali, Hindi, Odia, and Assamese depending upon where they live. Earlier these languages of the non-tribal were not vulnerable to them. They concentrated themselves within their own traditional language i.e. Ho language. This resulted in the misinterpretations of this community. And moreover, untouchability provided an impetus to these wrong interpretations.

In finding out the identity crisis of the Ho tribe in India, one cannot ignore the wrong definitions created so far by the non-tribals of India as well as the western people. As it is already said, the wrong definitions and descriptions have been created because of the obscurity of the Ho language, the cultural gap, untouchability as well as the fright of the non-tribals for the so-called indigenous and fierce tribe. Long ago, the tribes of Chota Nagpur plateau were known for their ferocious aggressiveness. In this respect, Ho people were not different from the other tribes. Rather, the Ho tribe was much fiercer because of its hunting nature. Their lives entirely depended on hunting and gathering from the forests. Probably for these reasons, the Ho people were called as the 'LarkaKols' or the fighting kols. So, this is one of the many reasons why there was a lack of communication between the Ho tribe and the other non-tribals. As a result, misconceptions and misinterpretations took birth about this tribe among the non-tribals and even among the researchers.

Conclusion

So far the untouchability is concerned; there was the effect of this curse too in the lives of the Ho people. They do not belong to any of the sects of *Varnashram* or *Chaturvarna* of Hinduism as they never belong to the Hindu religion itself. But still, there was the effect of untouchability. They were, rather they are still treated by the

Hindu orthodoxy as the outcastes or 'sudras'. Even now, in many places of India, though they work as the labourers in the fields of the Hindus. They are not allowed to enter the temples and houses of Hindus. Ironically, as mentioned earlier, some Hindu political organisations claim the tribes to be an integral part of Hinduism. So, untouchability can be mentioned as a reason for alienation of the Ho tribe and lack of connection between tribals and non-tribals which results in the misinterpretation of the tribal people.

Earlier, in this paper, the reports of census of India have been shown as the evidences of the tribes not being Hindu. But the census reports are also not free from corruptions. In several censuses, it is seen that the calculation or the counting of Hos or Kols as a distinct tribe is full of errors. As for example, in 1951, the total count of Ho or Kol people in West Bengal was 31; in 1961, it was 1075 and even in 1971 it remained unchanged. There was no change in numbers within ten years. It will be a foolery to blame only the census authorities as there was lack of awareness among the Ho tribe too about their identity.

So far, various aspects of identity crisis of the Ho tribe have been discussed. How the ethnic identity of the community is on the way of extinction. How their language, culture, food habit, rituals and dress code are under the clutch of 'civilization' and 'imperialism. How they are confused with Mundas and Santals. The Santals worship 'Marang Buru' and their script is called 'OlChiki', while the Hos or Kols worship 'Singbonga' and their script is 'Warang Citi'. Again, the misinterpretations of those Ho people by the census authority and the non-tribals have been portrayed. And as the reasons of these kinds of misinterpretations and identity crisis, various sides have been upheld like that of the lack of awareness among the tribes, errors in census, proselytism or conversion, language problem, untouchability, cultural and ethnic transformation of the tribe as well as the cunning 'Hindu method of tribal absorption'.

To conclude, this paper helps to get a clear idea about the unexplored and misinterpreted Ho tribe and their culture. It distinguishes the entire Ho community from the other tribal groups in terms of their culture, language and rituals. Moreover, it is shown how the tribes do not belong to Hinduism or Islam. Even this paper portrays the present cultural and economic situation scenario of this particular tribe. As stated earlier, the tribes are the aborigines of this subcontinent, but now they are facing various obstacles on the way to their progression as well as on the way to protect their culture. And thus, it can be concluded that if these kinds of misinterpretations continue, the once distinct culture and identity of the Ho tribe will reach its extinction.

Works Cited

Bawanda, Kartik Chandra. *Kol Bhasar Utsa Charit*. Medinipur: Kol Samaj Hayam Sanagom Society, 2013. Print.

Bhabha, Homi K. *The Location of Culture.* New York: Routledge, 1994. Print.

Bhowmik, P. K. "Tribal Situation in West Bengal." *Indian Anthropologist,* Vol.15, No. 1, (1985):1-19. *JSTOR.* Web. 2 August 2018.

Deogharia, Jaideep. Ed. *Times of India.*1 November 2015.Web. 25 July 2018.

<https://m.timesofindia.com/city/ranchi/All-tribals-are-Hindus-no-need-for-Sarna-code-RSS/amp_articleshow/49616469.cms>

Erikson, Erik H. *Identity, Youth and Crisis.* New York: W. W. Norton Company, 1968. Print.

Fanon, Frantz. *The Wretched of the Earth.* 1961. Trans. Constance Farrington. New York: Grove, 1963. Print.

Government of West Bengal. Backward Classes Welfare Department. *Ethnographic Notes on the Scheduled Tribes of West Bengal.* Kolkata: Cultural Research Institute, 2003. Print.

Grierson, George Abraham. *Linguistic Survey of India.*Calcutta: Government Press, 1906. Print.

Griffiths, Walter G. *The Kol Tribe of Central India.* Calcutta: The Royal Asiatic Society of Bengal, 1946. Print.

Houlton, John. *Bihar: The Heart of India.* Calcutta: Orient Longsman LTD, 1949. Print.

Murmu, Badal. "Warang Citi alphabet for Ho." *medium.com,* 23Feb, 2020,

<https//medium.com/@badalmurmu/warang-citi-in-browser-and-android-devices-

cb16957e745d>

Nayar, Pramod K. *Contemporary Literary and Cultural Theory: From Structuralism to Ecocriticism.* 2010. New Delhi: Pearson, 2017. Print.

Risley, Herbert Hope. *The Tribes and Castes of Bengal.* Calcutta: Bengal Secretariat Press, 1891. Print.

Sing, Santi R. *Men of Ho tribe dancing accompanied by musical instruments.*14 Jan. 2020, Author's personal collection.

.... *Women dancing in their traditional sarees.* 21 Dec. 2019, Author's personal collection.

Author's Bio-Note

Santi Ranjan Sing is currently an Independent Researcher working on Posthumanism(s) and tribal culture. He did his M.A. in English from The University of Burdwan (W.B.) in 2018. He qualified for UGC-NET, WB SET and UGC-JRF in 2020. His already published articles are on East Indian tribes.

8

Marginalization of the Tribal Populace: An Analysis of Hansda Sowvendra Sekhar's Select Short Stories

Rimpa Pal

Abstract

Adivasi literature refers to the literature in which life style and society of the tribals has been expressed. Tribal literature is literally very rich and priceless in its aboriginal languages. Adivasi literature depicts picture of the downtrodden people, their exploitation by the outsiders, their search for their own tribal identity and resistance. The beginning of the written Adivasi literature in India occurs in the early twentieth century when these indigenous communities come in contact with the modern education. Now tribal life has become one of the popular discourses in contemporary academia. Hansda Sowvendra Sekhar, an Indian author from Santhal community – one of the India's Adivasi group is a Sahitya Akademi Yuba Puraskar recipient. This paper attempts to portray the lives of those who are socially crushed, culturally deserted and economically exploited in his collection of short stories, *The Adivasi Will Not Dance*. In other words, this paper attempts to depict the deplorable conditions of the marginalized tribals in Jharkhand in these selected short stories: "November Is the Month of Migrations", "Baso-jhi" and "The Adivasi Will Not Dance". The paper investigates the migration of Santhal, one of the aboriginal communities in India, their agony and their painful reality. The paper also focuses on the mental trauma and physical hardship experienced by this marginalized 'other' in their native land. This collection of short stories *The Adivasi Will Not Dance* deals with marginalization, deprivation, social injustice, administrative indifference in an interesting way.

Keywords: Adivasi; Tribal; Marginalization; Exploitation; Migration; Aboriginal

Introduction

This paper deals with three major short stories of Hansda Sowvendra Sekhar. Hansda attempts to show how like any other tribal group, Santhals share a painful experience of social injustice and administrative negligence. These tribal people face an unequal battle with the government in order to survive. These poor people are exploited politically, economically and in the name of religion. As Hansda himself is from the downtrodden community, his characters are spokesmen of their strangled community. They share the common sentiments of the inhabitants of Santhal Pargana. The incomparable way in which Hansda writes is something striking and interesting and fascinates not only the common reader but also the literary world. The unending suffering and bitter reality gives birth to most important contemporary authors like Hansda.

Before going into the details of how Hansda's short stories deal with the problems of socially subjugated people, it is necessary to discuss their socio-political background. Inequality was the main source of this marginality which led to insecurity, injustice, and exploitation. Marginalized sections are always on the periphery and are distanced from the power centers. Santhals are always on the marginalized 'other' side of Indian society. So, when they started voicing after centuries of silence, there arose a literature depicting assertion of human rights, self-pride, revolt against social injustice, chronicles of personal and collective suffering, and hopes and aspirations for a new society devoid of discrimination. Adivasis are called by different names in different parts of India, invented by caste and all entailing insult and contempt. The native Santhals who are subjugated from the British rule, are now also exposed to the extreme dominance of the elite class. The Adivasis are victim of the exploitation since the establishment of British colonial rule.

Here, in this section, there will be a discussion on the substance of selected three short stories. His stories reflect on the personal and collective suffering of the Santhals. Hansda reveals his characters' inner state of mind as they are confined in a socially claustrophobic atmosphere. This would definitely help in a better understanding of the idea how Hansda familiarizes the characters of his stories with the story. The book *The Adivasi Will Not Dance* is a collection of ten stories dealing with Adivasis from Jharkhand. The book is an actual representation of Santhali life and culture.

"November Is the Month of Migrations" was published in the collection of short stories – *The Adivasi Will Not Dance* by Hansda Sowvendra Sekhar. This is one of the most heart-rending tale of poverty and utter helplessness. It is a story of migration of daily workers in order to struggle for existence. The poor people move from one place to another and work hard in order to fill their empty stomach. Talamai Kisku, a twenty year old girl is moving to Bardhaman district of West Bengal with her family members to plant rice and other crops in farms owned by the zamindars of Bardhaman. She was attracted by a young fair *Diku*, and a *jawan* of the Railway Protection Force. With a bread *pakora* in his hand, the policeman signals her to approach. The girl makes sexual intercourse with the *jawan* only for "two pieces of cold bread *pakora* and a fifty-rupee note" (Hansda 42). This is the bitter reality where we see a policeman, a government officer uses the girl's body and, in a way, objectifies her. This is the common fate of thousands of Adivasi women who have to accept this kind of sexual harassment just for some food.

The short story "Baso-jhi" was published in the collection of short stories by Hansda Sowvendra Sekhar – *The Adivasi Will Not Dance.* "Baso-Jhi" is a touching tale about Basanti and her dreadful experience with superstition in the Adivasi society – the picture which we still experience in the twenty first century modern India. She is ostracized from her community, from the society. At first, she is thrown away by her own sons accusing her to be a witch. Then the new refugee Pushpa abuses her as a *dahni* after three consecutive deaths taking place in Sarjomdih.

"The Adivasi Will Not Dance" is the title story that my paper deals with. It was also included in the collected short stories of *The Adivasi Will Not Dance* by Hansda Sowvendra Sekhar. This story is a moving monologue of Mangal Murmu, a Santhal performer and artist. The old man was the trainer of many dance groups for years but refuses to perform for an important prestigious function where elite class people come as chief guests. This story has a major inspiration from a real event. President Pranab Mukherjee visited Jharkhand to inaugurate an ambitious plant project. Due to that project, the original inhabitants of the land become homeless.

Mangal Murmu, a farmer of sixty year old, is the storyteller. The coal mining organization is established in the majority of the places in the native land of Adivasi. The story is set in Pakur district of Jharkhand. Jharkhand is a place full of natural resources. The story depicts the life style and struggle of the Santhals. The coal merchants have taken a large portion of their land in the name of progress. The coal company owners disown the Santhals from their roots and make so much profit by befooling the native aboriginals. Hansda shows how the outsiders take advantage from the simple and poor Santhals: "But we Santhals are fools, aren't we? All of us Adivasis are fools. Down the years, down generations, the Diku have taken advantage of our foolishness." (Hansda 170). Mangal's resentment is directed towards the stone merchants, all Diku-Marwari, Sindhi, Mandal, Bhagat, Muslim. They turn our land upside down, inside out, with their heavy machines" (172). Mangal also shows how the owners stole mine from their earth and sold them in faraway places – "Dilli, Noida, Punjab" (172).

Hansda shows us that there is a gulf of difference in the lifestyles of the coalmine owners and the Adivasis. Whereas, they have to fight for basic needs of life, the elite class is treated by the best doctors in Ranchi, Patna, Bhagalpur, Malda, Bardhaman and Kolkata. Murmu here bursts into despair. "What do the Santhals get in return? Tatters to wear. Barely enough food. Such diseases that we can't breathe properly, we cough blood and forever remain bare bones" (Hansda 172).

Murmu then tells about Muslim emergence in their homeland. He remarks, "Muslims barge into our homes, sleep with our women, and we Santhal men cannot do a thing" (172). Their homeland Santhal Pargana is overcrowded by the Muslims.

"Village after village in our Santhal Pargana – which should have been a home for us Santhals – are turning into Muslim villages" (173).

However, it is not that the story is antagonistic towards Muslim community only. Christian missionaries and high caste Hindu are also responsible for the wretched condition of the Adivasis. In the name of progress and making the original inhabitants of the Santhal Pargana superior and educated, Christian missionaries convert the Santhal children or rename them as "David and Mikail and Kiristofer and what not" (Hansda172). The rich Hindus want to make them forget their Sarna religion, convert them into Safa-Hor, and swell their numbers to become more valuable vote banks.

Here we see how the narrow religiosity intersects Santhal Pargana. Mangal Murmu remarks with despair, "We are losing our Sarana faith, our identities, and our roots. We are becoming people from nowhere" (173).

The adivasis are always victimized by the double standard of the society. They are disillusioned with the government policy and burst into grievance: "All our certificates and shields, what did they give us? Diku children go to schools and colleges, get education, jobs. What do we Santhals get? We Santhals can sing and dance, and we are good at our art. Yet, what has our art given us? Displacement, tuberculosis" (Hansda 178). His statement exposes the hypocrisy of the elite class.

The climactic moment of the story is when the performer and artist Mangal Murmu and his troupe are supposed to perform in front of the honorable President of India and other various important ministers and personalities. The ceremony is actually meant for celebration of a large thermal power plant. In order to fulfill their vested interest of the outsiders, the Adivasis are forcefully displaced from their native land. The Santhals are subjected to the whims and needs of the upper class society. The elite class makes most of the villagers of eleven villages in Santhal Pargana. Here Mangal Murmu questions: "And, I thought, how anyone can force Santhals to vacate their land in the Santhal Pargana? Didn't we have the Tenacity Act to protect us?" (Hansda 181). The villagers would have to vacate to make room for a thermal power plant. The villagers refused outrightly. Santhals, low-caste Hindu, and Paharias began fighting for their land. This is the true picture of shining India where government is indifferent to the basic necessities of life of the aboriginal community.

This paper brings to the forefront – how Hansda portrays that Adivasis are subjected to the administrative indifference, negligence, deprivation and forced displacements.

"November Is the Month of Migrations" is a poignant tale of a twenty-year-old Santhal girl Talamai Kisku. A railway *jawan* allured her and consummated her body. He trapped her and she succumbed to his enticing call only for two pieces of cold bread pakora and a fifty rupee note. The *jawan* satisfied his perverted carnal desire. It is a wonder that the girl accepts her lot without any protest as if loss of virginity does not matter to her. Hansda remarks:

> "Talamai knows what work he is talking about. She has done it quite a few times by the Koyla Road, where many Santhal women and girls steal coal from trucks. She knows many girls who do that work with truck drivers and other men. And she knows that on their way to Namal, Santhal women do this for food and money at the railway station, too" (Hansda 40).

It is the common lot of Adivasi women who migrated from their native land to other place in order to earn their livelihood. Thousands of Santhal women have to embrace sexual harassment just for food. Hansda depicts the grim reality of sexual intercourse in a moving manner: "Talamai takes care not to scream, or even wince. She knows the routine. She has to do nothing, only spread her legs and lie quiet. She knows, everything is done by the man. She just lies – passive, unthinking, unblinking – as cold as the paved ground she can feel through the thin fabric of the gamcha; as still as an inert earthen bowl into which a dark cloud empties itself" (41).

The way the railway *jawan* uses Talamai's body as an instrument of physical pleasure, we see commodification of a female body. This notion comes close to Kate Millet's basic arguments in *Sexual Politics* which begins with her saying that power is the cornerstone of politics. What patriarchy adopts is nothing more than the power dynamics which are exercised in a way that gender is discriminated summarily. Only to keep upper hand in the politics, men will do whatever is needed to keep patriarchy as an overarching influence on women.

Millet found a nexus between patriarchy and capitalism. In the advertisements, she found female body is presented as flesh in order to tempt the buyers. In this story, Talamaiis also represented in the same shrewd way. The society is basically gendered and patriarchy never fails to do it subtly.

"Baso-jhi" is the story where we see Basanti, an Adivasi woman is a victim to baseless superstition. She is excluded from her community because she is considered as a witch. After the successive deaths in the village, everyone doubts about Basanti's presence. Her new master Soren-babu screams at Pushpa, "So what do I do then? Tell her that she is a *dahni*, grab her by her hair and throw her out of the house?" (Hansda122). Baso-jhi is quite aware of such kind of accusation from her previous experience. Hansda expresses her mental state in a moving manner –"Baso-jhi knew. She was a *dahni* – a witch. She killed her own grandson and for that, her sons had disowned her. How could she expect strangers to accept her? She truly was a witch" (Hansda 122).

Basanti's grandchild succumbed to a bout of diarrhoea. Basanti attended the ailing child but his mother only yelled and blamed her for the child's sickness. After the death of the child, everyone including Basanti's own son held her responsible for that death. The son questions her "Tell us what you are up to inside your hut? Which evil gods do you worship, and how many children do you need for your sacrifices? (Hansda 127). Basanti was shocked to hear such kind of allegation from her own sons calling her a witch. She felt utterly helpless. Hansda describes the fate of Basanti in a pathetic manner: "Desolate, she watched her sons ransack her one-room hut. Her utensils, her clothes, her clay pots, her tin box, everything was thrown out. Not satisfied with all the damage he'd caused to his mother's hut and heart, the younger son threw Basanti on to the ground by her hair. Then he kicked her in the abdomen. The old woman screamed, in pain and in grief" (Hansda 127).

The sons kept hurling abuses and kicks. Many villagers gathered to witness the incident, but no one stepped forward to speak on behalf of Basanti. She was completely crushed in pain, grief, shock and humiliation. None speaks for her side. Here comes the notion of subaltern. Generally the term 'subaltern' refers to the class of people who are subjected to the hegemony of another powerful class. Spivak is especially interested in the fate of 'female subaltern' like Basanti. In her most provocative essay "Can the Subaltern Speak?" Spivak worries about the agencies of the subaltern to represent themselves. Her answer to her own questions is no. Spivak adopts the notion of subalternity in order to theorize the condition of the native in postcolonial state. The structure is doubly strengthened in the case of native women who are silenced through both patriarchy and colonialism (i.e. for both, her gender and her race). Spivak argues that subaltern cannot speak for herself because the double bind of colonialism and patriarchy silence her; only intellectual project must seek to make visible the position of the marginalized. Italian Marxist Antonio Gramsci used the very term 'subaltern' for peasants and workers, and Ranajit Guha has been at the helm of the subaltern chroniclers. Spivak questioned the authenticity of the discourse of the academicians who wrote and underpinned accounts of the subaltern. Spivak situates her argument towards the female space saying that when the male counterpart themselves cannot voice their own tales then it's almost ridiculous to think of a female voice while keeping the male-dominated society in the context of the discourse. The female subalterns are much more marginalized in this connection. Society may not be ready to listen to what the female subaltern have to say (Spivak 27).

It is no wonder that the incident of Baso-jhi is very much present in so-called modern progressive India. We still experience that a woman is not only ostracized from her community but also is killed sometimes.

The title story "The Adivasi Will Not Dance" is a tale of displacement where indigenous people of Jharkhand are dislocated from their homeland for an ambitious thermal plant. It causes a lot of troubles to the native inhabitants of the land. This aspect of industrialization exacerbated the separation of labour and capital. Those who owned the means of production become disproportionately rich, resulting in wider income inequality. Workers are forced to migrate to other places in search of job. They work long hours, are poorly nourished and live in overcrowded condition, which led disease and stress. Here comes Antonio Gramsci's concept of 'hegemony'. Gramsci coined the term 'hegemony' in 1926 in *Notes on the Southern Question*. He defined it as a system of class alliance in which a hegemonic class exercised political leadership over subaltern classes by winning them over. Hegemony is a sort of deception in which the individual forgets his own desires and accepts dominant values as their own. In this hierarchical power structure, Adivasis are powerless and outsider businessmen are powerful. The voice of the marginalized Santhals is too feeble to cope with the strategies of capitalist class. They are always at the margins and are subdued by the authoritarian voice (Anderson 45).

In the story "The Adivasi Will Not Dance", the outsiders and the elite capitalist class (who are building thermal plant) are the embodiment of hegemonic group over the whole of the Santhal community exercised through coercion and consensus. Capitalism concentrates power in the hands of a minority of elite capitalist class that exists through the exploitation and victimization of the majority of working class and their labour, prioritizes profit over social good, natural resources and the environment.

In this story, Mangal Murmu voices the emotions of the oppressed Santhals. Breaking the age-old tradition, Mangal Murmu remarks in a tone of defiance: "We Adivasis will not dance anymore – what is wrong with that? We are like toys – someone presses our 'ON' button, or turns a key in our backsides, and we Santhals start beating rhythms on our *tamak* and *tumdak*, or start blowing tunes on our *tiriyo* while someone snatches away our very dancing grounds. Tell me, am I wrong?" (Hansda 170).

At the end of the story, Mangal Murmu questions the double standard policy of government and how industrialization blossoms at the cost of tribal life: "You will now start building the power plant, but this plant will be the end of us all, the end of all the Adivasi. These men sitting beside you have told you that this power plant will change our fortunes, but these same men have forced us out of our homes and villages. We have nowhere to go, nowhere to grow our crops. How can this power plant be good for us?" (Hansda 187). Last lines of the story are very touching where the Santhals want to move away from their natural traditional practice of song and dance. Mangal Murmu exclaims: "And how can we Adivasis dance and be happy? Unless we are given back our homes and land, we will not sing and dance. We Adivasis will not dance. The Adivasis will not" (187).

Cultural erasure is a practice in which dominant and powerful group attempt to suppress, negate, demean and wipe out the culture of another community. The outsiders of Santhal Pargana want to erase the indigenous culture of the Adivasis. Santhal farmer and musician Mangal Murmu expresses this collective anguish in his monologue: "Was a farmer. Was a farmer is right. Because I don't farm anymore. In my village of Matiajore in Amrapara block of the Pakur district, not many Santhals farm anymore. Only a few of us still have farmland; most of it has been acquired by a mining company" (Hansda 170-171). Tribals are compelled to adopt foreign culture in order to live in a so-called civilized society.

To conclude, we can say that the culture of the outsiders of Santhal Pargana has completely destroyed the tribal lives socially, economically, culturally and psychologically. The present scenario of the descendants of Sidho and Kanho Murmu, the leaders of Santhal Revolution, are not leading a healthy life. This is painful reality after so many years of Indian Independence. The Adivasi children have no access to proper education. It is an irony that indigenous people who once fought against the British colonial power are today living in the most unfavorable condition being impoverished of basic necessities of life. They are still cut off from the mainstream society. The situation of the aboriginals remains the same. Poverty prevails in Santhal Pargana; underfed children are a known spectacle; deprivation and victimization are continuous phenomenon. Peculiarities in the social security scheme of government have become inevitable. In addition, state's role in facilitating land grabbing for companies in an effort to alienate the Adivasis from their roots, is thereby threatening their very existence. They are also dispossessed of natural resources of their own land. What remains unchanged is the utter poverty of these people. What we fail to understand is the motive behind the continued marginalization of the inhabitants of Santhal Pargana. The government is not at all interested in addressing issues of betterment of these poor people. In order to bring golden days for these Adivasi people, what is most needed is the development of the people who have been deliberately ignored by every possible theories and government. Development in the infrastructure in terms of electricity, road, and housing for the poor is not enough. Government should assure that all social security schemes are implemented properly and all Adivasis should benefit from the schemes rather than limiting to the coverpages of annual reports.

Works Cited

Anderson, Perry. *Las antinomias de Antonio Gramsci*. (1978).

Barry, Peter. *Beginning theory: An introduction to literary and cultural theory*. Manchester university press, 2020.

Chakraborty, Abin. "Examining Subalterneity in Hansda Sowvendra Sekhar's "The Adivasi Will Not Dance"." *Postcolonial Text* 12.1 (2017).

Nath, Keshav, and Neha Meena. "The Adivasi Will Not Dance: A Study in Dialectics of Tribal Voices from Jharkhand." *IMPACT: International Journal of Research in Humanities, Arts and Literature (IMPACT: IJRHAL)* 5.12 (2017): 143-150.

Nayar, Pramod K. *Contemporary literary and cultural theory: From structuralism to ecocriticism*. Pearson Education India, 2009.

Shekhar, Hansda Sowvendra. *The Adivasi Will Not Dance: Stories*. India, Speaking Tiger, 2015.

Spivak, Gayatri Chakravorty. "Can the subaltern speak?." *Die Philosophin* 14.27 (2003): 42-58.

Tripathi, Priyanka. Review of *The Advasi Will Not Dance: Stories*, by HansdaSowvendra Sekhar. *Rupkatha Journal on Interdisciplinary Studies in Humanities,* vol.9, no. 4, 2017, pp. 193-196.

Author's Bio-Note

Rimpa Pal graduated from Tarakeswar Degree College with Honours in English in 2015. She completed her post-graduation from the University of Burdwan in 2017. She joined Tarakeswar Degree College as guest faculty in September, 2018. She is now a state aided college teacher (SACT) at Tarakeswar Degree College, West Bengal.

9

Reading Indira Goswami's Fictional Works from a Subaltern Perspective: A Study

Ashmita Bora

Abstract

Indira Goswami is an Indian writer who has championed the cause of women in her works, about their suppression and domination by patriarchy and how services rendered by them are regarded as their duty as they are bound to the family structures. This paper enumerates several works of her that portray women both as victimised personalities and as unwitting agents of patriarchy, also defining the ways women negotiate the androcentric cultures through acts of self-affirmation and resistance. Indira Goswami has also done seminal work on the lives of Indian widows whose condition is even worse in the male-dominated society. This paper attempts to probe into the causes, the unquestioned beliefs, the practices and the rituals that perpetuate violence on women and seeks to ask questions and give voices to the women who have been rendered voiceless. Goswami's novels are dominated by female protagonists who struggle and protest against male dominance and break patriarchal order and reclaim their individualistic identities.

Keywords: Patriarchy; Society; Male-dominated; Women; Suppression; Widows

Introduction

One of the most reputed writers of North East India, Indira Goswami known mostly by her pen name Mamoni Raisom Goswami has been the recipient of the Jnanpith Award and Sahitya Akademi Award. She is a phenomenal personality who has tirelessly fought for the marginalised sections of the society through her writings. She brought forth the oppressed condition of women in Indian society under the dominant shadow of patriarchy. Being widowed less than two years into her marriage, she took a step of withdrawal with only the carefree memories of her childhood days, some letters of her father and a pen as her companions to distract herself from the tragedy that life had in store for her. She realised that Indian society, especially the Hindu Brahmin society she belonged to had no place for its widows, and with this realisation she came out stronger with a map of several social problems confronted by Indian women. In her works she gives space to a gamut of female characters who have been denied their rightful place by their families and the society at large. Their grim condition and miserable state form an important subject matter in her works.

Subaltern Women and Patriarchy: A General Overview

Gender has always been a rudimental determinant in the patriarchal backdrop of Indian society. Through history, women have been viewed as the subordinate class who lived at the mercy of her father from birth, and after marriage at the mercy of her husband and later in an event of her husband's demise, at the mercy of her son and in the absence of a son, the other male members of the household. Even her identity is always constructed only in relation to the men in her life. Married women were always required to make sacrifices, be docile and willing to be controlled, be dependent and always answerable to their husbands, who may be negligible, promiscuous or irresponsible. There has been a fixed destiny rigidly attached to an Indian woman through which her autonomy is restricted.

Traditionally the 'stronger' sex has been the heads of the household and the women were regarded as their weaker counterparts whose prime responsibility was to sacrifice themselves to the service of their husbands. Viewed through post-colonial lenses, their relationship is more that of the coloniser and the colonised rather than of wife and husband where the woman becomes the objective 'other', and slaves to their husband. "The subaltern theory takes the perspective of the "other" as one who has had no voice because of race, class or gender. It establishes the fact that norms are established by those in power and imposed on the "other" (Warner 2002). The inferior status given to women occurs in gender, racial, class and caste contexts through this otherisation.

Under the patriarchal order another important aspect is that women were seen as the physical goods of the society, the living rewards available to the men. They were supposed to be inherently submissive and docile, and could be sexually exploited by the males without misgivings. Furthermore, they were regarded reductively as reproductive objects, and many a time their value was based on this very consideration from beginning to end. This consideration led society to view the female body as an object as Foucault has discussed in at length in his work *The History of Sexuality*. Foucault calls this "the hystericization of the female body, the pathologization of the female body which is situated alongside women's responsibility to take care of children's health, the institution of the family, and the family's and society's health" (Foucault 104). He reviewed masculine and feminine positions as relations of power where the women are the subject to the patriarchal masters who rule over her.

Gayatri Chakravorty Spivak in her ground-breaking essay, "*Can the Subaltern Speak?" Marxism and the Interpretation of Culture* extends her argument about the colonial subaltern to the question of gender. Antonio Gramsci who wrote from a

Marxist perspective, used the term "subaltern classes" to describe those groups "subordinated by hegemony and excluded from any meaningful role in a regime of power" (Holden 202) Thus, we could say that the subaltern generally refers to a person or a group of persons who fall outside the hegemonic power structure of the society and thus their voices are silenced. "The Subaltern as female is even more deeply in shadow" (Spivak 83). Therefore, she is the gendered subaltern who is doubly colonised, firstly by the colonialist regime and secondly, by the patriarchal forces as she is a woman. She is subjected to oppression and subjugation and is rendered voiceless under the dominance of the men who hold the reins of her life thereby obliterating her liberty.

The plight of the women belonging to lower castes in a patriarchal set up is even worse. Apart from being a woman, when the stigma of caste is added, these women find themselves pushed to the periphery of society. There is nothing to console them, the age-old dogmas and stereotypes of caste, the principles of purity and pollution that are integrally built into Indian culture and belief system cause their exclusion from mainstream society. Such marginalisation pierce into their souls, and make their life pathetically bitter. There seems to be no escape from it.

The widows of Indian society are easy victims of the patriarchy. Their oppression is carried out through codified norms dictated by society. Their struggles are increased manifold by the forces that penetrate and perpetuate violence on the widows. Their presence is considered inauspicious on holy occasions, they are expected to change their food habits, dress patterns and their lifestyles thereby leading to their loss of position in family and kin groups. They are socially boycotted and victimised psychologically. Their collective identity changes from that of being a woman or a wife to a widow and they face exclusion from mainstream society being stripped off all the privileges hitherto enjoyed by them as married women.

Indira Goswami explores the social maladies that plague Indian society in her works. Her position as a woman and moreover as a widow enables her to understand to write about what women like her were subjected to, their sufferings, their struggles and their experiences. She realised that in the world of women, not only men but also the women themselves acted as agents of patriarchy who try to carry forward rules and regulations in the name of tradition and custom deemed necessary by society no matter how regressive they may be, especially to the cause of its women. Aware of this through her own experiences in the world she voiced out her concern about the plight of Indian women and sketched poignant female characters in her works to bring forth this issue of how patriarchy holds it women by fetters, making their existence suffocating and holding them accountable to the men in their lives for everything they do. Her characters often bow down to patriarchy, but rather reluctantly and they begin to question the means and methods that are used to enslave them, they protest against the injustice meted out to them by patriarchal forces and ultimately they emerge out stronger breaking the shackles that bind them in some way or the other.

Patriarchy, the Subaltern Woman and Her Empowerment in Select Novels of Indira Goswami

In the novel *The Moth Eaten Howdah of the Tusker* (2004) the plot revolves around three widows of a Hindu Brahmin family; Durga, Saru Gosani and Giribala. The eldest of the three, Durga acts in compliance with society's dictates. She is the subaltern woman who surrenders to the traditional beliefs mutely and never raises any questions about its validity. She is the epitome of tolerance, and have not learnt the language of rebellion. She is the representative of those women who never voices against the injustice of society for they do not recognise it as injustice in the first place. She is a mute spectator, an uncomplaining sufferer jealously sticking to tradition.

> "Her mind has become a graveyard. Day after day it is a tortuous task for her to find something tangible to hold on to, to hold on to her sanity. All those customary rituals of widowhood that she performed till a few years back without much effort are now a source of fear for her. Amoti is soon approaching. A wave of annoyance mixed with fear passes through her body........" (Goswami 11).

Soru Gosani develops sexual desires for the Brahmin caretaker, Muhidhor who helps her to collect rents.

> "She has observed for some time that this ripple of excitement would pass through her body whenever he came near her. She turned round and saw Mahidhar wearing the sane dhoti that she had got for him when she had gone to Pathaldia to meet her disciples...Mahidhar was a handsome man..... Like other days, today also, he looked at her wooden bed. It was covered with an old, tattered endi chaddar....Today too she could not fathom the meaning of his glance towards her bed." (Goswami 77-78).

Taking advantage of her position and her feelings towards him, he tries to cheat her by forging the transfer of most of her lands to himself. Patriarchy here appears in the form of the greedy caretaker who seeks to benefit himself by capitalising on the romantic weakness of a woman towards him. This betrayal destroys her dreams and shatters her to the core delineating how the actions of men destroy women's aspirations.

Giribala is a woman of the new generation who does not want to become an oppressed victim of patriarchy and makes every effort to break away from the traditions which threaten to choke her very existence. When women come to see her after she arrives at her father's home following her husband's death, she doesn't turn up in front of them or participate in their gossip about the escapades of her late husband or cry in his memory as they expect her to. She doesn't respect him or the customs that bind her, she lashes out at them in contrary to their expectations.

> "All the women had come with the sole purpose of hearing the harrowing tales of woe from Giribala'sownlips but she did not give them a chance. Like a streak of lightening she headed straight for the door of the room...........opened it with a jerk, entered and bolted the door from inside with the crossbar" (Goswami 30).

To whom girls are married off and how they are to lead their lives, even in the event of the death of their husbands was on society to decide for them. Both Durga and Giribala are forced into arranged marriages to men chosen by society represented by the male family members and even if the mother of the girl was not fond of the boy, she had no say in these matters. The subaltern's voice is always silenced, never allowed to speak for herself as Spivak has rightly delineated in her essay "Can the Subaltern Speak?":

> "The Gossainee spoke with a broken voice. "She (Giribala) never wanted this marriage. She behaved..........". The women.........reminded her: "But, Aie (mother), you were also not very happy with this marriage."
>
> "How could I be happy?...... ....That boy did nothing but roam about with Chaudhary's jatra party." (Goswami 30-31).

Unlike Durga, who pines to go back to her husband's home, Giribala actually feels liberated after her husband's death and has no wish to go back to her in-laws knowing it would be a suffocating existence to live with the remembrance of her dead husband who was engaged in extra-marital affairs when he was alive.

> "After I came of age, all those Gossainees on the river bank used to tell me: you are an Angel, you are a sweet Angel! But do you know? That husband of mine,... used to say, 'What's so great about your beautiful body?...You are nothing in comparison...I couldn't bind him to me with either my body or my mind." (Goswami 295-96).

Giribala eventually decides to revolt possibly to rid herself of her memories of her dead husband. Giribalaalso knew the lives of widows were hellish and their world was no lesser than that of a graveyard, and she wanted a life free from strict rules.

Durga wants Giribala to adhere to the societal rules that a widow is supposed to live with, thus showing that women themselves become the agents of perpetuating the violence of patriarchy on other women. They accept the laws as universal and could never imagine life without it. Durga was so given to the customary practices and rituals that she herself considers to be an outcaste.

> "She was considered inauspicious because of her so-called papagrahas-not one but three of them! Gradually these accusations and pointing fingers seeped into her mind and she really began to believe it herself" (Goswami 11).

When women go against the societal rules and norms they are cruelly punished as it happens with Giribala who is once beaten mercilessly when she gives in to the temptation and consumes mutton curry which is supposedly a sin for widows.

> "Giribala darted into the palanquin room and picked up the pot of mutton cooked with black beans. She forgot everything....religion and rituals, wisdom or restraint....she started gulping it down in great haste...After her widowhood, she had taken only rice and pulses boiled with some vegetables, adding a pinch of salt and a little Ghee made from Cow's Milk. Her tongue had become dull and dry. She was fed up with this diet" (Goswami 144).

The women internalised patriarchy and depended on the men so much so that when Indranath, Giribala's brother suggests that his mother and his aunt, SoruGosani move out of the house to take care of the land, they become horrified at the idea. To this he reacts angrily, "You are nothing but ghosts pretending to be human beings..." (Goswami 10).

> Girbala in a further act of defiance against societal norms develops an intimate relation with Mark Sahib, a British Christian monk but it ultimately results in doom. She confesses her feelings for him and her disgust at the society's dictates for widows "I cannot just exist, just for the sake of remaining alive, like Aunt Durga and SaruGossainee" (Goswami 198).

When her in-laws demand her return in view of her growing intimacy to the Sahib to save their family's honour, Giribala in an of act impulse enters Mark's room and declares her love for him, and proclaims that she would rather die than go back. Mark does not yield fearing the consequences, while villagers barge in and take her away. They perform a ritual to purify her where Giribala immolates herself as a last act of rebellion against a system that levies severe restrictions on the life of a widow. She prefers death instead of a life of bondage and in death she attains ultimate liberation from the constraints of the patriarchal system.

In the novel *The Man from Chhinamasta* (2005) Indira Goswami likens the women in this novel, Vidhibala, the daughter of a frantic worshipper of Goddess Kamakhya and Dorothy Brown, the betrayed wife of a professor to the animals offered as sacrifices to the deity as both become victims to the whims of patriarchal society. Vidhibala's father following the prevalent norms wanted to marry her off to a middle aged man of high caste before the onset of her puberty as opposed to his daughter's will. It is the voice of patriarchy represented by her father and she doesn't have any say in the matter nor her mother, "Her mother had retorted, "The man's hair and beard are already turning grey. Even those brahmins from Coochbehar were better. "Shutup!" Her mother could speak no more" (Goswami 94).

The objectification of the female body that was discussed by Foucault as "the hystericization of the female body" (Foucault 104) is brought out to the fore by Goswami during Bidhibala's Kumari Puja where the priest Shambu argues with two other devotees about her attaining puberty in the presence of the girl where she sits silenced as the men discuss about her body like they were referring to some object." "The girl seems to have crossed her twelfth birthday. Let's check her hands, feet and chest." "She has breasts!" "She must have reached puberty" (Goswami 47).

To celebrate the occasion of her marriage Bidhibala's father plans to offer a buffalo calf to the deity. Vidhibala voices her refusal by saying, "You cannot get buffaloes. You will not bring buffaloes. I shall not marry a man already..." (Goswami 121) only to be met with strong opposition from her father who doesn't even let her finish the sentence and flung his slipper at her.

"Singhadatta, furious at his daughter's audacity, lost control and threw his khadu, the wooden slipper he was wearing at her." The assault doesn't end there. "...without a word he grabbed her hair and began to kick her viciously...Bidhibala's grandmother was screaming. "You will kill her! She's only a child"..." (Goswami 123). When his decision is challenged, the father responded to it with violence because girls were never meant to question, they are only to abide by the rules laid down by the patriarchal regime while men were meant to exercise control.

Later when her father brings the buffalo calf, Bidhibala through the help of Ratnadhar who was in love with her, releases the buffalo calf to save its life. Her father grows angry at this and swears to sacrifice two buffalos instead of one. Vidhibala, unable to openly protest against her dominating father, as a form of silent rebellion leaves home and joins a group of prostitute who were sailing towards Shekhadari. She refuses to eat and dies within a month thus performing her final act of revolt against her father's unjust decisions. Ratnadhar mourns her rightly saying, "Bidhibala, they made a sacrifice of you instead of the buffalo" (Goswami 156).

On the other hand, Goswami sketches the tragic character of Dorothy Brown who separates from her husband, Henry Brown tormented by his adultery. Broken and hurt, she takes up a small house near the Kamakhya Shrine to get some mental peace. Viewing her as an object apparent through the concept of the male gaze, the priests in the temple hope to gain sexual favour from her, failing which they spread rumours about her character. Their sense of superiority and patriarchal honour is at stake when she fails to comply to their desires, similarly her husband could not come round to the fact that his wife could leave him. He reaches her house and wants to take her with him. When she refuses he verbally abuses her. "Come on out you stupid cow!" (Goswami 35). His attitude becomes further abusive when he grabs her by the hand and shouts "The buggy's waiting Dorothy. Stop this nonsense and let's go" (Goswami 35) and then calls her a slut and a whore before he leaves.

Dorothy connects with an ascetic, the jatadhari and becomes his disciple, "I shall be your shadow forever. Our relationship cannot be defined. It is a very special bond" (Goswami 174). However, being a White woman, she is again looked at suspiciously by jatadhari's other followers. They kept probing him thus, "O Reverend One, the English woman's presence is causing much distress... ask her to leave" (54). But Dorothy Brown stood up firmly for herself and said "I have come here of my own free will. No one can ask me to leave" (Goswami 55).

Dorothy's decision of leaving her husband was scrutinised by society and even though it was her husband who cheated on her but people considered her leaving him as lack of integrity on her part. Other men forbid their wives from giving her company and her own husband rebukes her calling her "mother of all whores" (Goswami 35). Her body is also discussed openly in public and a hermit from Torsa says, "he (jatadhari) will disrobe this white devotee... I know. He will have to touch her yoni for his experiments..." (Goswami 16). Her private space is invaded and becomes a matter of public scrutiny which is unacceptable.

Dorothy becomes pregnant and there was a great murmur on the shore about it. "Was Dorothy carrying the jatadhari's child? Apparently, the white men had come up here to find out the truth" (Goswami 165). But the scales for weighing are not the same for men and women because Henry Brown too has impregnated another woman which was the reason for his wife leaving him but that never caused the men to raise their eyebrows but Dorothy's pregnancy caused quite a stir.

Ultimately Dorothy Brown's revolutionary self was put to eternal rest by a bullet whose identity could not be established although it was conjectured to be by the husband. It was not only a bullet aimed at her body, it was a bullet aimed at all women who were bold enough to raise their voice, stand at par with men, and challenge patriarchy.

Conclusion

Rules, regulations and rituals have historically been the by-products of a long standing line of traditions and customs shaped by the influence of patriarchy. Indian traditions have often got away with justification about its regressive gendered practices by its claims that women are worshipped like goddesses. This is a hypocritical stance developed by the patriarchal forces as there is a huge contradiction between the pedestal offered to goddesses and the brutality to which women are subjected to in their homes and in society in reality. Indira Goswami through the portrayal of poignant women characters in her works, probes into the causes, the unquestioned beliefs, the practices and the rituals that perpetuate violence on women and resists male hegemony in the name of maintenance of tradition thus remonstrating against patriarchy. The treatment of women in Indian society often reflects a standard Victorian prejudice, namely that all women were inferior to men and they could be exploited without misgiving as they were inherently submissive and voiceless. Goswami seems to ask women to break free from the shackles of patriarchy and achieve self-fulfilment through subversive acts as and when the need arises.

Works Cited

Baruah, Nandini. "The Female voice in the novels of Mamoni Roisome Goswami: Ushered in of a new era of Women Empowerment." *The Criterion: An International Journal of English Studies,* vol. 07, no.2, April 2016, pp. 82-85.

Deka, Joyti Rupa. "Rebellious Singers: Mamoni Roisome Goswami's Women Characters." *Galaxy: International Multidisciplinary Research Journal*, vol. 02, no. 04, July 2013. pp. 01-05.

Foucault, Michel. *The History of Sexuality: Volume 1*. New York: Vintage Books, 1978.

Goswami, Indira. *The Moth-Eaten Howdah of the Tusker*. Rupa & Co., 2005. Print.

Goswami, Mamani Rayachama, and Prashant Goswami. *The Man from Chinnamasta*. Katha, 2006. Print.

.... *Selected Works of Indira Goswami (Mamoni Raisom Goswami)*. Delhi: B.R. Pub., 1988. B.R. Pub. Corp. Web. 11 May 2019.

Holden, P. "The Subaltern: Political Discourse – Theories of Colonialism and Post colonialism". *Singapore: National University of Singapore*, 2002, pp. 202.

John R. Warner, Jr. "The silence of women, the voices of women." *International Third World Studies Journal and Review,* Volume XIII, 2002, pp. 458

Kishor, Neena. "Women In Indira Goswami's The Man From Chinnamasta: An Analysis." *Research Journal of English Language* and Literature (RJELAL), vol. 4, no. 4, Dec. 2016, pp. 699-704

Sharma, Malavika. "Indranath And Giribala – The Young Adult Dystopian Characters In The Moth Eaten Howdah Of The Tusker." i-*Manager's Journal on English Language Teaching*, vol. 5, no. 2, June 2015, pp. 19-27., doi:10.13140/RG.2.1.2449.5526.

Spivak, Gayatri Chakravorty. *"Can the Subaltern Speak?" Marxism and the Interpretation of Culture.* Ed. Cary Nelson and Lawrence Grossberg. Urbana: U of Illinois P, 1988. 271-313. Print.

Author's Bio-Note

Ashmita Bora is a Research scholar at IITG. She is a post-graduate in English Literature from EFLU. Her areas of interest include Gender and Women studies. She writes poems and short stories and has won prizes in various inter-university competitions. She was campus ambassador for Campus Inc. India in 2018-19.

10

The Character of Karna in *The Mahabharata*: A Study from a Dalit Context

Mamta Mahendru

Abstract

Dalits are the oppressed, broken or marginalised people of the society who suffer oppression and victimisation because of the rigid social structure in a traditional and discriminating society like India. The present paper is an attempt to study the character of Karna in *The Mahabharata* as a dalit character who, in spite of having a marvellous talent of archery, always faces discrimination in the hands of upper class like any other dalit in modern India. With the help of facts and statistics, I have tried to analyse the condition of dalits in India, compared it to the position of Karna in *The Mahabharata* and then found him too at the marginalised position. But in spite of all odds, he has emerged as a true hero who never succumbs to the atrocities and discrimination forced upon him.

Keywords: dalit; marginalised; Karna; discrimination; casteism; society.

Since the ancient times, our society has been divided into different sections on the basis of gender, religion, caste, creed etc. No division can be considered absolutely flawless and each one has become the reason of hatred and discrimination at some or other time. In India, the issue of casteism is the most delicate and serious since it has damaged the identity of Dalits or low-borne i.e. an essential fabric of society. The word 'Dalit' literally means "oppressed" or "broken". Jyotiba Phule, the founder of Satya Shodak Samaj is believed to have coined the term "Dalit". He refers the term to the outcasts and untouchables as the victims of the caste based social division of the Indian society. According to a definition given by Singh and Jain, "a Dalit is one who has suffered *dalan* and *daman*, oppression and victimization; one who has been suppressed; one who has been oppressed; one who has been exploited; one who is on the margins of society; one who is considered abhorrent; one whose human rights have been denied" (Singh). Time and again, the world has been proved very harsh towards them. They were continuously tortured, oppressed and humiliated in the name of ancient laws and practices.

"Dalits face discrimination at almost every level: from access to education and medical facilities to restrictions on where they can live and what jobs they can have" (Haseena). With the passage of time and the spread of education, the consciousness among such people started to appear. Few amongst them like B. R. Ambedkar, Jyotiba Phule and Savitribai Phule raised their voice through their writings, later known as Dalit Literature. It is the literature written by Dalit people to show the oppression and plight through which they have been going for ages. This should be considered as the space they are able to create for themselves after years of struggle in an extremely discriminating society like India. In spite of having talent, intelligence, and skill they feel marginalised and bordered by the privileged section of society on the basis of caste. "Dalits are daily victims of the worst crimes and atrocities, far outnumbering the other sections of society" (Haseena). Karna from the epic *The Mahabharata* was one such character who despite having tremendous talent and unmatchable skill of archery was considered not more than a sut-putra or low-borne as he was the son of a charioteer. This research paper is an attempt to present the character of Karna in the light of Dalit context since he is judged and marginalised on the basis of his upbringing by a low-born charioteer.

"It is not difficult to fall in love with Karna. He has all the elements of a hero but he is not allowed to be one – by his mother, his brothers, his teacher, even God. Our heart goes out to him" (Pattnaik). When he was born, his royal ancestry was snatched because of his mother's mistake. He was thrown into the web of the ruthless world of those times based on rigid caste system where everybody would get his share as per the ranking of his cast. Dronacharya refused him to teach archery. He was not allowed to take part in the graduation ceremony of Kuru princes and even in Draupadi's swayamvar. In addition to this, his own mother Kunti wanted him to withdraw himself from the war to save her other Kshatriya sons. He had to undergo all this just because of his low caste status like any Dalit in present day India. His situation can be compared to other Dalits through the findings of a report. It is conducted by the National Campaign on Dalit Human Rights – *Dalit Arthik Adhikar Andolan* and supported by UNICEF in 41 primary schools, 36 middle schools, and 17 secondary schools in of Bihar, Uttar Pradesh, Rajasthan and Maharashtra and shows the worst face of the conditions of Dalits in India. The report says "the morning assembly was invariably always conducted by upper caste children. In the class, Dalit children were made to sit at the back and in some schools of Bihar on the barren floor while mats were given to upper caste children. Even the notebooks and homework of the Dalit children were not checked by teachers" (Jamanadas 44-45).

The whole tragedy of Karna began from the decision of the princess Kunti, his biological mother, to abandon Karna at the time of his birth as he was born before Kunti's marriage to a Kuru prince, Pandu. "She uses a magical formula given to her by a sage to summon the sun-god, Surya, who is compelled to give her a child" (Pattnaik). Kunti abandoned Karna to save her own reputation but forever spoiled her first born's reputation. Thereafter life treated him a low-born. "Kunti places the child-born with natural armor and divine earrings – in a wicker basket and leaves him afloat to a river's whim" (Pattnaik). That river takes Karna into the household of a suta, Adhiratha. He was a charioteer of Kuru household. He took the child and gave him to her childless wife, Radha. From here began Karna's painful journey as 'Radhey', a sut-putra. Being a low-caste, humiliation and insult at every step had become his fate like other Dalits who "regularly face discrimination and violence which prevent them from enjoying the basic human rights and dignity promised to all citizens of India" (Haseena).

At heart, Karna knew that he was a warrior, "why else would he be born with an armor if he was not fated to fight?" (Pattnaik). Desperate to learn archery, he went to Dronacharya, the teacher of Kuru Princes but he was turned away. "Karna, like the other heroes in *The Mahabharata*, forces us to look at ourselves and at our frailities. When Karna is not allowed to train in weaponry because he is a suta, it makes one ask, "What if my child had been denied entry into college because of his birth?" (Das 180). He was told to stick to his caste duties and learn his father's trade. "Dalits are subjected to social, economical and cultural exclusion deeply embedded in social practices" (Haseena). But he was determined to win a respectable place in society based on merit. Unwavering in his spirit to learn archery, he went to Drona's teacher, Parshuram, as a disguised Brahmin because Parshuram was ever willing to teach Brahmins the use of weapons to stand up against Kshatriyas. Here, we find the case of Karna's Dalit consciousness. "He was not dare enough to claim him a sut-putra but introduced himself as a Brahmin boy.....Karna fears he might have rejected again if he admits his caste and so he lies" (Lakshmi). Karna was accepted and soon became the favourite student of Parashurama but soon his true identity was revealed and he was cursed to forget his knowledge at the time when he needed it the most. "But when Parashurama notices his ability to withstand intense pain silently, Parashurama concludes the boy is a Kshatriya by birth. Feeling he has been made a fool of, an enraged Parashurama curses Karna" (Pattnaik).

The Graduation Ceremony was organised by Bhishma to showcase the talent of his grandsons and all the Kuru princes but Karna because of his unparalleled flair proved the show-stealer. He showed his talent in a truly incredible way. Everybody wanted to know about him but his biological mother Kunti recognised his natural armor. She dared not speak anything. Once more, she chose to remain silent leaving him to his pitiable fate when Adhiratha, his foster father came to hug him in public and only because of his low upbringing "The great warrior is no warrior at all. He is a lowly charioteer" (Pattnaik) though his archery skills were unbelievable. Being the son of a low borne charioteer he was not allowed to take part in that ceremony. "Bhimsena took Karna for a charioteer's son, and said by way of ridicule – O son of a charioteer, thou dost not deserve death in fight at the hands of Partha----even as a dog doth not deserve the butter placed before the sacrificial fire" (Roy 325). When nobody was on his side, Duryodhana took his side and anointed him the king of

Anga country, giving him the powers equal to a Kshatriya king thus making him a Kshatriya by merit if not by birth. For this, he remained eternally grateful to Duryodhana but no one took his royal title seriously. The Pandavas argued quoting Dharma-Shastras that a man should be what his father is. As Karna's father was a charioteer, he could not be a king. Such treatment resembles the treatment Dalits meet even today in the Indian society. The interview data from the National Institute for Economic and Social Research has shown that caste awareness and differentiation in UK based Indians, "My brother used to get sworn at because of his caste when he was at work-with comments like 'you are not even equal to our shoes" (Metcalf & Rolfe). Though a Dalit or low-born gets opportunity to work at some respectable place, he has to endure humiliation and insults there. His ability is not at all recognised like that of Karna. Only Duryodhana speaks in favour of Karna and asks others to give him due respect and regard. He says, "Your own birth, ye Pandava princes, are known to me. Can a she-deer bring forth a tiger (like Karna), of the splendour of the Sun, and endued with every auspicious mark, and born also with a natural mail and ear-rings? This prince among men deserveth the sovereignty of the world, not Anga only, in consequence of the might of his arm and my disposition to obey him in everything" (Roy 326). But the high born Kshatriyas were not ready to accept him as their equivalent.

All through his life Karna remained loyal to Duryodhana because Duryodhana was the only Kuru prince in the whole epic who unconditionally loved and supported him irrespective of his low cast. He sided with Duryodhana even when he did wrong. No other person from the Kuru clan liked him. Duryodhana's mother, Gandhari, would resent his association with the son of a lowly charioteer. Even Bhishma did not like him. He would think Karna was a bad influence. Dronacharya hated him as he thought him to be a better archer than his favourite Arjun. Moreover, he did not want a sut-putra to be the rival of a Kshatriya prince Arjun. Thus, "although he is among the mightiest of warriors he is underestimated and insulted by Bhishma, Drona, Kripa and Ashwathama" (Guptan).

When Karna appeared in the archery contest organised by the king of Panchaal for the hand of his daughter, Draupadi, he was disqualified by the bride herself on the grounds of his low cast. "But seeing Karna, Draupadi loudly said, – I will not select a suta for my lord! Then Karna, laughing in vexation and casting a glance at the Sun, threw aside the bow already drawn to a circle" (Roy 425). She said that a person from the unknown origin and low rank could not even contend to be her groom. All through his life Karna endured taunts, insults and humiliation for being a sut-putra. That hurt him grievously. The insult by Draupadi was like a raw wound in the heart of Karna which could never heal. However, the Pandavas also came in disguise as mendicant Brahmins due to their exile and the competition was only for Kshatriyas. Even then Draupadi preferred Arjun over the sut-putra, Karna.

All through his life, Karna carried in his heart the raw wound of the unrecognised greatness. "The many insults and humiliations he had to endure were because of his supposedly low class birth led to a lifelong quest for recognition as the mightiest Kshatriya of his age and this fuels his feats of great heroism, his bitter rivalry with Arjuna and his ultimately self-destructive *daanveerta*" (Guptan). Thus, he tried to earn merit by becoming the lord of charity. He secured the title of 'Dan-veer' for himself. Indeed in that feudal society "if Karna had not possessed outstanding talent and a burning ambition, he might have led a reasonably well-adjusted life as a charioteer's son. But he was a Kshatriya warrior who, the epic tells us, had an inborn *svabhava*, 'natural inclination' for a heroic life" (Das 157). Karna does never show himself as the victim of the bad times and always shine as a victorious legend. Not only his mother and brothers but God himself in the form of "Krishna takes advantage of his charitable nature and gets Indra, king of the gods, to ask as charity Karna's natural armor. Karna donates this leaving himself vulnerable" (Pattnaik). In the Mahabharata war, Krishna even told Arjuna to take advantage of the situation when Karna was unarmed trying to free the wheel of his chariot. Arjuna released the arrow and Karna died in the back at the moment when he could not even defend himself. "The wheels of his life were stuck in misfortune much before the wheels of his chariot stuck in the bloody quagmire of Kurukshetra" (Guptan).

In spite of all the curses and humiliation Karna never gave up. He knew he would die one day defenceless and unarmed but all this could not lessen his love for archery. He worked towards achieving the excellence in this field but his skill was never acknowledged by the upper class of his times. "Karna has to be the wrong person in the wrong place'-this is what Karna symbolizes to many minds today. Life may have been unfair to Karna but he rises above pity. Despite his flaws we admire him" (Das 181-182). Karna never became the victim of caste rather emerged as an unconventional hero who did not belong to a royal class. He never presented himself a pitiable figure rather a revolutionary spirit who stood above all the boundaries created by caste and society. Karna embodied a man who refused to submit to the social system imposed upon him by the society. Irrespective of all the public opinions about *Dharma* and *Adharma*, Karna put his friendship and loyalty towards Duryodhana above everything else. He presented himself as a valiant who fought till his last breath and truly proved that heroism lies not in caste and status rather in deeds, bravery and determination. He challenged the popular notion of Dharma through his charitable nature that charity is not always the attribute of kings and royals. "Karna challenges their traditional understanding of dharma – as inherited status – and offers a new notion of dharma as deserved status" (Das 180). Even Indra came to him for charity. He felt so proud when Krishna approached him in the battlefield as a Brahmin to get his righteousness to redeem himself. His resolve to learn the art of archery leaves the message that learning is above every caste and rank. He was sent away by Dronacharya but he did not leave his resolution and ultimately fulfilled his wish and became the best archer in the world irrespective of his cast. Only his presence on the side of Duryodhana gave him the courage to fight with Pandavas with even Krishna on their side.

Though casteism is deeply rooted in the psyche of Indian society because of its importance mentioned in the religious scriptures, the things are getting better for Dalits. Education brings awakening in the minds of traditional and uneducated Indian masses. Ghuman has tried to show a recent picture of social creativity which can be considered a ray of hope. After millions of conversions by Dalits and untouchables to other religions, now they have "stopped trying to convert to other religions, but have resurrected and strengthened their own religions.....This has led to a resurgence of pride, and a 'sense of self-worth' among Dalits. There is renewed cultural, religious and political movement of Dalits" (Ghuman). We have seen the same attitude of 'sense of self-worth' in Karna also who even after knowing his real identity as a Kshatriya, never claimed his royal status; rather, he wanted to be known as suta-putra. He carried this very identity till his last breath. Krishna wanted Kunti to make her relation with her first born publicly so that he could at least die with the pride of being a Kshatriya and get his life-long due respect and admiration because he knew very well that the society would never approve a suta-putra's archery skills and charitable nature. But Karna insisted on dying with his older identity as 'Radhey'. "Karna's search for identity reminds one of the terrible mistakes that society makes in forcing individuals to privilege one identity over all the others. Karna has many identities: he is a caring son, an outstanding warrior, a father, a husband, an extremely generous person, a loyal friend of Duryodhana. Why must his father's background trump his many rich-perhaps, far richer-identities and become the sole basis of his status in society" (Das 169).

Actually, Krishna was right in his perspective since casteism has been innate in our society and it works according to the hierarchical pattern. The basic structure of our society is based on casteism. A child knows about caste from his elders who teach him the concept and existence of casteism in society. Children are often asked to maintain a distance with and to treat badly the low-caste people because Indian society considers caste system as something hereditary, hierarchical and justified according to the ancient Hindu scriptures. But the need of the hour is to adopt a more sensitive and sensible point of view regarding Dalits and untouchables. Creating humanism and awareness in upper caste people is the only solution to eradicate the problem of casteism and this can only be done by creating a casteless society where all the citizens will be treated equally. They must be treated as human-beings not the instrument to satisfy the false ego of the twice-borns. They have their own identity which need not be changed for anything or anyone on this earth. They consist more than one third of the total population of India which has resulted into a huge number of people. Collectively, they can change the fate and fortune of any society and can also add a lot more colours to the Tricolour. From sports to defence and industry to ministry they have proved their worth in almost every field.

Conclusion

The Mahabharata happened long back in which a valiant hero Karna suffered due to the prevalent vice of casteism in society; but 21st century India must not repeat her inhumane mistake. An undeserved wrong done to Karna resulted into the rivalry between the brothers, dishonouring the women, ruin of kingdoms and the utter devastation of *Dharma* but time is giving us an alarming signal now. We must not tolerate the atrocities done to any person irrespective of caste, religion and gender. All of us should work collectively in order to fulfil the dream of casteless India which Rabinder Nath Tagore envisaged long ago in his book *Geetanjali.*

> "Where the mind is without fear and the head is held high/Where knowledge is free/Where the world has not been broken up into fragments by narrow domestic walls------Into that heaven of freedom, my father, let my country awake."

Works Cited

Das, Gurcharan. The *Difficulty of Being Good: on the Subtle Art of Dharma*. Penguin Books. 2012. pp. 169-182.

Guptan, Madhu. "Karna and Arjuna" *boloji.com,* March 17, 2007, www.boloji.com/articles/1435/karna-and-arjuna. Accessed Jan 30, 2019.

Ghuman, Paul. "Reaching out to the Untouchables." *The Psychologists,* Vol 28 (2015): 564-567. Nov 29, 2018, thepsychologist.bps.org.uk/volume-28/july-2015/reaching-out-untouchables. Accessed Jan 11, 2019.

Haseena V. A. "The History of Dalit Culture and Their Deplorable Situation in India". *Historical Research Letter*, vol. 23, 2015, ISSN 2225-0964, pp14-17, www.iiste.org/journals/ index.php/HRL/article/view/24700. Accessed Jan 09, 2019.

Jamanadas, Dr. K. *Dalits in 21st Century Ambedkarite Perspective.* Kalpaz Publications. 2014. pp. 44-45.

Lakshmi, S. Jothi. "A Study on The Mahabharata Character, Karna in Dalit Context in the light of *Karna's wife* by Kavitha Kane." *Research Journal of English Language and Literature,* vol 6 issue 4, Oct-Dec 2018, ISSN 2321-3108, pp 258-261, www.rjelal.com/6.4.18/258-261%20s.jothi%20lakshmi.pdf. Accessed Jan 10, 2019.

Metcalf, H. And M. Rolfe. "Caste Discrimination and Harassment in Great Britain", *National Institute of Economic and Social Research.* Dec 22, 2010.

Pattnaik, Devdutt."A Boy called Karna" *devdutt.com.* devdutt.com/articles/indian-mythology/mahabharata/a-boy-called-karna.html. Accessed Dec 8, 2019.

Roy, Pratap Chandra translator. *The Mahabharata of Krishna-Dwaipayana Vyasa,* vol 1 Adi Parva. www.holybooks.com./Mahabharata-all-volumes-in-12-pdf-files/ Accessed Jan 19, 2019. pp. 325-425.

Singh, Vikas and Vikas Jain. "The Development of Theoretical Principles of Dalit Literature." *Fortell,* ISSN 2394-9244. www.fortell.org/content/development-theoretical-principles-dalit-literature. Accessed Jan02, 2019.

Tagore, Rabindernath. *Geetanjali.* Mahaveer Publishers. 2008. pp. 49.

Author's Bio-note

Dr. Mamta Mahendru, M.A., UGC-NET, Ph.D, having experience of 14 years of teaching in different colleges, has presently been working in Khalsa College, Amritsar as an Assistant professor since 2015. Her research papers have been published in various edited books and journals.

11

Subaltern Images of Women in Anita Desai's Novels: A Critical Study

L. Sangeetha

Abstract

Anita Desai occupies a prominent and towering place among the postcolonial female writers. She presents the perplexed situation of females who are victims of patriarchal set-up in which the females are neglected as well as treated inferior to men. Women are treated as tools and objects, and men try to silence their voice which is suppressed by the male-centred ideology. Females are treated as objects and others in the postcolonial set-up. The vision presented by Anita Desai reflects the confrontation of women against the oppression and suppression of male-dominated world. In most of her novels, middle-class women in contemporary India strive to overcome societal limitations imposed by male-centred society.

Keywords: Changed woman, patriarchy, recognition, image, system, discrimination, inferior.

It is an established fact that the women studies have been receiving increasingly academic and disciplinary recognition throughout the world. It has emerged as a different genre in English literature. Contemporary writers choose to present a varied image of women in their writings to situate the position of women in the society. In this way, every write puts on record his or her response and reaction to the place of women in the social system, giving way to an image of new women. The purpose of the present paper is to propose a model of Indian feminism to redefine the role or image of women in the postcolonial Indian English literature. The Indian model of feminism is not based on revolt against the difference, inequality and operation; but on the other hand, it is based on the rhythmic, mutual, complementary and welfare – oriented approach.

In the postcolonial society, various writers have drawn a parallel by comparing women as colonized and men as colonizers. Men are seen as the 'norms' and women are the 'other'; he is rational and assertive, she is emotional and submissive. In the same way, man is considered as primary, and the woman as secondary. In such male-dominated societies, there is always, as Troil Moi also observes, "intellectual, emotional and physical victimization of women by men." There are many other critics who claim that women "in many societies have been neglected to the position of 'other' and 'marginalized.' They share with colonised races and people, an intimate experience of the politics of oppression and repression. On the other hand, some critics say: "all women live in an 'imperialist' situation in which the men are colonialist and women are native. Some basic relations of inferiority and superiority of powerlessness and power prevail between women and men in all countries.

There is no doubt that Indian women writers have added a new dimension to the postcolonial Indian English fiction. The female writers contributed a lot to the development of the English fiction including new themes dealing with feminism. Their feminine sensibility made them capable to break new ground in Indian English fiction making an approach from the external to the internal world filled with extraordinary sensitive beings. Women writers of Indian English fiction attempted a lot to exhibit the eternal quest of their female characters for a meaningful life. The journey of Indian English women novelists gradually reached to such a distinction which brought the concept of a 'changed women' out of her view point towards man, society and life.

Among the female novelists in Indian writing in English in the postcolonial period, we come across a galaxy of women writers in which Anita Desai, Ruth Prawer Jhabvala, Kamala Markandaya Namita Gokhale, Nayantara Sahgal and Kamala Das are worthy of detailed consideration. Whereas, other women writers explore the feminine sensibilities, Anita Desai delineates the inner world of her hypersensitive female characters. She started with psychological novels and got excellence in this particular field. Her female protagonists suffer greatly because of their futile attempt to get emotional response. Anita Desai depicts female characters caught in the gulf between the inner and the outer world, expectation and reality which resulted in the deep anguish of a sensitive soul.

It goes without saying that Anita Desai's novel, *Cry, the Peacock* explores powerfully the concept of man-woman relationship, quest for identity, marital discord, and a sense of meaninglessness in life. The author deals with the complexities of modern Indian culture from a feminine perspective. It highlights the female predicaments of maintaining self-identity as an individual woman. The novel is a tale of a highly hyper-sensitive, cultured woman, Maya who is romantic by temperament as M. K. Bhatanagar in his book, titled, *The Novels of Anita Desai: A Critical Study* also observes that Maya is "romantic related with ideal, egoistical and self-indulgent, pursuing fancies and fanciful feelings... a 'toy' ---- 'princess' living in a world of elusive happiness" (Bhatanagar 4).

This novel is a story about a woman and told by a woman. Regarding this, D.S. Maini in the essay, titled "*The Achievement of Anita Desai*" in *Indo-English Literature: A Collection of Critical Essays* has aptly observed that *Cry, the Peacock* is "a typically feminine novel because it is a story of a woman told by a woman but because... it is the of feminine sensibility" (Maini 67).

Cry, the Peacock gives expression to the long suffocating sad cry of the wounded psyche, the painful tale of blunted human relationship being told by the chief protagonist herself. In this context Meena Belliappa, in her book, titled *Anita Desai: A Study of Her Fiction* has remarked that this novel is "a remarkable attempt to fuse fantasy with perceptual experience" (Belliappa 25).

In the present work, Anita Desai delineates beautifully the saga of a highly sensitive girl, Maya, obsessed by a childhood prophecy of disaster. The novelist has projected her extreme loneliness the way in which she is sensitive to the core. Maya cannot get over the trauma of a prediction that an albino priest forecasts death for Maya or her husband in the fourth year of their marriage. She is married to a man who is not only double her age but temperamentally quite different from her. Maya has been completely neglected by her husband.

Anita Desai delves deep into the feminine psyche of Maya from childhood through youth to death as she probes psychologically into the mind and heart of the protagonist. Desai has very rightly used the stream of consciousness technique to describe the cause and growth of Maya's disappointment. In this novel, Desai has described the pain, suffering, and depression suffered by Maya on the death of her pet dog, Toto. Maya was very attached to her pet dog Toto. When the dog died, she was alone at home. She was in great pain. She thinks that she will be soon gone mad. She feels alienated after the death of her pet dog, Toto as she says in this connection: "I am moving further and further from all wisdom, all calm and I shall soon be mad, if I am not that already" (*Cry the Peacock* 45).

Similarly, in one of her most celebrated and famous novel, *Voices in the City,* the female protagonist of the book, Monisha wants to break all the traditional shackles to free herself from domestic slavery. It is not an easy task for Monisha to liberate herself from family's obligations and moral duties as in this regard, Monisha remarks: "... life follows a subdued pattern of monotonous activity without acquiring any meaning" (*Voices in the City* 252).

Like Gautama and Maya, both Jiban and Monisha are poles apart. Monisha is highly sensitive like Maya. Monisha's expectations from her husband lead to dissatisfaction as her husband belongs to a traditional and orthodox Hindu family. Jiban's family is rooted in traditional and orthodox conventions where the family members are supposed to follow customs, certain restrictions and customs for everything. Jiban also believes in orthodox role of woman like, "cutting vegetables, serving food, brushing the children hair" (VCT 115). Monish is very fond of reading books of different subjects, but her intellectual aspirations amuse the women of the house with "indoors minds, starless darkies" (VTC 81). The ladies of the house always have an eye on her.

Whenever Monisha gets time, she wants to read the books but unfortunately, she has no time at all for reading her books. She is always busy in kitchen to prepare fresh chappatis and serving her uncles, listening to her mother-in-law. Although living in a joint family, Monisha craves for privacy; but even in her bedroom she is not able to enjoy the same as she frequently finds children playing all around. The ladies in the house are indulged in gossiping all the times which also does not provide her comfort. Monisha wants loneliness and solitude from such dominating relatives. She completely feels suppressed. Even when her sister Amla comes to meet her, she is surrounded by the children. This clearly shows that Monisha has lost her individuality in the house of her husband. Her in-laws don't think about Monisha's expectations and aspirations. She is like a cog in the machine, a log of wood who works day and night. Even her husband Jiban, like Gautama, is completely indifferent to her feelings.

Monisha's death is a "desolate liberty" which provides new vistas of understanding for Nirode. It brings him knowledge and reality. Only after the attainment of this awareness, Nirode is able to see the duality of his mother, the duality of the city, and the duality of existence. He says to Amla: "She is kali, Amla, I know her know. She is Kali, the goddess and demon is one...Mother, mother-kali is the mother of Bengal, she is the mother of us all. Don't you See, Amla how once she has given birth to us, she must also deal us our deaths (VTC 255-256). Monisha's tragic end redeems her from her "one dimensional existence" for she becomes conscious of the duality implicit in all existence. It is Monisha's death that brings the family together.

Like Maya and Gautama, and Monisha and Jiabn, the relationship between Sita and Raman is distorted due to their incapability to understand each other. Raman is patronising and commiserating towards Sita. Her fifth pregnancy throws her into outburst. She does not want to deliver her fifth child nor is she ready to abort it. She turns neurotic. She cries, smoke cigarettes, tosses clothes and books into her suitcase. Raman remarks: "It was an expression that was not infrequently fitted on to his face. Now and then exclaimed, – Don't be silly, and – Sita, don't behave like a fool, and – Think of your condition. What do you know about my condition? She flared. – I've told you – I've tried to tell you but you haven't understood a thing, and hurled slippers, papers, nightgowns" (WSWGTS 33) Similarly, Usha Pathania in her book titled *The Fiction of Anita Desai and Kamala Markandya* has remarkd about the different attitudes of Sita and Raman:

> Sita is a dreamer and a romantic visionary, whereas Raman is a down-to-earth realist...Raman, on the other hand, favours sanity, rationality and an acceptance of the norms and the values of the society. He is an average, busy, practical man of the world who avoids extremes...He does not understand what Sita means when she describes her friend and relatives – as pariah you see in the streets (Pathania 36).

Sita is highly subjective and introvert, has no experience of outer reality. Even the day-to-day common happenings make her react sharply and passionately. Regarding this D.S. Maini in the essay titled "*The Achievement of Anita Desai*" has observed: "Several symbolic little scenes of her bruised life are flashbacked in succession – the lone young eagle set upon and torn to ribbons by an assembly of raucous, rasping crows, the tearing up of the sketches by the cold, clinical Menaka who'll have none of her mother's sympathy or advice etc" (Malini 228).

Like Maya and Gautama, both Sita and Raman are spiritually apart. Raman has capability for accommodation and compromise, but Sita's overdramatic manners upset Raman and her children. She shows little respect to cleanliness, orderliness, tidiness. Raman is a responsible man while Sita is careless; yet he compromises and continues his relations with her. He finds her uncooperative at times. In spite of this, he is unable to shatter their weak relationship for the fear of insecurity and scandal. Sita fails to praise all this. Being self-centred and vain, she doesn't understand anything as the novelist puts it as: "Her husband with a greater capacity for accommodation than most had – even in the society with a truly remarkable capacity for accommodation, as long as it made for comfort, for security, continuity and safely from change or scandal had grown, over the years, immune to the shocks and suspicions she contrived to create" (WSWGTS 130).

Sita had the imagination to offer it an alternative – a life unlived, a life bewitched. She had cried out her great "NO" but now the time had come there epitaph to be written" (WSWGTS 139). This epitaph saves her from being explosion and violent like Maya. She has turned a different personality through her temporary but painful experiences. Her experiences realise Sita her moral responsibilities and duties along with the necessity of her inner-self. The outward appearance of her house is full of companions, her children and husband where no one can enter her inner world. It is only the island that fills her yearning for life. It is very clear that Sita must retreat to Bombay and admit her life as it is. This acceptance puts an end to breaking down of the family and they can be united again.

Through the portrayal of all the female characters Nanda Kaul, Raka, and Ila Das in the book *Fire on Mountain*, Anita Desai has propounded the idea how the patriarchal society leaves a void in their lives. Like Sita in *Where Shall We Go This Summer*, whose alienated life in the city, dominated by her husband, compels her to retreat to her father's island, but for a temporary relief. Nanda Kaul permanently departs from the city to retire in Carignano in order to enable herself to live "outside time" and also, away from the masculine law that rules the city which signifies the man:

> The old house, the full house, of that period of her life when she was the Vice-Chancellor's wife and at the hub of a small but intense and busy world, had not pleased her. Its crowding had stifled her..., She had suffered from the nimiety, the disorder, the fluctuating and unpredictable excess. She had been so glad when it was

> over. She had been glad to leave it all behind, in the plains, like great, heavy, difficult book that she had read through and was not required to read again (FM, 29-30).

She remembers nothing but duties and responsibilities that existed in that house. The only one bond that existed between her and her husband was her duties in the house, she always saw as "his house, never hers" (FM 18).

Nanda Kaul is gravely self-isolated as Victor George in his book titled *Invisible Men: Faces of Alienation* has very rightly observed: "Alienation from the self is a tragic condition... for those who are severely alienated, the loss is usually obviously. Their feelings range from apathy to grinding despair.... Many live apparently ordinary lives until with advancing years, there comes a missed chance of a wasted existence... others spend a large part of their lives in institution" (George 83). In her final years, Nanda Kaul realises that she has lost so much happiness of her family. She also feels that her previous life is completely void. Now she wishes to go away from her busy life and expects that she can lead an isolated and peaceful life at Carignano. She wants to spend her life like an institution without any trouble. She would like to be alone at Carignano among pine trees and cicadas. She has completely inhibited herself from the outside world of 'bags and letters, messages and demands, requests, promises and queries" (FM 44).

A contemporary issue facing every country is the question of women weather in Western or Indian literary traditions. The women are seen as launching themselves for their identity. The concept of 'new women' today challenges the traditional notion of 'Angel in house' and 'sexually voracious' image. The idea of 'emerged woman' is no doubt, a woman of awareness and consciousness of their choices. Anita Desai's female characters are new and different as she says in this connection: "the feminist literary criticism has developed as a component of women's movement and its impact has brought about a revolutionary change in literature or literary studies". Anita Desai's emerging new women is contemplating about her predicaments and chooses to protest and fight against the general accepted norms and currents. The difference that one witnesses is that they are prepared to face the consequences of their choices.

Clear Light of Day is one of the important novels in which female characters can be categorized into division: the females who do not surrender and so keep the conventions alive; and the second, those women who do not want to surrender and be coward, but break the convention to face their situation and take up a new direction where no one is there to dominate them.

Bim, the central protagonist of the novel, *Clear Light of Day,* is presented with two-fold ambition: to be emotionally and economically independent. She does not want to marry as she says in this connection: "I can think of hundred things to do instead. I won't marry,... I shall earn my own living-and look after Mira Masi and Baba and be independent." She would not depend on anyone, not even on her father.

Had she depended on her father for education, she would have been an illiterate as she asserts: "for all father cared, I could have grown up illiterate-and cooked for my living or swept. So I had to teach myself history and teach myself to teach."

Her desire to be independent, to be courageous, and to dress and smoke like a man, enables her to grow up both strong and confident. It is only because she has trained herself to be different. The much admirable characteristic of women, that is, weak will, dependence and shyness are alien to her perception. Bim refuses to confine herself to her role as a traditional woman, showing an insignificant victim or object for other's use and pleasure.

Bim emerges as a new woman with the passage of time. She is independent and liberated and yet there is no mark of arrogance of superiority in her personality. Bim is very clear about the aspirations, yet she is not able to roll in pity about her alienation. She felt cheated and stranded, and thought Raja and Tara to be selfish. She was ready to forgive them. She was ready to see every flaw of others in the light of understandings.

Bim and Tara, in their quest for identity, liberty and individuality act and react in radical ways to the set conventional construct. Tara was certainly not unhappy in obeying her husband, but the question which finally perturbs her is "how long"? She realises that she does something that she never likes as the author says: "She felt she had followed him enough, it has been such an enormous strain, always pushing against her grain, it had drained her of too much strength, now she could only collapse, inevitably collapse."

If we draw a comparison and contrast, we find in comparison that Bim has everything that Tara does not have. And, in that she has all this, and not what the society and tradition expect her to be, she is most of the times misunderstood as the novelist says in this context: Now I understand why do you not wish to marry. You have dedicated your life to others-to your sick brother and aged aunt and your little brother who will be dependent on you all his life. You have sacrificed your own life for them."

But, despite this gloomy and dismal atmosphere prevailing all around, Bim is determined to fulfill the responsibilities of her house. She breaks the established conventions and rules to establish her identity. Anita Desai seems to suggest the significant sign of emerging a new woman.

Anita Desai's female protagonists are all reflective about their condition. Their protest is not for equality, but for the right to be acknowledged as individuals, capable of intelligence and feeling that do not look for freedom outside, but within without painting their lives in various artificial shades of emotions.

In this way, the foregoing discussion leads to conclude the idea that the very concept of emerging women is central to Desai's fiction. The emerging woman that has been explored in the book reveals that she is not the ideal or the best women. She is new in the dimension of time by being a rebel against the general current of the patriarchal society, and in exploring her true potential, along with the struggle to fulfill her urges and needs.

Conclusion

In this way, after making a close and incisive study of Anita Desai's fictional works and the female protagonists, we can safely and rightly aver the fact that her heroines oxillate between attachment and detachment. Anita Desai's protagonists are the victims of injustice, suppression and inequality in their life. In fact, she is interested in the characters who are not average, but who have been treated or been driven into some extremity of despair and turned to fight against all odd situations. Anita Desai's women protest just for the right to be acknowledged as individuals and to get their due place in the family and society. It cannot be said that the concept of changed women as revealed in some of her works is to be taken as the model of the ideal women, but they are new and challenging in the dimension of time.

Works Cited

Atrey, Mukta and Kirpal Viney. *Shashi Deshpande: A Feminist Study of her Fiction*. Delhi: B.R. Publishing Corporation, 1998.

Bande, Usha. *The Novels of Anita Desai: A Study in Character and Conflict*. New Delhi: Prestige Books, 1988.

Belliappa, Meena. *Anita Desai: A Study of Her Fiction*. Calcutta: Writers Workshop, 1971.

Jain, Jasbir. *Stairs to the Attic: The Novels of Anita Desai*. Raipur: Printwell Publishers, 1987.

Pandey, Surya Nath. *Contemporary Indian Women Writers in English: A Feminist Perspective*. Atlantic Publishers and Distributors, 1999.

Prasad, Madhusudan. *Anita Desai: The Novelist*. Allahabad: New Horizon, 1981.

Ram, Atma. *Essays on Indian English Literature*. Aurangabad: Parimal Prakashan, 1984.

Sebestian, Mrinalini. *The Novels of Shashi Deshpande in Post-Colonial Arguments*. New Delhi: Prestige Books, 2000.

Khan, Fawzia Afzal. *Cultural Imperialism and he Indo-English Novel: Genre and ideology in R.K Narayan, Anita Desai, Kamala Markandaya, and Salman Rushdie*. The Pennsylvania state University Press, 1993.

Noami, Black. *Virginia Woolf as Feminist*. New York : Cornell University press, 2004.

Bande, Usha. *Validating the self: The Female Hero in R.K. Narayan's The Painter of Signs*. New Delhi: Manohar publishers, 1998.

Desai, Anita. *Fasting, Feasting*. London: Vintage, 2000,

Chitnis, Suma. '*Feminism: Indian Ethos and Indian Convictions*.

Author's Bio-Note

Working as an Assistant Professor of English and Head of the Department at Government Arts and Science College, Kallakurichi, (Tamilnadu), Dr. L. Sangeetha got her Doctorate from Periyar University, Salem. She is the author of three books, 10 research papers and 4 book chapters. She has also organized 30 online National Level Webinars.

12

Representation of Subalterns in Shashi Deshpande's *The Dark Holds No Terrors*

Prachi Bhongale and **Varsha Vaidya**

Abstract

Shashi Deshpande is one of the iconoclastic writers of post independent India. She is famous for her sincere and true depiction of the middle class educated women. Shashi Deshpande has explored the complexities of man-woman relationship in the context of marriage and has attempted to break the traditional moulds which trapped women. She has been successful in generating her characters who claim their uniqueness by showing their talents and abilities in their individual careers. In *The Dark Holds No Terrors*, Saru, the protagonist, plays role of an ideal Indian housewife who limits her self-development. This novel narrates the evidence of subaltern demonstration against the male-chauvinist society. A subaltern is someone who is lower in rank or position. Saru is the victim of patriarchal society despite her successful career. She becomes a victim of marital rape. She is deprived of her individual freedom which is why she is treated as a subaltern. Due to such treatment, she feels disillusioned and her individual freedom is lost. Saru plays two roles, one of being a doctor during day and other of a trapped animal at night at the hands of her husband. This paper investigates Deshpande's *The Dark Holds No Terrors* from a subaltern perspective.

Keywords: Subaltern, Individual freedom, Marital discord, Internal struggle, Tradition.

Introduction

The first person to use the word 'Subaltern' was Antonio Gramsci (1891-1937). He was of the view that subalterns were underclass upon whom the dominant class exerts its power. India was no exception to this. For ages, women haven't been considered as humans. A woman was treated as a subordinate sex only entitled to have offspring. They were treated as delicate, weak, and marginalized and had no right to serious thinking. As Simone De Beauvoir quotes "She is not regarded as an autonomous being. She is defined and differentiated with reference to men... She is called the sex… He is the subject. He is the absolute. She is the other" (*The Second Sex* 76).

In traditional Indian society, women were enclosed in the four walls of their home. They were deprived of equality when it came to careers. Women have always been considered as the second sex. Traditionally, marriage was the ultimate goal of a woman's life. In the process of marriage, women were not even given a chance to choose their husbands. Shashi Deshpande's depiction of the plight of women sandwiched between subaltern treatment by traditional patriarchy on one hand and their quest to self-realization and their aspirations on the other, marks the real contribution to Indian English literature. Indian women, in particular, are bound to serve their husbands with utmost dedication and devotion. However, Saru, being a modern woman is aware that her aim in life is not to please her husband.

To begin with, *The Dark Holds No Terrors* is the story of Saru that depicts her small-town upbringing, a dominating mother, a jealous husband and a marriage on the rocks. Shashi Deshpande throws light on the silence, loss, disappointment and cruelties caused by the subaltern treatment to women in the novel. Saru faced gender inequality right from her childhood. She was always treated as inferior to her brother just because she was a girl. Since childhood she was reminded of how unwanted she was in the family. She was treated as a liability whereas her brother Dhruva was treated as an asset. Duc to this sense of gender discrimination, Saru believed that only education will relieve her from the clutches of this discrimination. Hence, shc worked hard to become a doctor. However, her belief gets shattered when she faces the same kind of subaltern treatment under the disguise of 'an ideal wife' at the hands of her husband, Manohar (Manu). Vern Bullough observes:

> "The very word woman… emphasized [a] passive anonymous position. It derives from the Anglo-woman separate from wifehood. As individuals, with few exceptions, women did not account. They are mothers, wives, daughters, sisters" (*Subordinate Sex: A History of Attitudes towards Women* 3).

Humiliation Faced by Saru during Childhood

Saru, as a girl child faced parental rejection only for the reason that she was born as a girl and that too because of no fault on her part. She is made to feel that her birth was a horrible experience to her mother just because it rained heavily the day she was born. It seemed later to Saru that it was her birth that was terrible to the mother and not the rains. The birth of a son is happily accepted in Indian families whereas the birth of a daughter is unwelcomed. The reason for this discrimination is the fact that birth of a daughter brings burden to the lives of parents as they take away dowry to their in-laws' place. Saru was no exception to this. Her mother treated her as second sex. She recalls the excitement in the house on the occasion of naming ceremony of her brother. The fact that she is a liability to her parents is deeply implanted in her mind. She is not given any importance. She is always ignored in favor of her brother.

Dhruva's birthdays were always celebrated with joy and excitement with all the religious rituals. Later, after the death of her brother Dhruva, her birthdays went unacknowledged as if she killed him. Even small scale celebration on her birthdays stopped after his death. On receiving a small gift from a friend Smita, Saru feels so pleased. There was no one in the family whom Saru would share her feelings. Her father never spoke to her though he used to have conversations with Dhruva. This indifferent behavior from his end implies the fact that daughters are mother's business and have nothing to do with fathers. Saru's brother Dhruva died due to drowning and this was a major loss in the life of her mother. She couldn't bear the loss of her son and blamed Saru for his death. This is evident from following lines. "You killed him. Why didn't you die? Why are you alive, when he's dead?" (*The Dark Holds No Terrors* 21).

Saru's mother surprises her by gifting a pair of earrings on her fifteenth birthday. The gift was presented not because she cared for her daughter but for the sake of society that what they will think about a grown-up girl of fifteen without any ornaments of gold. The biased attitude can be attributed to the unhappy childhood of Saru's own mother. Saru's maternal grandmother was deserted by her husband, leaving her with the burden of raising two daughters. They were sheltered unwillingly by her parents. The ways with she was treated like a burden had conditioned her to such an extent that she started considering girl child as burden. Kamala, Saru's mother, does not complain about anything to her husband. She suffers from stomach cancer and is not able to tell her husband about it. She never eats food properly and never reveals the same to her husband. Even when she is asked to visit a doctor, she refuses to do so and Mai Kaki appreciates her refusal just because Kamala is not like new generation women who rush to see a doctor for every small reason. As Sarbjit Sandhu observes:

> The mother is very attached to her son. Her attitude is a typical one, all he is a male child and therefore one who will propagate the family lineage. In another sense also, the male child is considered more important than a girl, because he is qualified to give 'agni' to his dead parents. The soul of dead parents would otherwise wander in ferment (*The Images of Woman in the novels of Shashi Deshpande* 72).

Her mother's constant criticism gets on Saru's nerves. Hence, Saru decides to work hard and become a successful doctor. This decision is not appreciated by Saru's mother. Had she been a boy, her parents would have taken pride in her achievement of passing the exam with the first class. Behind Saru's fortitude was the internal aspiration to prove her mother wrong and her unquenchable thirst for acknowledgment. She had to literally fight for her career.

> And don't forget, medicine or no medicine, doctor or no doctor, you still have to get her married, spend money on her wedding. Can you do both? Make yourself a pauper, and who will look after you in your old days?... Let her go for a B.Sc.... You can get her married in two years and our responsibility will be over (*The Dark Holds No Terrors* 144).

Saru is deprived of her mother's love, affection and care. This incident strangulates the mother-daughter relationship. Her mother used to comment on Saru's complexion all the time and that she is too dark to be beautiful. Saru suffers a jolt by her mother's constant criticism of her appearance. This reflects the typical Indian inclination towards fair complexioned girls. Everyday we witness various advertisements endorsing the fairness creams. The rejection by her mother in her childhood days leads to a psychological insecurity in Saru. The exhaustive list of do's and don'ts make Saru more obstinate. The stress is given on the passivity and sublimity.

You will never be good looking, you are too dark for that...looking at yourself in the mirror! I'll give you a certificate to say that you're beautiful. Will that satisfy you!... A wedding in midst of approving relations. Bowing down dutifully to all of them (*The Dark Holds No Terrors* 25).

Women are not unequivocally taught about sex and this is evident in following lines.

Wanton... as girls they told us never to sit with our legs apart. We wondered why. Until that first day when he said to me... Open your legs, my love, or I can do nothing. And then I knew (*The Dark Holds No Terrors* 209).

Marital Discord

Marital discord is as old as the organization of marriage itself, even if it has diverged from time to time and from person to person. In the pre-industrial period, men and women who came jointly in marriage shared intellectual values, mutual dedication, belief and hope which subordinated the interests of the individuals resulting in the smooth relationship of the family. There were tensions in their marital relationship too, but the ethical and religious convictions, economic belief and the fear of social condemnation kept them together (*Sharma* 86).

As rightly explained above, traditional Indian working women are no exceptions to it. Saru meets Manu at college and is bewitched by his charm. They eventually end up having an affair. They try to culminate this relationship into marriage. When Saru discloses her love affair to her parents, her mother asks. "What caste is he? I don't know. A Brahmin? Of course not" (*The Dark Holds No Terrors* 96).

Saru had no freedom to choose her career and life partner as well. If a girl decides to marry by her own choice or marry outside the caste, she is labelled as threat to the family's reputation and honor. However, a man is free to marry as many times as he wants. This reflects subaltern treatment. If a well educated Saru is not allowed to marry the partner of her own choice then one can very well imagine the plight of illiterate women in Indian society.

By this Shashi Deshpande reflects the typical attitude of post independent Indians where caste consciousness prevailed. It was obvious for disapproval of their match. Despite the disapproval, they get married. Saru feels that after her marriage she will be a free bird. However, her wishes are shattered.

Marriage is a union of two souls. It's like two wheels running in parallel and the burden has to be shared by both husband and wife together. Both husband and wife are equally responsible to hold the relationship together. However, there is always subaltern treatment towards women in male chauvinist society.

K.M. Kapadia, while discussing the concept of marriage, writes: "Marriage was a social duty towards the family and the community, and there was little idea of individual interest. The social background provided by the authoritarian family afforded no scope for the recognition of any personal factor, individual interest and aspirations, in the relation between husband and wife" (*Marriage And Family In India* 169). Thus, Saru's individual interests remain unacknowledged.

Saru's total dedication in treating the victims of an accident in a nearby factory gained her fame and there are greetings and smiles. People looked up to Saru because of her profession. However, this view of Saru being respected in the society due to her highly respected profession made Manu uncomfortable. This was because Manu has been moulded in a way where women never had a supreme position than men. In society, it is expected that woman's earning as well as her educational qualifications should be less than man's. Also, a woman's existence is based on man. She is some way or the other connected to a man. A woman plays various roles – as a daughter of her father and then wife to her husband. There is no individual identity as such. Tradition has bound women to be dependent on men. This was not Manu's fault but the culture into which he was brought up into.

Manu is unable to digest the fact that his other half is more financially sound than he is. This financial imbalance makes Manu insecure. Saru's professional career turns out to be so strong that Manu is unable to impose his male superiority over her. His belief that man is always at the center and woman is at the periphery is shattered. Things become terrible when a columnist from a magazine tries to question Manu as to how it feels to have a wife who earns more than him. This query drifts the husband and wife relationship apart.

The growing fame of Saru becomes a cause of humiliation for Manu. This jealousy makes Manu to become a sexual sadist. He becomes violent stranger at night. What makes it worst is the fact that Saru's consent is not even sought in the matter. He believes that the license of marriage bestows him with right to humiliate his wife sexually as much as he wants. Thus, Saru is victim of marital rape and discord. Saru is unable to fight back. In Saru's weakness he finds his strength. This is a reflection of his inferior complex as an underpaid lecturer. Disillusioned Saru goes back to her home to escape from the torture.

Another aspect of subaltern treatment is represented in behavior of Padmakar, Saru's classmate. Padmakar wants favors from Saru on one hand and does not respect his wife on the other. He dislikes his wife just because of the fact that she talks every now and then about her children and family. She always cooks food based on her husband's likes and never calls her husband by his name. Thus, we see that women can earn respect by not following the traditional ethos but by asserting their individuality.

Internal Struggle and Self-realization

Saru shows a sheer disapproval for the established traditional norms. The deprivation of parental care and affection makes her decision of marrying Manu even stronger. She feels that after her marriage with Manu, she will be happy. However, her dreams suffer a jolt when people start acknowledging her profession more than Manu's. This makes Manu a sadist. Saru is unable to openly retaliate against the tyranny of her husband as she has children. She feels lonely after Dhruva's death. She passively endures the pain inflicted on her. Her guilt consciousness makes her unable to talk to Manu openly about his sadist attitude. Saru feels that in some way she is also responsible for her husband's failure. Every time she decides to talk to Manu, she is unable to do so due to underlying guilt. However, as an educated woman she is unable to fight against her husband's torments. Saru wanted a refuge due to the torture that she had faced in her parental home. However, the same feeling of suffocation is felt by her at home which she has chosen as a refuge. She realizes that her cruelty to her brother, mother and her husband makes her guilty of what she has done to them.

When she arrives at her father's home, she carries out an honest self-appraisal. She detaches all the identities of wife, mother and a doctor that defines her. She tries to ponder upon the situation that she is in. This helps in her self-discovery. That Saru who was initially identified as a daughter and later a wife is now just Saru who tries to search her own identity. She realizes that there is no point in running away from the problems. The only way to get out of the same is to face them audaciously.

She is able to perceive her faults against Manu, only after her going away from him. Her rebellion against the age-old tradition ends up in her realization of accepting the reality. She is torn between the obligation to her profession as a doctor and her duty as an obedient wife. Her story is the story of every Indian woman. Her education makes her to resist the unreasonable and irrational things. Thus, Saru realizes that there are no terrors in the dark; rather, those lie in her only. She learns to accept her faults, flaws and decides to return to her husband Manu. She learns that the only way out is to balance her professional and personal life. Marriage to Manu turns Saru timid and gentle who unquestionably follows the traditional ethos. However, after much self-introspection she attains a stage of looking towards life with an optimistic approach.

Conclusion

The internal struggle of the protagonist, Saru, in *The Dark Holds No Terrors*, goes from the life of an unhappy childhood to facing her husband with courage and confidence. Subaltern aspects are quite clearly represented in this novel of Shashi Deshpande. Saru somehow tries to come in terms with self-realization through sincere contemplation. Since childhood she is treated as unwanted due to her gender. She is criticized for her complexion. After marriage, she is treated as a trapped animal just because of her profession and that her husband is an underpaid lecturer. These aspects highlight the subaltern perspective in which movements and thinking of women are controlled according to their gender to mould their personalities. Saru undergoes humiliation, neglect as a child, and after marriage as a wife, she feels lost. Saru is humiliated emotionally during childhood at her parental home and physically by her husband after marriage. Since childhood she feels neglected and after her meeting with Manu, she feels loved. She feels someone is there to listen to her and share her feelings. However, her bliss is short lived. Despite her highly recognized profession, she is tortured by her husband. Being educated, she rejects the caste and religious rituals. It is her education that transforms her personality. She realizes that it's her life and she is the maker of her own destiny. Saru emerges strong and confident enough to face her husband. At the end of the novel, she accepts the reality and looks for solution with an open mind. The novel ends with a positive hope for change. Saru makes herself ready to face the upcoming challenges and derive harmony in her marital life. Shashi Deshpande tries to convey that women should no more be treated as subaltern and they should try their ways out and surpass all the obstacles without losing their individuality.

Works Cited

Deshpande, Shashi. *The Dark Hold No Terrors*. New Delhi: Penguin Books, 1990.

De Beauvoir, Simone. *The Second Sex*. New York: Vintage Books, 1989.

Bullough, Vern. *Subordinate Sex: A History of Attitudes towards Women*. New York: Penguin, 1973.

Kapadia, K.M. *Marriage And Family In India,* 2nd edition, Bombay: Oxford University Press, 1958.

Sandhu, Sarbjit K. *The Images of Woman in the novels of Shashi Deshpande,* New Delhi: Prestige, 1991.

Sharma, Mohini. "Marital Discord in Anita Desai's Novels." *Global Journal of Human Social Science Linguistics and Education*, vol. 13, issue 10, Version 1.0, Publisher: Global Journals Inc. USA, 2013, pp. 86.

https://www.google.com/url?sa=t&source=web&rct=j&url=https://socialscienceresearch.org/index.php/GJHSS/article/download/737/684/&ved=2ahUKEwjclbaS6KXvAhXK8HMBHS3aD7gQFjAGegQIDBAC&usg=AOvVaw1QwNzprJPV6748BOJjThCK&cshid=1615383643722

Author's Bio-Note

The author is a registered research scholar for Ph.D program in English in Rashtrasant Tukadoji Maharaj Nagpur University, Nagpur. She is pursuing doctoral research on topic *'Conflict between Tradition and Modernity in selected novels of Shashi Deshpande'* under guidance of Dr. Varsha Vaidya since May 2019. She has published some research papers in various reputed National/ International journals and has also attended various seminars and conferences.

13

Subaltern Voices through Feminine Sensibility: A Study of Kamala Das' Selected Poems

Prafulla Kumar Panda

Abstract

Women in India enjoy a subaltern status in every walk of life – social, political, economic, and cultural. The patriarchal society has taken away their fundamental rights making them objects of men for sensual or sexual gratification unleashing trauma and bitter anguish to them for ages. In the post-colonial period, the influence of the feminist movement is clearly reflected in Indian writings. Kamala Das being herself the subject of womanly experiences effectively gives voice to the aspirations, frustrations and emotional upheavals of a woman in the Indian social milieu. She gives voice to feminine desires, hopes, fears and frustrations of women in their journey from tradition to modernity. A speciality of her poetry is the depiction of women in patriarchal family as a subaltern Indian woman. She represents the modern woman's voice who wants to free herself from the religious and social convention, from marginalization and exploitation. This paper investigates, how Kamala Das has raised the feminine issues and has become the voice of the subaltern through her disclosure of her private life. She depicts her personal trauma, childhood suppression, unfulfilled love and her sensual desire, frustration, etc. hoping to represent such universal problems of women that lie dormant and inexpressive for ages in a patriarchal family or society. Kamala Das receives much respect and praise from her readers and critics for her independent thinking, frankness and bare-dare expression of the problems of woman. Further, her works enable the readers to understand how subaltern voices speak and about what they speak for establishing their self, their dignity and social status.

Keywords: Patriarchal, feminine sensibility, womanhood, subaltern voice, self-realisation, dignity.

In India, we witness scenes of women's subjugation that has kept them out of the reach of social, political, economical and cultural equality with their male counterparts. Such inequality has taken away their fundamental rights making them objects of men for their sensual or sexual gratification. The picture of ancient India where we find Aryan's depiction of the goddesses of the *Shakti-cult* remaining under subordination of male Gods, for instance, Goddess Lakshami as a devoted wife sitting at the feet of her husband Vishnu, or Sita bearing the burden of Rama's exile or even undergoing rigorous expiation like *Agniparikshya* (walking on fire), shows the attitude of society towards women. However, it was observed that, women enjoyed considerably a good status in some cases, especially, in socio-cultural milieu then. They had the right to choose husbands in *swayamvara*, and to divorce; also had the liberty to take part in religious activities and even widows were allowed to remarry in certain conditions. But, the status of women deteriorated during the post-Vedic age when women were denied any kind of freedom and suffered subordination and subjugation soon after Manu established a patriarchal system. *Manusmriti* prescribed that women to remain under the control of men: in childhood, under her father's control; in youth, under her husband's; and when her husband dies, under her sons' (*Manusmriti*: 51481) debarring them from intellectual, philosophical and spiritual pursuits.

Further, invasion of the Muslims and the establishment of Islamic regime by the Mughals in the sixteenth century aggravated their status to a greater extent with the imposition of rigid codes of conduct in the name of religion reducing their status to mere puppets in the hands of men and could not voice their feminine urges, feelings, emotions or sensibilities. The observation of *purdah*, self-sacrifice, tolerance, etc., was severely imposed on them forcing them to remain within four walls. Afterward, they also enjoyed a subdued inferior status during the British regime and throughout the eighteenth century. With the advent of Indian social reformers like Raja Ram Mohan Roy, Ishwar Chandra Vidyasagar, Jyotirao Phule etc., and formation of new laws in the 19th century, British government curbed such social evils like the practices of *sati,* child marriage, polygamy and discrimination towards female education, etc. to a great extent. In the words of Sunanda P. Chavan "The new social situation led women to assert, for the first time, their full identity as independent, self-made individuals in the man-oriented society."

The women's assertion of equal rights – the rights of freedom, education, equality of opportunity, expression, and equality of socio-cultural status began in the post-colonial India after the implementation of the constitution. The urbanization and the influence of the western culture have brought many changes in the socio-cultural life of modern Indian women. But unfortunately, common women are still victims of patriarchal mindset and are being humiliated, harassed and oppressed in homes and at workplaces as well. As Clara Nubile states, "in modern India the situation of women is still far from an ideal, liberated, democratic model. They keep on struggling against the burden of tradition, against the legacy of the past and the orthodoxy of patriarchal system". The male chauvinism has created gender discrimination; religious taboos, etc. making them become victims of crimes like dowry killing, physical and mental torture, sexual harassment, trafficking, *purdah*, *pativratadharma* (husband worship), or female infanticide, etc. The denial of education, domestic violence, arranged marriage or denial of female's participation in certain socio-cultural activity, etc. are the burning issues that a majority of women face in India, now. In fact, in modern times, they are no longer to be borne by the subaltern and wait for western feminists or someone here to speak for them as a representative; rather, they feel fit to voice their issues by themselves without hesitation and the same has been coming out like an outburst, or as a volcanic eruption.

Indian feminist theorists like Gayatri Spivak, Chandra Tolpade Mohanty and Mandakranta Bose deal with the issues of women hoping to improve the condition of Indian women – family violence, education and female sexuality, female infanticide, etc. Women who have been reprimanded, rejected or dismissed by the patriarchal societies have taken up the pen and write their own destiny, thus establishing a feminine perspective exposing patriarchal hegemony. Such women writers even bear the brunt of male aggression time to time while writing down women's stories of oppression, harassment and their physical and mental trauma. That's why; many of them even write using male pseudonyms in order to hide their identities.

In the post-colonial period, the influence of the feminist movement of the west is clearly reflected in Indian writings, especially in poetry, majority of which are of subjective of all literary genres. The writers like, Toru Dutt and Sarojini Naidu, or writers like Sharat Chandra and R. N. Tagore have expressed concern about the pitiable condition of women living in our society under lot of restriction and pressure. Modern Indian poets, like Nissim Ezekiel, A.K. Ramanujan, Imtiaz Dharker, Gauri Deshpande and Mamta Kalia, Eunice de Souza, Sujata Bhatt, Mukta Sambrani, Menka Shivdasan, Suniti Namjoshi, Lakshmi Kannan, Tara Patel, etc. have also powerfully portrayed Indian women, their whims and aspirations, their love and pain, their sorrows and suffering, etc. Kamala Das being herself the subject of womanly experiences effectively gives voice to the aspirations, frustrations and emotional upheavals of a woman in the Indian social milieu. Being influenced by the feminist trends, she gives voice to feminine desires, hopes, fears and frustrations of women in their journey from tradition to modernity. She revolts against the restraints in the patriarchal society and expresses the pathos of a woman emerging from a passive role to the point of discovering and asserting her individuality, identity and freedom in the society. With her creative imagination, she has brought a different picture of Indian women entirely different from that of her predecessors on account of her voice for women – for their dignity, status and equal treatment on both individual and social fronts.

Kamala Das (1934-2009), born in Punnayukulanam in Thrissur district in Kerala, is considered as an iconoclast in her generation who has become a very significant voice for women's freedom and their status in the society which is governed by men. She used to write in two languages – English and Malayalam, and honestly revealed her personal life and experience through her poetry. Throughout her writing, she has been very brave, candid and honest in expression while dealing with women's issues and female sexuality-completely free from guilt and inhibition. She has feminist concerns through her writing articulating the sadness and longing of women, free from male accusations and wants only to free women from their stereotypical status. 'She talks about the subject of "woman" and the revelation of female experiences, trauma of an unhappy marriage or humiliation of unwanted surrender in sex or disgust at the male domination. Pursuit of love and afterward striving for its realization is certainly the recurrent theme of Kamala's poetry. Her treatment of love theme is characterized by increasing depth and intensity' (Tilak 106). In a society dominated by men, she has tried to highlight her feminine identity in her autobiographical poems exposing her sufferings, mental trauma, anguish and sensibility. Her confessional poetry is a poetry of rebellion which expresses her humiliations, the result of all psychological dissatisfaction and trauma, suffering, the tortured soul, of women's sensitivity making herself miserable and "a misfit everywhere" (Das 109). Harimohan Prasad has rightly remarked about Kamala Das's poetic works: 'Her poetry has often been considered as a gimmick in sex or striptease in words, an over expose of body or *"snippets of trivia"*. In a modern society, she is not to be subdued by the patriarchal social order rather finds a medium through which she can raise voice to her pent up feelings and emotions' *(35)*.

In post-colonial era, Kamala Das is one of the most prominent and debated poet who writes with honesty and candour; and such frankness is rarely seen among other Indian writers. Unlike her predecessors like Toru Dutt and Sarojini Naidu, in her poetry we find a conflict between tradition and modernity at various levels – social, cultural, national and cosmopolitan. A remarkable feature of her poetry is that, she blends her personal experiences and observations in her poetry in such a way that appears universal. A speciality of her poetry is that, her depiction of women in a patriarchal family has been the voice of the subaltern in Indian society. She represents the modern woman's voice who wants to free her from the religious and social convention, from marginalization and exploitation. She admits her readers into the arena of her private life and discloses the delicate facts of her personal trauma and childhood suppression, unfulfilled love and her sensual desire, incompatibility with the inadequacies of life, frustration, etc. hoping to represent such universal problems of women in general that lie dormant and inexpressive for ages in a male dominated society. She tries to present women who struggle to shatter the patriarchal taboos and hold an unbiased position to maintain their 'self' and dignity. In other words, she has become the voice of the subaltern and depicts their universal sufferings through her own, and asserts their struggle to establish their own identity and their self-realisation in the society in a rebellious way breaking the social taboo fixed by men.

Kamala Das is essentially known for her bold, frank and open expression of her feelings. All poems of Kamala Das are her quest for identity in a traditional society. *'An Introduction'*, an autobiographical poem by Kamala Das, deals with feminine sensibility. In the poem, she introduces herself as a typical brown coloured Indian who tries to establish her 'self' – her identity:

'I don't know politics but I know the names
Of those in power, and can repeat them like
Days of week, or names of months, beginning with Nehru.
I am Indian, very brown, born in Malabar,
I speak three languages, write in
Two, dream in one.' (*An Introduction*, L. 1-6)

Further, she talks about the traditional role of woman and traditional look and she wishes freedom from it. She struggles to break the chains around her which has been put by patriarchy and wants to be free from the established tradition and custom of time and glorify her passion – her real self as she says:

'…I wore a shirt and my
Brother's trousers, cut my hair short and ignored
My womanliness. Dress in sarees, be girl
Be wife, they said. Be embroiderer, be cook,
Be a quarreller with servants. Fit in'. Oh
Belong, cried the categorizers. Don't sit
On walls or peep in through our lace-draped windows.
Be Amy, or be Kamala. Or, better
Still, be Madhavikutty. It is time to
Choose a name, a role'. (*An Introduction*, L. 33-42)

In '*An Introduction*', Das universalizes her private experiences, suggesting that whole womanhood has some personal feelings of yearning and loss that is being checked by manhood. According to Kamala Das, womanhood involves certain collective experiences (Verma and Dhar 2013). A young girl's dilemma, fear and loss of freedom and her suffering as a young girl, is revealed here when she says:

'He drew a youth of sixteen into the
Bedroom and closed the door. He did not beat me
But my said woman body felt so beaten'. *(An Introduction, L. 28-30)*

These lines also symbolize her loss of freedom to live her life in her own way. Actually, in this poem she portrays her physical and emotional agonies when she was growing up as an immature girl. But the poet is not to be subdued by male dominance and opts to rebel against male supremacy.

She speaks of male domination an important cause of her unhappy marriage, the humiliation of a desireless surrender in sex, and her brave desire to free herself from the shackles of stereotype subaltern status as a woman.

'I met a man, loved him. Call
Him not by any name, he is every man
Who wants a woman, just as I am every
Woman who seeks love. In him… the hungry haste

Of rivers, in me... the oceans' tireless
Waiting'. (*An Introduction*, L. 45-50)

The above lines imaginatively present the basic difference between a man and a woman and invite men for better understanding of womanhood. Both have their whims and passions, desires and pains. So, both need to understand this and also mark the underlying differences that exist between themselves.

Kamala Das is quite open, honest and bold about her talks of her passion. She is one of the very few poets who speak so openly about her passion, and her desire. Obsession with love is one of the predominant features of her poems. She is deeply shocked and wounded when she failed to attain love and her emotional fulfillment. So, she revolts against the society that has brought gender bias blocking her emotional, intellectual and spiritual development. She realizes that both man and woman are equal and have equal rights to learn, enjoy and please their senses and establish their 'own selves'. So, in this respect, there is no question of male only to get a better edge over female.

'I have no joys that are not yours,
No aches which are not yours I too call myself "I". (*An Introduction*, L. 60-61)

Although, she talks of incompatibility and the inadequacies of life, frustration and gender complex, marginalization and exploitation of women, unlike other feminists, she shows her concern for social and cultural construction of gender, and does not question the importance of men while talking of her equality, individuality and emancipation. Hence, she articulates the 'man-woman relationship' for consummation of life as well as spiritual satisfaction which can only be realized through a balanced and perfect union of the two. In order to lead a contended life both need to listen and respect each other and obey each other as she says in *'Composition':*

'Husbands and wives,
Here is my advice to you,
Obey each other's crazy commands,
Ignore the sane.
Turn your home into a merry
Dog-house,
Marriage is meant to be all this
Anyway',... (*Composition, L.* 181-188).

"I do not know politics" is a confession of ignorance that has brought to her by a society due to her subaltern status which she ironically exposes.Her present status is such that, even if she possesses knowledge of politics and knows the political heads it can put no impact on her personal life. In *"Composition"*, she talks of the degenerating condition of women when her school building turns into a brothel where common women become the victims of politics of the male hegemony in a prejudiced culture where they are forced to sell off their bodies and are treated insignificantly as mere as toys.

'My first school-house
Is now a brothel,
And
The ladies sun themselves on the lawn
In the afternoons
With their graying hair,
Newly washed,
Left undyed.
Who can say, looking at them,
That they are toys,
Fit for the roaring nights'? *(Composition, L.163-173)*

The life of an Indian woman is not free and easy like that of her male counterpart. She has to walk on a path created by man with lot of do's and don'ts. Womanhood is a curse that looms as a burden on our society. Das has better realised this truth when she boldly expresses:

'But my sad woman-body felt so beaten.
The weight of my breasts and womb crushed me.
I shrank pitifully.*(An Introduction, L.31-33)*

The social code of conduct formulated for women by a society dominated and governed by men, does not allow them for their self-realization. In fact, this ends in a sort of self-negation of woman increasing her dependence on men in spite of their apathy, sexual exploitation and betrayal. Das realizes that, lack of love in man-woman relationship is an improvised form of male dominion and oppression.

Obsession with love is one of the dominant themes of Kamala Das' poetry. The failure to arrive at its peak in the company of her man leaves her emotionally wounded. There are some poems such as 'The Freaks', 'The Old Playhouse', 'The Looking Glass', 'The Sunshine Cat', 'Conflagration' and 'The Stone Age' which poignantly express her helplessness in not finding true love which ultimately brought to her feeling of loneliness, fear of separation and emotional breakdown. She shows her loneliness, nervousness and her emotional break down when she doesn't find intimacy and love from the man she loved but only lust. Hence she questions the existence without love:

'Who can
Help us who have lived so long
And have failed in love'? *(The Freaks, L. 12-14)*

Her experience of pain in love is due to her unfulfilling of passions and her drifting towards a feeling of loneliness and disappointment in *"The Testing of the Sirens"*:

'I shut my eyes, but inside eye-lids, there was
no more night, no more love, or peace, only

the white, white sun burning, burning, burning.
Ah, why does love come to me like pain
again and again and again'? (*The Testing of the Sirens*, L. 42-46)

It can be marked that in the midst of her disappointment, the poet aspires to raise herself and her emotions in this vast unfeeling, apathetic world.

The theme of failure and frustration in love and marriage which is a recurring theme of Kamala Das' poetry gets a better expression in her '*The old Play House*'. Her feminine sensibility is at its height which has forced her to expose the temperament and disposition of her husband. Her inexpressible plight as a housewife with an egocentric and male chauvinist husband has summarily reduced her aspiring self into a mere entertaining toy. She has been reduced to be a mere caged wife by the male ego. She realizes that her freedom is encroached upon. Her life is supposed to be the old playhouse where her mind is stifled and crippled and her spirit crushed. The poet ruefully speaks:

'....There is
no more signing, no more dance. My mind is an old
play house with all its lights put out'.
(*The Old Playhouse*, L. 23-25)

The concrete and evocative imagery and imaginative symbols that she has used brilliantly expresses an individual's suffering. *The old Play House* is a poem which is permeated by Das' feminine sensibility which revolts against her husband's manner of making love to her. In fact, his love making for her is full of lust only and shows no love at all. She is bold enough and thus expresses her disgust with a husband who only engages in the gratification of his lust, his carnal desire in the pretext of making love. She dislikes such a mechanical and unemotional way of making love which does not show love to her, or even shows no concern about her feminine sensibilities. As a result, her desire to grow, to attain self-knowledge and self-realization is totally checked. She is reduced to become a mere helpless hanger-on on her husband – nothing more than a sex object:

'You dribbled spittle into my mouth, you poured
Yourself into every nook and cranny. You embalmed
My poor lust with your bitter-sweet juices. You called me
wife...' (*The Old Playhouse*, L. 10-13)

Her feminine sensibility and her voice become so powerful and poignant in her poems that the poet seems to be a mouthpiece of feminine movement in India. '*The Old Playhouse*' presents the pathetic and gloomy condition of a girl in a patriarchal home. A girl comes to the house of her husband with great expectations of love and happiness which she rarely finds because of the lustful but unconcerned attitude of her man turning her life into a hell and her new home into a graveyard. In her helpless state, she compares herself to a *swallow* which her husband wants to tame and keep her fully under his control by the power of his love making. Further, the poet says, in this suffocating atmosphere of her new home the woman loses her all "will and reason, freedom and appetition".

'You planned to tame a swallow, to hold her
In the long summer of your love so that she would forget
Not the raw seasons alone, and the homes left behind, but
Also her nature, the urge to fly, and the endless
Pathways of the sky'. (*The Old Playhouse*, L. 1-5)

She is bold and loud when she speaks to her unfeeling, uncaring husband to 'be kind' to her and not to treat her as a mere lifeless object of pleasure and lust which displeases her and suffocates her in the house in his presence in the poem *"The Stone Age"*:

'Fond husband, ancient settler in mind,
Old fat spider, weaving webs of bewilderment,
Be kind. You turn me into a bird of stone, a granite
Dove, you build round me a shabby room, *(The Stone Age, L. 1-4)*

The woman's spirit of rebellion against male domination and ego is found in the poem "*The Conflagration*":

"Woman, is this happiness, this lying buried
Beneath a man? It's time again to come alive.
A world extend a Pot beyond his six foot frame" (qtd. in Iyer 214).

Her womanly spirit rebels against male domination and ego and wishes to go beyond them for 'happiness and freedom'. The womanliness in her "desires to extricate from this 'soul killing' subjugation" *(Iyer, 371).*

'Woman, is this happiness, this lying buried
Beneath a man? It's time again to come alive.
The world extends a lot beyond his six foot frame*' (Conflagration).*

Loveless relationships are unbearable for a woman as it hinders the upliftment of her 'self' and brings imbalance to her emotional and spiritual fulfillment. '*The Looking Glass*' symbolically mirrors her hurt-self and shows her struggle to achieve identity and individualism as a woman.

The poet ironically portrays her man as the stronger part in the pair and not praising the qualities of a woman because if she does not praise him, she may not obtain his love. The fear of loss and the helplessness of the woman is understood when she says, '...but living/without him afterwards may have to be/Faced...' *(The Looking Glass, L. 17-19).* As a result, the absence of man may bring her suffering from loneliness and lack of love. The dependence of woman is reflected in these lines as she needs to accept the man's presence for admiration and praise of her physique. Even if he leaves her, she has to undergo humiliation and suffering as she is unable to realize the worth of her 'self':

'...All the fond details that make
Him male and your only man'. Gift him all,
Gift him what makes you woman,... *(The Looking Glass, L.11-13)*

The Looking Glass presents to the readers with the image of Indian womanhood and the feminist sensibility. The mirror is a complex symbol of reflection of societal attitude that warns a woman against the possibility of loneliness and suffering living without her man. It shows the gender bias, of male superiority.

'...Stand nude before the glass with him
So that he sees himself the stronger one
And believes it so, and you so much more
Softer, younger, lovelier. Admit your
Admiration. Notice the perfection
Of his limbs,...' (*The Looking Glass*, L. 03-08)

The poet makes a realistic description of a woman in this male-dominated society where her main job is to please her man. A woman should admire her man's ego standing naked with him before a mirror exposing her soft, and smooth and lovely body that is so tender before the stronger muscular male body.

In the poem *The Sunshine Cat,* it is feminine sensibility which compels her to describe and expose her husband as a selfish and cowardly man who never loves her nor has had emotional attachment but uses her as a mere object of lust to satisfy his sexual desire. While she craves for love and care and support for her emotional and spiritual uprising, her husband as well as her so-called lovers have remained cold and treat her like a prisoner reducing her to become drab and useless *'a cold and half dead woman, now of no use at all to men'* needing sexual satisfaction.

The young lovers simply use her for their sexual gratification forcing her to "build walls with tears...walls to shut herself in" when she fails to get love and emotional support. There she could only find a ray of hope – is the streak of sunlight – the sunny impulse in her which reduces also in the passage of time. The poem focuses on unconcerned and ruthless attitude of the society towards woman making her an object of sexual gratification of man.

'Her husband shut her
In, every morning, locked her in a room of books
With a streak of sunshine lying near the door like
A yellow cat to keep her company,...
...that the cat of sunshine was only a
Line, a half-thin line,...' (*The Sunshine cat*, L. 14-20)

The confessional tone of the poet is not only an authentic tone of her expression of her tortured soul but also a voice of the subaltern in the contemporary Indian society in which they seek a harmonious relationship between the two sexes.

With the arrival of Kamala Das on the horizon of Indian English poetry, the tone of poetry as well as the portrayal of women has drastically changed. Kamala

Das frees herself from the metaphysical and romantic traditions of Indian English poetry written by women poets such as Toru Dutt or Sarojini Naidu. Unlike her predecessors, her poetry centres round her own feelings of love and her suffering, her unfulfilled sexual desire bringing in mental trauma to her, and her loss of dignity and self-glorification as a woman which, in the context of Indian poetic scenario are often considered brave and surprising. Through her poetry she not only expresses her own inner feelings and her sufferings but also projects herself as a feminist poetic voice who is always asking for a dignified place of honour for the subaltern. Her predecessors, Toru Dutt and Sarojini Naidu talk of man-woman relationship and woman's plight but on a lighter vein. Toru Dutt is fully aware of the sufferings and plight of women, the sorrowful condition of widows of her time in Indian society. While narrating a woman's suffering, in *"Savitri, Ancient Ballads and Legends of Hindustan"* she has tried to create women's free identity which is essential in society:

"He for his deeds shall get his due
As I for mine: thus here each soul
Is its own friend if it pursue
The right, and run straight for the goal;..."

(*Savitri, Ancient Ballads... Canto*, 31).

In "Love Guerdon", Naidu speaks of woman's suffering in her lover's hands but the ladylove is prepared to accept and bear such suffering and humiliation:

"Fires were the wounds
You struck me O my love
And bitter were the blows!
Sweeter from dear hands all suffering
That rich love tokens other comrades bring
Of crimson, Oleander and of rose." *(Love's Guerdon, L 50-55).*

Similarly, Toru Dutt's woman, Savitri pleads for her husband's life. She is fully aware of the pain and suffering that separation can bring to her life without her husband.

'I bear my husband, by the faith
That looks from earth to heaven above',...

(*Savitri, Ancient Ballads... Canto*, 30).

Like Toru Dutt's "*Savitri*" in "Caprice" Naidu talks of man-woman relationship. While talking of a man-woman relationship, she is soft in her tone and temperament. Though the woman protests against the discrimination of man, she does so but on lighter vein:

'You held a wine-cup in your fingertips,
Lightly you raised it to indifferent lips,
Lightly you drank and flunk away the bowl....
Alas! It was my soul'. *(Caprice, L. 5-8).*

The poems of Toru Dutt and Sorojini Naidu breathe an Indian air which is mellifluous and their projection of woman is an ideal Indian woman of Ancient times. Naidu's poems like *"Indian Love Song", "Village Song", "Pardanashin" and "Indian Dancers"* portray the life of Indian women of different sects – their hopes and aspirations, their joys and jubilance in love. So, they are seen dancing, enjoying and are happily engaged in the thoughts of their lovers and wait patiently for them, too. Love is the dominant theme of Sarojini Naidu's poetry where women are shown as the worshippers of love who are ready to surrender before their lovers for the sake of love and its consummation. *"If You Call Me", "The Path of Tears", "The Sanctuary" and "The Worship of Love"* represent the role of women as lovers in various moods. They are ready to sacrifice their happiness for the sake of their lovers' happiness. Even, if a woman complains about negligence, she shows it differently, readily accepting all the insults and suffering in her lover's hand as a sweet gesture of her love. On the other hand, Kamala Das' poetry is a protest against the lovers for their wrong doing and ill-treatment towards the beloved for which she demands correction. The projection of woman, beloved, or wife in her poetry seeks correction and justice against the convention of society which favours patriarchy. She never glorifies love like other Indian women poets rather to bring forth the pains and sufferings of a woman for not finding true love from her man or lover. Her poetry centres round on her own experience while playing different roles at different times – Kamala as a woman, as a wife, as a sexual partner for many men besides her husband and as a mother. Her disillusionment in love, her unfulfilled desire, and feminine sensibility, etc. are the motivating and governing factors which give her poetry a distinctive tone and character as well. Her poetry is confessional in tone and what Parthasarathy says, "is distinctively feminine (22)" and her feminine sensibility ranging from the subject of love in its various forms and moods is a form of protest against the male-dominated society which is rarely found among other Indian poets.

Das protests against the restraints and restrictions imposed upon women by the patriarchy in general and husbands in particular and for which she seeks freedom. She seeks justice and certain corrective measures for the Indian womanhood and wants equal rights and dignity of living for them. Thus, Kamala Das can be described as a feminist, who talks of the cause of the subaltern's rights in order to free them from the chains of slavery put by men for ages. Although she "has never tried to identify herself with any particular version of feminist activism" (Raveendran, 1994), but it's quite pertinent to label her as "a feminist" because of her candour in dealing with women's needs, desires, and their sensibility. Her voice is the voice of Indian women who were neglected, suppressed and silenced for ages by patriarchy. She is regarded as a representative, a fervent feminist voice and a spokeswoman of the victimized subaltern in the Indian society. Her main concern lies in the plight and pathos of women. Hence, she tries her best to lead the victimized mass into consciousness, making them realize their own potential, their self and dignity. "What Das has done is dare to express in her own life, as well as make the claim in writing, that not only do women have sexuality, but that we deserve the right to proactively, freely, express that sexuality" (Kafka, 2003). Because of such frankness and bare-dare expression, her work is considered as a crucial link to understanding how subaltern voices speak and about what they speak and receive much admiration and praise among her readers and critics.

Searching for the self and dignity are the important features of her poems. She also says: "One's real world is not what is outside him. It is the immeasurable world inside him that is real. Only the one, who has decided to travel inward, will realize his route has no end" (Das 109). Her study of the inner world, the 'self and her psyche' is what makes her quite distinct as a poet. In many of her poems such as "The Freaks", "My Grandmother's House", "A Hot Noon in Malabar", "The Old Playhouse", "The Conflagration", etc. the readers find 'the journey of the self' towards consciousness – the ultimate – that is what makes her so prominent and distinct from other Indian poets. Kamala Das is frank and bold enough to raise her voice against humiliation and the neglected status of women in the society and revolts against the conventional label on Indian womanhood. In this respect, C.R. Nambiar has rightly stated his observation on the essence of Kamala Das' poetry, "She becomes a feminist writer by making her women conscious and providing them wings to rise and flutter… The essence of her poems is struggle about her own self and… is a cry for freedom" (Nambiar 122). She expects society to understand women, and their rights and to provide them equal status and opportunity vis-a-vis men realizing their sensibility and emotional cravings. Devindra Kohli aptly observes, "Her poetry is in final analysis an acknowledgement and a celebration of the beauty and courage of being a Woman" (Kohli 89). The image of the woman that is mirrored in the whole gamut of Das' poetry strongly expresses the problems and pathos of Indian women rising out of the dungeon of patriarchy which has assigned them a passive role in the society and has crippled their self and their dignity as well for ages, and asserts their freedom, identity and dignity in the present socio-cultural scenario.

Works Cited

Chavan, Sunanda P. (1984). *The Fair Voice: A Study of Indian Women Poets in English.* New Delhi: Sterling Publishers.

Das, Kamala. *My Story.* New Delhi: Sterling Publisher Pvt. Ltd., 1976.

Dutt, Toru. *Ancient Ballads and Legends of Hindustan.* Ed. A. N. Dwivedi. Bareilly: Prakash Book Depot, 1976.

Dwivedi, A. N. 2006. *Kamala Das and Her Poetry.* New Delhi: Atlantic Publishers.

Iyer, Sharda. (2001). "Das, Kamala: Split-Self in the poetry of Kamala Das", *Encyclopaedia of Literature in English, Vol.II.* Ed. M.K. Bhatnagar. New Delhi: Atlantic Publishers & Distributors.

Kafka, P. (2003). "Outsiders Silenced: On Domestic Violence and Suppression and Denial of Female Sexuality." *On the Outside Looking In(dian): Indian Women Writers at Home and Abroad.* New York, NY: Peter Lang, 2003. 138.

Kamala Das: Selected Poems. Ed. Devindra Kohli. India: Penguin Books India, 2014.

Kohli, Devindra. (1980). *Contemporary Indian English Verse.* Ed. Chairntan Kulshresha. New Delhi: Arnold Heinemann.

Kohli, Devindra. *Kamala Das.* New Delhi: Arnold Heinemann, 1975.

N. Clara, 2003. The danger of Gender: Caste Class and Gender in Contemporary Indian Women's Writing. Sarup & Sons Publishers, New Delhi.

Naidu, Sarojini. *The Sceptred Flute.* Allahabad: Kitabistan, 1943.

Nambiar, C.R. (2000). "The Quiddity of Kamala Das". *Modern Indian Poetry in English: Critical Studies,* ed. Nila Shah and Promod K. Nayar, New Delhi: Creative Books, 2000, 122.

Paranjape, R. Makarand. 'Love's Guerdon' *Sarojini Naidu.* India: Rupa Publications, 2010.

Parthasarathy, R. Ten Twentieth-Century Indian Poets. New Delhi: OUP. Ed. 2004.

Pathak, R. (2009). "Indian Writing in English and Kamala Das". Boloji.com N.P.,7 June, 2009.

Pathak, R.S., 2003. "Quest for Identity in Indian English Poetry". Indian English Literature: Marginalised Voice. (Ed.) Avadhesh K. Singh, New Delhi: Creative Books, 2003, 22.

Prasad, Harimohan. (Ed.) *Indian Poetry in English.* New Delhi: Sterling Publishers. 1991.

Ramakrishnan, E. V. "*Kamala Das as a Confessional Poet*". The Journal of Indian Writing in English, Vol. 5, No. 1. Jan, 1977.

Raveendran, P.P. (1994). "Text as History, History as Text: A Reading of Kamala Das'Anamalai Poems." *Journal of Commonwealth Literature* 29n2, 47-54.

The Old Playhouse and Other Poems. Mumbai: Orient Longman Private Limited, 1973.

Tilak, R. (2009). *New Indian English Poets and Poetry.* New Delhi: Rama Brothers India Pvt. Ltd., p.106.

Verma, S. and Dhar, Ravi. K. (2013). "Confessionalism and Extrasensory Detachment in Kamala Das' Poetry". *International Journal of Applied Research & Studies., 1-12.*

Author's Bio-Note

Dr. Prafulla K. Panda, MA in English & Education, M. Phil, Ph. D (English) & B.Ed., is a teacher, poet, editor and researcher. He has written articles on English Language & Literature and has published them in different National and International Journals. At present, Dr. Panda is working as a Lecturer in English at Udala College, Udala, Mayurbhanj, under Deptt. of Higher Education, Govt. of Odisha, India. His area of interest lies in English Language Teaching, and Cooperative Language Learning.

14

Subalternity in Amitav Ghosh's *The Hungry Tide*

Natabar Jena

Abstract

The post-colonial writings are marked by the exploitation, humiliation, pain, suffering of the people of lower rank by the hegemonic structure of the society. These people have been marginalized and suppressed from the main stream of social life for their insecurity of living, position, habitat, power, colour, caste and influence. The term 'Subaltern' was popularized by Antonio Gramsci, an Italian Marxist in the 1920s and 1930s as a surrogate for the term 'Proletarian class'. It refers to the colonized and oppressed people whose voice has been silenced. Subaltern literature reflects the pain and suffering undergone by the people who have been deprived of the facilities of living, showing their identity and importance in social, political, and economic setup. Under the leadership of Ranjit Guha, a group of South Asian historians made effort to rewrite the history of reading the silenced voice of the Subaltern. The great writers like Mulk Raj Anand, Arundhati Roy, Amitav Ghosh echoed the voice of the neglected and suppressed human beings in social setup.

Amitav Ghosh's *The Hungry Tide* represents the voice of the homeless subalterns who take shelter in Sundarban forest in West Bengal. As marginalized people, they face oppression of Nature, government and the so called laws of the country. They wish to have their own home and identity. They are treated as 'others' and even inferior to animals. The paper aims to explore the traumatic and miserable condition of the homeless settlers in the novel.

Key words: Sundarban, Morichjhapi, dispossessed, refugees, settlers

Introduction

> Each slow turn of the world carries such disinherited
> Ones to whom neither the past nor the future belong (*The Hungry Tide* 165)

Subaltern studies occupy a significant place in postcolonial theory. Etymologically, the word "Subaltern" is originated from the Latin word "Subalternus" in which "Sub" means under and "alternus" means every other. The word "Subaltern" means person of inferior rank. According to *Oxford Advanced Learners Dictionary* the word

"Subaltern" means "any officer in the British army who is lower rank than a captain (Hornby 1541). It is primarily a British military term used for a junior officer below the rank of a captain, literally meaning "Subordinate". Indian Marxist theoretician Antonio Gramsci (1891-1937) first used the word, "Subaltern" in Civil sense or in non-military sense as a part of the Marxist theory during 1920s.

The meaning of the word "Subaltern" keeps on hanging from the medieval times to present times. During 1920s, Gramsci used it to refer non-elite social groups outside the power structures like industrial workers. In 1980s, Subaltern Studies Group (SSG) began using the term "Subaltern" for the peasants of Indian freedom struggle, then slowly it included the colonized sections of the South Asian Societies. The term has increased its range from small section to a broader section of the colonial and postcolonial society. The idea of subaltern studies began in 1970s, when a group of Cambridge based South-Asian scholars in Britain started to revisit the history of post-colonial societies of India and South Asian countries with different perspective. These subaltern scholars, who are very much interested in the post colonial societies of South Asia in particular and the third world countries in general are called Subaltern Studies Group (SSG). The founders of the SSG are Ranjit Guha, Partha Chatterjee, Dipesh Chakraborty, Gyanendra Pandey, Goutam Bhadra, David Hadriman, David Arnold, Sahid Amin etc. Amitav Ghosh was influenced by this group and their influence appears in the novels like *Sea of Poppies*, *Antique Land* and *The Hungry Tide*.

Homi K. Bhaba in his theoretical essays emphasizes the importance of social power relations in defining the minorities as subaltern. He feels the presence of the oppressed or minorities as essential for the self-definition of the majority group. An Indian literary theorist Gayatri Chakravorty Spivak's best known essay, "Can the subaltern speak?" is treated as the founding text of post colonialism and subaltern studies. This essay popularizes the concept of subaltern worldwide. The word 'Subaltern' is used in broad perspective as a synonym for minorities, refugees, colonial subjects, the illiterate, helpless women and children whose voices and actions have been muted. The postcolonial writers have been trying to bring enlightenment to the oppressed, marginalized or so called 'Subalterns'.

Amitav Ghosh's *The Hungry Tide* echoes the voice of voiceless and the helpless migrants who struggle in Morichjhapi as subaltern category. Through the character of Kusum, the novelist talks about the plight and suffering of the settlers at Morichjhapi and island of Sundarbans.

Interpretation

The novelist describes the pathetic situation of the struggle of settlers for living and its consequences. At the end of the struggle, Kusum sends Fokir along with Horen. On the final day when the police attack the settlers, many people die. A few women along with Kusum are taken away, raped, killed and thrown away into the water of the tide country which she loved so much.

Amitav Ghosh's *The Hungry Tide* reflects the miserable living condition of the Dalit refugees who live "at the door of a small shack – of the usual kind made with bamboo and plain leaf thatch" (161). In the novel, Ghosh has successfully brought out the silenced history of the subalterns like Kusum. The subaltern voice of the migrants can be heard in their cries wafting across the water "Amrakara? Bastuhara. Who are we? We are the dispossessed" (255).

Shouket Telwani observes in *The Hungry Tide* that Amitav Ghosh sketches the outcaste Dalit refugees from Bangladesh in Sundarban forests. *The Hungry Tide* registers the response to the social and political concerns of the marginal sections of the society. The novel mentions the events of Morichjhapi in 1978 and the subaltern consciousness arising out of the post partition movement of persons from East Bengal to West Bengal. Morichjhapi incident takes place when these refugees are fighting for survival and habitation. They are forced to leave the place and their struggle is strongly repressed by the government forces. They stopped food and water supply to the island. The refugees came to India after partition from Bangladesh.

They had been among poorest of the rural people, oppressed and exploited, both by Muslim communalists and by Hindu of the upper castes. 'Most of them were Dalits, as we say now', said Nilima. 'Harijans', as we used to say then (118).

Kusum appears to be the representative of the oppressed and downtrodden community. Her father was killed by a tiger while foraging for firewood. Her mother does not get compensation from the Government. In assurance of job, Dillip, the landowner sells her to a brothel house. Inspite of Nirmal's persuasion, she is forced to take the help of Dillip. They have no means of living. In 1978, Rajan died in a train accident leaving Kusum and Fokir to their fate.

A helpless person longs to come back to their own land. Kusum longs to come back to the tide country. She dreams of the land which will give her shelter and satisfaction. She says:

> "walking on iron, we longed for the touch of the mud; encircled by rails, we dreamed of the Raimangal in flood .... We thought of high tide, and the Mohanas mounting, of islands submerged like under water clouds. By night we remembered, we talked and we dreamed by day coal and metal were the stuff of our lives" (169).

She hears about a group of people moving towards east along the Railway tracks secretly in darkness. They are refugees going from Dandakaranya to the tide country. Kusum joins them and comes back to her homeland.

The settlers in Morich Jhapi are represented by Kusum and they fight against the police, laws for their settlement and living. Nirmal Bose and Horen are sympathetic to Kusum and other settlers. She with others lives the life of uncertainty, fear and poverty. She says:

> The worst part is not the hunger. And the thirst it was to sit here. Helpless, and listen to the police making announcements, hearing them say that our lives, our existence was worthless than the dirt or dust (261).

The novelist through the character of Kusum, representative of Subalterns, raises the question about the island 'as a part of reserve forest' which has to be saved for its trees and animals like tigers. She criticizes the government rules and regulation of saving animals at the cost of poor neglected community. She demands the equal freedom and rights for them.

I wondered, who love animals so much that they are willing to kill us for them? Do they know what is being done in their homes? Where do they live? These people, do they have children, do they have mothers, fathers? As I thought of these things it seemed to me that this whole world has become a place of animals, and our fault our crime was that we were just human beings always have, from the water and the soil.' (262).

Pooja Raj Srivastava quotes B.K. Sharma in her article to show Ghosh's moral support to subaltern community and their struggle to establish their identity. "Ghosh's major concern in this novel is to universalize subaltern history. These subaltern figures therefore are made the real heroes by their sheer power of resistance to unbearable odds and adversities rise to the status of real maker of history" (qtd., in Sharma 195).

Nirmal, a character in the novel is a revolutionary since his youth and supports the settlers of Morichjhapi. He "was in love with idea of revolution" (*THT* 119). He decides to record everything in his notebook so that history can get certain publicity through Kanai. He has worked for the dispossessed to possess something of their own. As a Marxist, he believes in breaking the barriers of class, wealth, power, community and to bring subaltern people and elite together which later Piya repeats with Kusum' son Fokir.

> Kanai, a man of education and sophistication scolds Fokir with obscene language like "Shala, banchod, Shuorerbachha" (326). His anger arises out of "the master's suspicion of the menial; The pride of caste; the towns man's mistrust; of the rustic; the city's antagonism to the village" (326).

Fokir, the fisherman visualizes Kanai, a representative of "a great host of people – a double for the men who had destroyed Fokir's village, burnt his home and killed his mother: he had become a token for a vision of human beings in which a man such as Fokir counted for nothing, a man whose value was less than that of an animal" (327).

Fokir, a boatman and rustic finds the so called educated urban people as harmful and lack human values. In the same way, Kusum raises the question of love and protection of animals at the cost of human beings like them. When people kill animals, it becomes crime but when the poor people become victim of animals, nobody pays attention to it. Piya praises Fokir's ability, "I've never met anyone with such an incredible instinct: it's as if he can see right into the river's heart" (267).

The rustic people have their own beliefs and tradition. Fokir tells her mother's words about dolphins which live in water "were Bon Bibi's messengers" and "they brought her news of the rivers and Khals" (307). He also says that his dead mother has told him in dream to see his son and to bring him Garjontala. He further says that in dream she has told that she is glad to see Fokir's son and asks him to take his son to home and come back there again to be together. Fokir also says that his mother has talked about the place where he has to learn not to be afraid and he may get the answer to his troubles.

Conclusion

Morich Jhapi is found to be a place of brutal violence and the people of low caste and position fight for their habitation and identity. The voice of the common men, their struggle and sacrifices which are unknown to others, get prominence in the fiction of Amitav Ghosh in a different way. It depicts a real picture of subaltern and their survival in the given shelter. "It is an unimaginable challenge for the poor and voiceless people who run their lives with tiger, crocodiles and other dangerous animals in Sundarbans" (E. Suresh).

Amitav Ghosh presents the realistic picture of the position and condition of refugees after the partition of Bengal. The refugees trying to settle at Morichjhapi Island belong to subaltern community. They are harassed by the government and even educated community of India. They have to bear the scolding and torture reconciling to their fate. The novelist draws the attention of the readers as well as government to consider the plight and miserable condition of the settlers for the sake of humanity.

Works Cited

Bhabha, Homi k. "Unsatisifed: notes on vernacular cosmopolitanism". *Text and Nation: Cross Disciplinary Essays on cultural and National Identities.* Ed. Laura Gracia – Morena and Peter C. PF eiffer. Columbia, Sc: Camden House, 1996. pp. 191-207.

Ghosh, Amitav. *The Hungry Tide*. Delhi: Ravi Dayal, 2004.

Hornby, A.S. *Oxford Advanced Learners Dictionary.* 8thed. New Delhi: oxford university press, 2010.

Sarkar, Sushil. "Subaltern perspective in Amitav Ghosh's Novel *The Hungry Tide*". *International indexed and referred research journal.* vol.3, issue 35. Aug 2012 pp. 55-56.

Srivastava, Pooja. "Amitav Ghosh's perspective on Subalternity and his Novels", *IJELLH.* Vol – II, Issue – IX, Jan. 2015.

Suresh, E. "Survival is a Quest for subaltern in Amitav Ghosh's *The Hungry Tide*". *Pune Research* Vol-II, Issue-5, Sept-Oct. 2016.

Telwani, Shouket. "Subalternity: A question in Amitav Ghosh and Khaled Hosseini". *Third front Journal of Humanities and social sciences.* vol. 1, issue 1, Feb 2013, pp. 113-27.

Thieme, John. "Amitav Ghosh". *A companion to Indian fiction in English.* Ed. Piero Paolo Piciucco. New Delhi: Atlantic Publisher, 2004. pp. 251-75.

Author's Bio-Note

Natabar Jena is working as a Lecturer in English at T.S.D. College, B.D.Pur, Ganjam, Odisha. He has published twelve research articles in different international journals published in India. He is doing research on the works of Salman Rushdie, Amitav Ghosh and Rohinton Mistry. His focus areas are Diaspora Literature, Post Colonialism, Translation Studies and Language Teaching and Learning.

15

Articulating Resistance: Bama's *Sangati* as a Celebration of Dalit Womanhood

Aneeshya V.

Abstract

Dalit women writers sought to challenge and protest against the male hegemonic canons through their protests. The established voices in Dalit writing are many, but only a few among them chose the genre of autobiography as a tool for articulating resistance. Most of these autobiographies have been written in regional languages, and then translated into English. Dalit autobiographies are not a mere narration of their quotidian life, rather a form of quest for identity, and a tool of protest. The quest for establishing the identity of an individual is mixed with the anguish of the whole community. Bama's *Sangati*, challenges the brahmanic patriarchy and articulates the lived experiences of caste and gender. It also reveals the powerful female solidarity which could bring the individual women experiences and articulations together to a collective whole and thereby celebrate the dalithood as well as womanhood. Sangati replaces feminist ideals by womanist ideals.

Keywords: Dalit; subaltern; woman; marginalization; resistance; articulation

The novels of Bama, the Tamil – Dalit writer, challenge the hegemony of the narratives of oppression as a default frame of reference in dalit-feminist discourses. They articulate the lived experience of caste and explore the new dimensions of the battles of the Dalit woman. Bama's *Sangati* analyses Dalits women's oppression by double patriarchies – the covert patriarchal stance subsumed within the gender relations of their own community and the overt patriarchal system of the upper castes. Absolute power rests with men in the community and in the institutions led by them – the caste courts, the Church, the *panchayats*. Domestic violence is one of the major issues foregrounded. The text simultaneously brings forth the patriarchal attitude of the upper castes who equate the visibility of the dalit woman with availability. But *Sangati* is not merely yet another tale of the pain of a oppressed Dalit woman. Bama highlights the "difference" of Dalit women from the privileged upper caste women and more importantly, celebrates their "identity" in their strength, labour and resilience. Though Dalit women are oppressed, subjugated and looked down upon as inconsequential creatures both by the upper-class people and by their own men, these women exhibit an amazing strength of resistance and survival potential.

Karukku (1992) depicts the sufferings of an individual Dalit woman; whereas *Sangati* (1994) transcends from the individual to the community. *Sangati* means news, and the book is full of interconnected events, the everyday happenings in the Dalit community. Lakshmi Holmstrome, who translated *Sangati* into English, describes it as the autobiography of a community. It portrays the collective struggle of the Dalit women against all kinds of oppressions and the assertion of identity with their collective consciousness. Bama, in the Preface to Sangati, writes:

> In *Sangati*, many strong dalit women who had the courage to break the shackles of authority, to propel themselves upwards, to roar (their defiance) changed their difficult problem – filled lives and quickly staunched their tears. Sangati is a look at a part of the lives of those women who dared to make fun of the class in power that oppressed them. And through this they found the courage to revolt (Bama vi).

In *Sangati,* Bama shouts out the sorrows, tears, and anger of Dalit women. She further documents their lively rebellious culture, their strong will to swim against the tide, their self-confidence, self-respect and the resolute efforts not to let life shatter them. We hear the voices of many women, some in anger, some in pain, some in despair, some in frustration and some lacking courage. The text, at length, dwells on the gender bias faced by a Dalit woman right from her infancy. The girl child in a dalit community has a very brief childhood. The boys play freely. The girls are saddled with responsibilities. She has to look after her siblings, help with the domestic chores, fetch water and firewood and even bring home a wage.

The nurture of the girl child is neglected but "if a baby boy cries, he is instantly picked up and given milk. It is not so with girls...a boy is breast-fed longer. With girls, they wean them quickly, making them forget the breast" (Bama 7). The sense of inferiority of being a Dalit girl is thrust upon her right from the childhood. Girls get no time to play, and if at all they get time, they have to be satisfied with the girls' games like thayam and not boys' games like kabadi. Maikkanni, in *Sangati*, is the typical Dalit girl child for whom childhood is a fleeting experience while forced labour and surrogate motherhood are the realities of life.

While the condition of a Dalit girl is pitiable, growing up as a Dalit woman is an excruciating torment. They are abused by their own men, and are subjected to sexual molestation by the upper-class. The grandmother of the narrator of *Sangati* warns the young girls who go out to gather firewood, "...women should never come on their own to these parts. If upper caste fellows clap eyes on you, you're finished" (Bama 8). The story of Mariaamma, narrator's cousin, provides ample testimony for the double oppression suffered by Dalit women. Mariaamma faces sexual advances from an upper caste landlord, Kumarasami. Though she manages to escape from his hands, Kumarasami who fears that the news would tarnish his reputation fabricates a story about her misconduct with another Dalit boy. Ironically, the males in her own society choose to believe Kumarasami's version without paying any attention to the anguished appeals of the girl. She is charged with a fine of two hundred rupees, while Manikkam, allegedly her fellow sinner, has to pay only one hundred rupees. This gender bias and the consequent shame force girls to remain silent even when an upper caste male misbehaves with them, as in the case of Paralogam.

Codes of morality are brow-raisingly different for men and women. Mariaamma's father has extra marital relations, but it never ruffles the moral feathers of the village court. Thus, justice itself is gender based. The Dalit woman's anger at their own males who cannot and will not protect or support them is expressed by Soosayyamma. The Dalit male remains a silent sufferer in the presence of the all-pervading power of the upper caste and takes out his frustration on the female. The curious reversal of the roles, the tormented becoming the tormentor, is effectively brought out by Bama in *Sangati*. The Dalit male who is pushed into peripheries as an inferior being in the society, and is oppressed by the upper castes becomes the superior being in the context of family. The dominated becomes the dominant. "Within the home, they lay down the law, their word is scripture" (Bama 59). But the Dalit woman consistently remains an object, both in the society and family.

> From the moment they wake up, they set to work both in their homes and on the fields. At home their husband and children pester them; in the fields there is backbreaking work besides the harassment of the landlords. When they come home in the evening, there is no time even to draw breath. And once they have collected water and firewood, cooked a kanji and fed their hungry husband and children, even then they can't go to bed in peace and sleep until dawn. Night after night they must give into their husband's pleasure. Even if a woman's body is wrecked with pain, the husband is bothered only with his satisfaction. Women are overwhelmed and crushed by their own disgust, boredom and exhaustion, because of all this (Bama 59).

Males enjoy the freedom to love and marry girls of the sub-castes like Chakkiliyar or Pallan. But a Dalit woman would be ostracized if she does so. Even conversion to Christianity does not free them from humiliations. The church proves not to be different from the caste-courts when it comes to the treatment meted out to women. The Dalit woman learns the painful truth that churches, as well as caste courts, are male oriented and male dominated.

Another problem addressed in the novel is the gendered inequality that prevails within the system of labour and wages. Most dalit women are wage earners and bread winners for the family. They are as hard working as the men folk and struggle along with the men in agricultural fields and construction sites. But they are paid less. This disparity in their earnings becomes a crucial factor in the well-being of a Dalit family because the society approves of the male's right to spend his wages as he pleases; while the family has a claim over the female's earnings.

Thus, the novel interrogates caste and gender issues but it transcends the limits of the routine narrative of oppression by foregrounding the indomitable will and strength of the Dalit women. Very importantly, they are narratives of cherished solidarities. The women stand by each other to help each other when there is injustice meted out to them in societal and family circles.

Sangati also portrays the dignity and self-respect of Dalit women. In spite of all the humiliations they are subjected to, the dalit women consider themselves superior to the upper class women. Within their close circles they choose to be irreverent of the upper class women. By enjoying the simple pleasures like swimming or bathing in the pond, which is denied to the upper caste woman, the dalit woman assert her freedom. They are also proud of their financial independence and physical prowess which help them do tough work.

Bama makes a very powerful statement when she discusses the colour of the skin which has always been one of the components that goes in to the making of the great divide between the upper and lower castes. She challenges the common, very old, notion about the Dalits' inferiority complex when she shows how a Dalit woman considers her dark skin beautiful and how she feels superior to the fair skinned upper class women.

> Black is strongest and best, like a diamond. Just go to their streets and look about you. Yes, they might have light skins, but just take a close look at their faces. Their features are all crooked and all over the place, inside out and upside down. If they had our color as well, not even a donkey would turn and look at them (Bama 114).

Another factor that makes the Dalit women proud of their status as Dalits is the absence of the dowry system among Dalit communities. Marriage is not an expensive affair for the Dalit women. In Dalit community, it is the bridegroom who gives 'parisam' (gift) to the bride while the hapless bride is victimized in the name of dowry among the upper castes. In most rural homes, a Dalit woman is an earning member and hence widow remarriages are possible and *tali* or *mangalsutra* is not the binding symbol as in other communities. In the novel, the narrator's grandmother Vellaiyammakizhavi gets married at the age of fourteen, and is deserted by her husband Goyindan at a very young age. She symbolises the mental strength of a Dalit woman who can bring up her children single handedly. The narrator speaks about a very bold gesture made by her. "When there was a terrible famine, she took off her tali and sold it" to feed her children. The tali, which is of infinitely sacred magnitude in the case of her upper caste counterpart, is a very ordinary ornament to the Dalit woman and she refuses to attach any undue importance to it.

Sangati further reveals a powerful female solidarity that empowers the individual Dalit woman and her community. In the midst of all the misery, there is an inalienable liveliness in the Dalit women. They would always laugh and chatter "even though they left at dawn and hardly ever came back until after dark, they still went about laughing and making a noise for the greater part" (Bama 76).

Though the narrator, Fathima, is initially mournful about the oppression faced by Dalit women, she gradually transcends this state of depression and frustration.

She emerges as a representative of the Dalit woman who is confident of becoming an achiever relying on her inner resources.

Sangati, thus, celebrates the fortitude of the Dalit women who can actualize their potential even though they are oppressed by the male dominated and caste ridden society. The feminine ideals of fear, shyness, innocence and modesty are replaced by the womanist ideals of courage, fearlessness, independence and self-esteem in the Dalit woman's ultimate quest for identity.

It can be concluded that Bama serves victorious in voicing out Dalit women experiences, narrating their resistance, celebrating their womanhood, articulating their female solidarity. She also suggests that it is only by helping and supporting one another, which the Dalit women will be able to swim against the torrential flood of oppressions and exclusions. The tool and the weapon suggested is nothing other than voice, articulation. It is by voicing out one's lived experiences, the reader or the listener will be able to identify with the author or the speaker. This acts as a chain and can bring more similar individuals together, which can thus bring about a radical change in the society and in the lives of the oppressed and the excluded. Thus, as depicted in the text, there is a hope for collectivity, for inclusions.

Bama concludes that women have to take up their lives into their own hands and thus help each other live a better life. In order to cease oppressions, the society has to be inclusive. If the society is reluctant to be inclusive, the oppressed and the excluded shall join their hands together for the claiming their own space. Bema's *Sangati* offers hope to the reader, and to the wider public and it also urges the importance of articulation and resistance, which makes the oppressed object the independent subject of their lives, the master of their own experiences. The text urges the need of this realization and asks the reader and the wider public to tell their tale and establish their own space.

Works Cited

Bama. *Sangati: Events*. Trans. Lakshmi Holmstrom. OUP, 2005.

Ghosh, Anita. "Dalit Feminism: A Psycho-Social Analysis of Indian English Literature" Dalit *Literature: A Critical Exploration*. Eds. Amarnath Prasad and Gaijan. Sarup and sons, pp.47-59.

Patel, M F. *Indian Women Writings in English*. Mark, 2011.

Sekhar, Ajay S. *Representing the Margin: Caste and Gender in Indian Fiction*. Kalpaz, 2008.

Author's Bionote

Aneeshya V., is an Assistant Professor of English at NSS College Ottapalam, Palakkad, Kerala with seven years of teaching experience and pursues her PhD at Avinashilingam University of Home Sciences, Coimbatore, under the guidance of Dr. Christina Rabecca, Professor of English.

16

Marginalization of Culture and Identity and Building up the Discourse of Resistance: A Comparative Study of the Select Works of Meena Kandasamy and Temsula Ao

Manik Mandal

Abstract

Theme of marginalisation in literature has reached to a new height in literature throughout the centuries. The common factor of such marginalization arises due to the incapacity of people to fulfil the needs of the society. The people who are incapable of serving in valuable socio-economical, political and cultural sectors feel themselves insignificant and alien within the society. In a country like India, we have several times come across such marginalization almost everywhere. Irrespective of their cultural roots, the process of marginalization still exists in society. Among the greater marginalized communities of India are schedule castes, schedule tribes, women and children. In this study, my focus will be on exploring the concerns of the minority, low caste marginal, Dalit women as voiced through the poetry of South Indian Tamil writer Meena Kandasamy. An attempt will be made to study the contemporary Dalit feminist writings and how Dalit women at large use literature as their weapon of empowerment. On the other hand, the focus will be on Temsula Ao, a major voice of North East in Indian English Literature. A clear picture of how her poetry interconnects and combines the oppression of women and nature will be the focus of this discussion.

Keywords: Empowerment, Marginalization, Patriarchy, Subjugation, Trauma, Violence

Introduction

It has been clearly mentioned by Indian Government in the national portal of Culture and Heritage: "The Indian literary tradition is the oldest in the world. It is primarily one of verse and essentially oral. The earliest works were composed to be sung or recited, and were so transmitted for many generations before being written down." Among this versatility of themes, marginalisation is one of such having been the key focus of Indian literature whether in ancient time or in present day. In *The Mahabharata* and *The Ramayana*, we have found such marginalization too. Women born in low caste or the uneducated people were among the marginalized. Not only that, even the concept of racism plays a very crucial role in terms of marginalization as it is clearly discussed through the character of Satyavati for having black complexion. She has to agree to the demands of the sage Parashara for sexual union and to marry Santanu, the king of Hastinapur. Even the other characters Vyasa, Krishna, Arjuna and Draupadi are considered outside the Vedic community due to their dark skin and therefore marginalized. But they knew really well how to empower themselves from their marginalized status and became successful asserting their identity. Similarly, in *The Ramayana,* we have experienced such marginalization and specially the women who elevated their position by placing them in the centre of action fighting against patriarchy, male dominance and male chauvinistic culture.

Indian writing in English started during the colonial period with the hands of Raja Ram Mohan Ray. He worked a lot for the empowerment of women in India. But the field of English poetry started with Toru Dutt. Apart from her, Michael Madhusudan Dutt, Sarojini Naidu and Rabindranath Tagore are some of the colonial stalwarts in Indian English poetry who write about the demands of the social, political, economical and even of the intellectual sphere of the country. Literature of post -colonialism gave scope to all groups of society which had borne the yoke of slavery silently for centuries. It touched various intimate aspects of the colonized native societies and tried to find out the answers of their problems. One such was the problem of 'marginalisation'. According to Gayatri Chakraborty Spivak, "The study of colonial discourse, directly released by work such as Said's, has... blossomed into a garden where the marginal can speak and be spoken, even spoken for" (Spivak 56).

Marginalized literature reflects various themes such as oppression, gender discrimination, subjugation of lower and working classes, disregarded women, deprived sections of society. In the era of globalization, Third World countries like India and many others are encountering the state of poverty and oppression. From the marginalized section of the society, women poets proved their presence in the spectrum of Indian writing in English. Their poetry delivers how marginalization occurs in a society depicting examples such as the segregation of depressed classes in India.

Marginalization of Culture and Identity in Kandasamy's Poetry

Ilavenil Meena Kandasamy (b.1984), one of the first women writers of South India to write in English, has raised her voice that not even a single Dalit community is entirely free from inner contradictions and practices rather they are doubly marginalized and are being oppressed and suppressed not only by a caste ridden structure but also by culture and society. Her writings, on the contrary, asserted rights and justice of Dalits. Kandasamy fights against the existing system which is against the marginalised that is women, Dalit, low caste etc. without any hesitations exposing all the traumas and difficulties that encircled the life of common as a result of ineffective, corrupted and unjust social structure. Her poetry arises not out of reading and knowledge, but out of active engagement in real life. Her three poetry collections; *Touch* (2006), *Ms Millitancy* (2010) and *This Poem Will Provoke You and Other Poems* (2014) portray real picture of the marginalized in Indian society.

Kandasamy in her first poetry collection *Touch* boldly uses various strategies to fight against the prevailing society where women, dalit, low castes etc. are among the marginalized classes. The title of the collection itself bearing two simultaneous references at one point reminiscing us how the lower castes are denied of even touching the upper castes and on the other hand while going through the poems in the collection we have found that how Kandasamy criticizes them causing havoc on the idea of Brahmin supremacy, digging the roots of religion to uproot such belief by demystifying the Hindu ideologies. In the poem "Songs of Summer", Kandasamy raises her voice against the maltreatment of male in a patriarchal society. In a society, a woman has been given various identities like a daughter, sister, wife, daughter-in-low, mother, a goddess like figure and many more. Their deplorable psyche has been prominently delineated by Michel Foucault as "[T]he body as object and target of power... the body that is manipulated, shaped, trained, which obeys and responds... A body that may be subjected, used, transformed and improved" (Foucault 136). But the society fails to understand the real self of a woman as a woman. Kandasamy sheds her tears thinking about this society where women are treated as their object of merriment or slaves:

"You are trespassing on my territory
You guarded it with LoCs and walls
And barbed wire fences where hatred
Danced like high-voltage electricity...
You killed creatures and cleared forests
And wiped away the darker people...
A collective manhood of nuclear warheads
That explode and penetrate..." (*Songs of Summer* 17-29).

In a poem entitled "My Lover Speaks of Rape", Kandasamy analyses the untold sufferings and agony of a woman. A woman sacrifices her freedom and enters into husband's house leaving the care of her parents and family hoping of a happy conjugal lovable life. Instead of love, she receives negligence and lack of reciprocation. Her husband or lover treats her as an object of appeasement and sensuous pleasure:

"Flaming green of a morning that awaits rain
And my lover speaks of rape through silences,
Swallowed words and the shadowed tones
Of voice. Quivering, I fill in his blanks" (*My Lover Speaks of Rape* 1-4).

Not only the married women even the unmarried women in Indian society are also the worse sufferer of such physical as well as mental exploitation. The scenario is more severe in a dalit community where they are the double-oppressed section in the first hand by the upper-class people and by the people of their own. It is a matter of great sorrow that if a dalit girl is sexually assaulted by an upper class people the society will raise their finger against that victim girl and she endures humiliation and stigmatization and ultimately having no other way to cope with that, she commits suicide. Kandasamy portrays such a brutal picture in her poem "Shame" where an untouchable young woman becomes the victim of a gang rape and without getting justice, she chooses the path of suicide.

Kandasamy also points out the threefold oppression faced by these women i.e., patriarchy, race and domination by first world feminists. Spivak asserts that the 'subaltern' should favour to write their own body and stories. Similarly, Meena Kandasamy materializes her urge to express and fight for non-dominant caste women: their desires, dreams, and independent views and speak for themselves rather than always be spoken for or of by the existing patriarchal social order and their male counterparts. Her spirit of rebellion resonates through the poem, "Aggression" against the prevalent injustice in society:

"Ours is a silence
That waits. Endlessly waits
... But sometimes,
The outward signals
Of inward struggles takes colossal forms
And the revolution happens because our dream
Explode" (*Aggression* 1-2, 7-10).

Kandasamy's fight against the subjugation and atrocities of the male dominant society is a constant one. Her resistance is always directed against the multi-faceted oppression accusing both the society and its gruesome patriarchy. In her second poetry collection *Ms Militancy*, Kandasamy uses her poetry to empower women who are marginalized in every sphere of life. The descriptions of each poem bear the testimony of her experience and her commitment. Kandasamy believes in the innermost urge of the women. Like a calm and quiet volcano, they can be violent enough to withstand with the world where they are subjected to be marginalized. They will assert their position in the way by which they are condemned by the society. They will answer every humiliation they have bestowed upon by the males of the society. In one of his poems named "Backstreet Girls", Kandasamy overtly reports the society's moral police defending all the women against their acute criticisms and accusations of women.

"And I am a shrew with summers in my name…
There will be no blood on our bridal beds.
We are not sure that ones you will choose for wives.
We are not the ones you can sentence for life" (*Backstreet Girls* 6-14).

Here, Kandasamy protests the institutional and traditional system of Indian society, like marriage where women are subjected to various atrocities. One such is inquiring whether the girl is virgin or not seeing the blood on the bridal beds. Here, Kandasamy indicates the revolution of the modern Dalit women, in each and every word and revolutionary language, she inspires her readers to protest against the exploitations and injustices suffered by them.

In another poem "Big Brother: An epic in Eighteen Episodes", Kandasamy shows how males are jealous of their wives. In the poem, she talks how males are careless about their possessions when they involve themselves in gambling, they bait almost everything. They become unconscious of what they are losing and how their life is going to be affected by this. But these males become very conscious when they see their ladies try to do the things for their amusement. They become tactful, sneaks their ladies like the spy cameras observing them all day and night as the Big Brothers in George Orwell's novel "1984". This reminds us of the condition of Indian women in our society where they are confined within the four walls with plenty of restrictions. In *Manusmriti,* we have found such references that "as a girl, she should obey and seek protection of her father, as a young woman her husband, and as a widow her son" (Olivelle 98). The males become discreet about their positions and meticulously they start subduing them with humiliation and tortures:

"His sanity – untouched by poker dons –
Slipped when he saw his lady leave for work:
A high – heeled item, a stripper queen.
Jailed and exiled, the brothers served their tem
With mafia shootouts on the streets, and then
There were none but the Storyteller and the Slumdog" (*Big Brother* 4-10).

Caste, class and gender are among the major problematic issues prevalent in Indian society. The society is predominantly run by the male patriarchal ego where males have the liberty of doing all misdeeds without having any kind of stigma to their characters. Instead of living in the same society, their society is larger than the females. In this context, we can trace the treatment how women have gone through in Virginia Woolf's book *A Room of One's Own*. Woolf wisely observed that while it is 'unpleasant to be locked out... it is worse, perhaps, to be locked in' (Woolf). A severe criticism of this has been made by Kandasamy in the poem "Celestial Celebrities". She first talks about how our society has been shaped very much male centric giving males an established reputation where they have the free will of their choice of female partner. They treat their partner as the object of their pleasures. When this object becomes very habitual and monotonous, they wish to have a new attractive object of their pleasure. As a result, the object has been thrown to the dustbin. Similarly, when the males lack amusement and pleasure from their females they deprive them in search of coarser pleasures. Kandasamy here criticizes that these males who have the entrance ticket for heaven but the women who are the worse sufferer of it have to face the denial into heaven. Their life is in astray in Kandasamy's words:

"… Fallen women exiled to earth
When the heavens found them
Too bloody hot to handle" (*Celestial Celebrities* 26-28).

According to Kandasamy, patriarchy is more dangerous to Dalit women. They are exploited physically and psychologically in the male dominated society. They are caught between casteism and patriarchy. Here, in this poem Kandasamy depicts the misfortune and pitiful trauma of the subjugated and deserted women in the hands of their males and society.

The victimization of Indian women at the hands of the men is the prominent issue against which Kandasamy has penned down again and again. She was strongly against the stereotypically male bound society where a girl is judged assessing her potential being a possible bride for man. Apart from dowry problem, patriarchal burdens, domestic violence, women are subjected to various atrocities and sexual harassments from their males. Their position is of a doubly marginalized; whose lack of social and economic power endangers their education and freedom. In "Dead Woman Walking", Kandasamy presents a heart-wrenching picture of Indian married woman. A woman who was once accepted pompously by her prospective husband and family as a suitable bride, becomes unpalatable for him after some time. She is subjected to negligence, deprivation and torture. Even the burden of society does not give her space to breathe a fine air. She goes through the death-in-life experience:

"I am a dead woman walking asylum corridors,
With faltering step, with felted, flying eyes,
With hollowed cheeks that offset flying eyes,
With welts on my wrists, with creasing skin,
With seizures of speech and song, with a single story
Between my sobbing, pendulous breasts" (*Dead Woman Walking* 1-6).

Almost in every poem of Kandasamy, we have found an utmost urge to counteract against the unrelenting marginalization and subjugation of women in a caste ridden Indian society. Through her poetry, she always provides her readers a great taste of both auditory and visual effect catching their attention letting them aware of their palpable conditions and arousing their need for immediate withstanding against such atrocities. Through her poetry, she exposes the so-called refined and just face of the society. She not only highlights the unjust treatment given to women but also discuss how women suffer the most whether at the hands of gender, culture or caste.

Temsula Ao, a Major Voice of North East India

Marginalization has its numerous facets and one of such reasons is geographic location and environment of that particular region. Similarly, we have come across North East of India suffering from severe identity crisis. The Indian Government, instead of looking after the concerns of its marginalized people empathetically, has played the role of an oppressor so far through its repressive policies and draconian acts. Insurgency, ethnicity, violence, illegal migration, governance deficit, underdevelopment, unrest centring the proposed big dams, among many others, are some of the key areas drawing wide spread attention in recent times. Temsula Ao (b.1945), from Nagaland always tries to bring back the lost cultural identity through her writings. Her poetry also focuses on the issue of centre and margin.

Ao seeks to alleviate her existential loneliness in the feeling of communal togetherness, in specifically identifying with her gender, her tribe, and then with identity. While she cannot recollect when she began writing, her first collection of poems was published in 1988, when she was in her forties. She has published five collections of poems namely *Songs That Tell* (1988), *Songs That Try To Say* (1992), *Songs of Many Miles* (1995), *Songs From Here and There* (2003), and *Songs From Other Life* (2007) and two collections of short stories apart from her academic work and her collection of Naga folk tales. Her poetry also focuses on the issue of centre and margin along with the oppression of the natural world and the women by patriarchal power structures.

In her first poetry collection *Songs That Tell*, Ao presents herself as a lyricist who like a bard presents the inherent story of North East. Almost in every poem, we have seen her scarching for the cultural roots where once the pride of their society belonged. But the changes which befell in the state throughout the years have been revealed not only in the geography of the state, but also in the characters of their people, in their sense of uprooted condition, their sufferings and pains. In "A Lover's Prayer", Ao portrays how the women are themselves going through the process of confusing state of mind. She critically presents women in comparison with nature mother. Both are the very close to the human beings. As the nature shows its withstanding and own stance when we violate it with the excessive rough use of it, similarly woman also separate themselves in their own state when they are perturbed due to the continuous subject of subjugation and negligence in the hands of their husbands:

"But when you wake
To find
The dreams gone
The regrets done
You may need someone
To light your way,
Then I'll say sweet heart
Let me be the spark
To feel the fire
Of the present need." (*A Lover's Prayer* 16-25)

In her next poem named "Coming of Age", Temsula once again becomes very much critical about the present state of North East. But the paradox lies in her delineation of the poem. She presents the poetic persona with a deep rooted conflict with her mind. She presents different shades of time: first as a twenty years youth and forty years of experienced lady. She presents the dichotomy of the two simultaneously here, as a very youth there was so much turbulence, ebb and flow of spirit which does not abide by any restriction of life and which indulges her as the free flowing of water. But on the other hand, when the same lady reaches at her age of forty it seems that lot of maturity has gathered within her and she becomes relatively adjusted and stable. Similarly, Ao thinks their cultural roots are now evading due to the modernization and she fears of not only having the faith among the people in their culture throughout the ages:

> "But forty came
> Unbid unwelcome
> To initiate
> A reluctant novice
> Into knowledge that
> The coming of age
> At twenty one
> Was but the prelude
> And the etude
> To the symphony of life
> Beyond forty." (*Coming of Age* 14-24)

Temsula Ao, a major proponent of the society with her artistic poetic style points out how a society has been plagued due to the greed of power structure. Her poem, "A Strange Place", here stands out as a social critic critiquing society's degrading state. According to her, the people residing in it are in race with each other. It becomes a chaotic dystopian place where justice has been mocked, the protector of people, army men become the object of diplomacy. She was very much perplexed seeing how her own dwelling place North East has been marginalized due to the geographical surroundings and the age old tradition of having tribal culture.

Ao in her next collection of poetry voices the cry of the marginalized people specially the women and how they have played major roles in the society. In the poem "The Creator", Ao points out how generation after generation, women are subjected to suppression at the hands of their male dominated society. Even staying in this ultra-modern society, Ao believes that women are not still whole heartedly free. Similarly, her poetic persona in this poem feels apathy being born as a woman out of another woman. But she does not lose her hope; she determines not to be dominated by the males of her society like her mother. She breaks the tradition of choosing a suitable husband for her. But in the conjugal relationship what she thought has not been fulfilled due to the male dominated patriarchal society. That's why she desires to have her daughter become successful in creating her own identity which she and her mother have failed to achieve:

"I am a woman
And woman creates.
Therefore
I shall create
The real me
And a brave new world." (*The Creator* 27-32)

In the poem, "Earthquake", Ao portrays the heart-stricken condition of women during their childbirth. She clearly views here that woman are the other self of nature. Like Mother Nature, women are fertile. They are the harbingers of the society. But it is to her dismay that nobody knows how much pain and risks both nature and a woman adores during the days of their bearings:

"When the earth rumbles
And controts
To throw up her secret
Like a pregnant woman
After conception,
It is no protent
Of new life.
But of death and disaster
For those who dwell
Upon her swell. (*Earthquake* 1-10)

Ao speaks out the desolate and degraded state of women in the vile institution of Indian society, marriage. She describes in her poem "Confessional" that both males and females have their long lasting desire of youth to mitigate their sexual urge at the time of their marriage. It is the social construction where they can express their desire to each other. But, being a woman, she has experienced that this spark does not stay for long days rather it's flame ceases out after few days of marriage. She condemns the males who have the nag of leaving their females and fantasize upon other women:

"But one day
The fires met
And in our conflagration
We burnt down
The sign-posts and name-plates
Tagged on to unawakened fires." (*Confessional* 14-19)

Sexual harassment is another key element of marginalization may operate in any circumstance and at any place. But Ao tells that it can even be occurred in our private places too like a love relationship or in a married life. She dramatically represents this in one of her poems named "The Serpent and I" where she has identified males as the serpent and 'I' with the entire victimized woman who are the victims of it. She portrays how males pursuit the females to have sexual gratification and how hypocrite the males are. They manipulate them with their tricks and leave them alone after the satisfaction of their lust or sexual desire:

"My resistance breached
I accepted
The promise
And at once felt
The earth heave
The spring melt
To reveal my nakedness". (*The Serpent and I*, 39-45)

Ao speaks how women throughout the years have become the prey of this male dominated society in her one of the best feministic poems named "Woman". Women are seen as the subject of torture, subjugation and negligence. Even, she also describes how nature has formulated women with her artistic hands. It is true that women are the germinator of the society, but it is very sorry to say that we have failed to treat women as they should be. They are cheated and forced to bend down in front of their males. Not only their males, even religions, customs, dogmas have crushed them down in every respect in such a way that even when women cry and wail in protest, the men cheat them without supporting their cause. But Ao believes that nothing can be subdued until it has no calibre of its own. In this way, she has an ardent belief in women empowerment. She has faith that howsoever the burden of patriarchy be, women know how to survive it. It is due to their tender heart like a caring mother that they act submissively serving their males. But this submissiveness is not their weakness; rather, it is their modest and humble personality. When the nature gets wounds, it will not let the doers to wound them once again and we have plenty of experience how nature can create havoc when it becomes hostile. In similar way, women know really well how to rebel against this mean minded male dominated society. Ao in this poem, similarly, has figured out how in past, women have rebelled against such marginalization through their empowerment:

"So woman begat
Such deviates
To spurn man
And custom:
Boedica and Godiva
Clytemnestra and Cleopatra
Medea and Borgia
And etcetra... " (*Woman* 30-37).

Ao propounds in the poem "Judgement" about an accelerated judgement by the women that does not require a trial and in which the court's interpretation of the pleadings forms the basis of judgement. She describes the dejected state of women with the title "the adulteress". She compares them with the ancient Jewish like Pharisees and Sadducees as they are often seen by the males:

"The man looked at them again
The Pharisee and Sadducee
And the woman accused of adultery
And saw only erring humanity.
They in their pride and vanity
And she in her frailty." (*Judgement* 42-47)

She even changed her tone in the concluding part of the poem where she sarcastically asks women as the evils of the society instead of the males:

"Woman, go home
And sin no more.
The Judgement of one
Who know
What it meant
To be human." (*Judgement* 75-80)

Ao's another finest poetry advocating women's segregation and the inherent need of their empowerment is "Requiem?" The poem is one of the best examples of feminist text where she speaks against the evil custom of dowry system:

"Who will mourn this blackened mass?
This charred carcass
Roasted on the pyre
Of a avarice
Lit by gluttony
Of the scavengers
And abetted
By the kitchen stove" (*Requiem* 2-10).

According to Ao, women being the society's most integral part, they have to suffer in all respects. Whatever sacrifices they may have done, nobody will stand there in favour of them. Even when a woman dies during her service, their males does not even mourn over her death. Rather, they venture out for another woman for the substitution. A very glaring example of is found in Robert Browning's all-time favourite dramatic monologue "My Last Duchess" where the duke of Ferrara after the demise of his former duchess is in search of a new duchess.

Conclusion

To sum up, it is clear to us that the women are not unequal to men; rather, it is our social structure, caste, class, male super ego which pushed them to the margin. We have seen how Kandasamy subverts the tradition using her language and poetry as a weapon. On the other hand, Temsula Ao through her poems portrays a way of life which has been under constant threat of violence where ordinary people are the worst sufferer of it. Thus, after a comparative discussion of their poetry, we may conclude that both of the poets' subject matters are same but they differ in their own way of delineation. One chooses the highly bold and explosive approach and on the other hand the later prefers bold approach but in lesser degree like an eco-feminist does.

Works Cited

Ao, Temsula. *Book of Songs: Collective Poems 1988-2007.* Nagaland; Heritage Publishing House, 2013.

Foucault, Michel. *Discipline and Punish: The Birth of Prison.* Translated by Alan Sheridan. Vintage Books, 1995.

Joseph, Soya. *The Touch is not simple: An Exploration of Meena Kandasamy's Poems.* Research Journal of English Language and Literature. Vol.3.3.2015 (July-Sep).

Kandasamy, Meena. *Touch.* New Delhi; Navayana, 2010.

.... *Ms. Millitancy,* Mumbai; Peacock Books, 2006.

Olivelle, Patrickk. *Manu's Code of Law,* London; Oxford University Press, 2005.

Spivak, Gayatri Chakravorty. *Critique of Postcolonial Reason: Toward a History of the Vanishing Present.* London; Harvard University Press. 1999.

Woolf, Virginia. *A Room of One's Own.* Mariner Books; 1st Harvest/HBJ Edition: 1989.

https://knowindia.gov.in/culture-and-heritage/

https://www.springmagazine.net/marginalization-versus-empowerment-in-the-mahabharata/

https://roundtableindia.co.in/index.php?option=article&id=9093:caste-shambuka-and-marginalized-reinterpretations-of-the-ramayana&catid=119&ltemid=132

https://feminismindia.com/2017/07/24/meena-kandasamy-ms-millitancy/

Author's Bio-Note

Manik Mandal is working as a State Aided College Teacher at Egra S. S. B. College. He has cracked NTA NET twice. He also has cleared WBSET. He has attended and presented numerous papers in national and international seminars and journals.

17

Intrusion of Proverbs and Representation of Women in Tendulkar's *Silence! The Court is in Session*

Dipak P. Ganmote and **Umesh Jagadale**

Abstract

Subjugation of women is an age-old problem in Indian cultural context. Traditionally, women are considered inferior to men in Indian culture. It is evident in every walk of life be it any area of socio-cultural exchange. It's an unfortunate yet a common observation that women in India are confined to kitchen and children. This marginalization of women is reflected in various socio-cultural contexts. Even in literary works, the oppression of women has been very obvious. There are specific abusive expressions solely attributed to women in all cultures and the Indian culture is not exception to this. Expressions like proverbs are full of ethnic information that mirrors the working of the society. The subjugation of women, unfortunately, finds place in these culturally loaded expressions without fail. The present article examines the proverbs used about and for women in Vijay Tendulkar's play, *Silence! The Court is in Session*. The subjugation of women counter attacked by the central character Ms. Leela Benare is precisely the focus of the present assessment. It becomes clear from the study that the proverbs used about and for women in the play both glorify and dishonor women. It is evident in the present exploration uncovering a mock court trial in which Ms. Leela Benare is made a culprit and her private life is exposed by others intentionally or unintentionally resulting in her psychological subjugation.

Keywords: Subjugation; Oppression; Emancipation; Marginalization; Proverbs; Gender

Introduction

Gender discrimination is an issue handled by many writers across the world. It was a movement called feminism which brought into focus the concept of equal opportunity for the person belonging to female gender. Women have been the victims of so-called male supremacy in the society and it was first publically discussed by Katherine Hepburn in the film *Woman of the Year* (1942). Yet the term *Feminism* or

Feminist did not receive popularity until 1970s. The term feminism is associated with a movement which supports gender impartiality towards women and works for women's rights aiming to theorize the socio-political welfares concerned with issues of gender difference which is predominantly present in the society. The gender discrimination is evident not only in the form of physical subjugation of women but in the form of words as well. Many abusive words make use of women at their core. The 'F' words are generally associated with women inevitably when someone tries to abuse the other person. So is the case of certain proverbs which both glorify women as well as put limits on them. The play *Silence! The Court is in Session* by a celebrated Marathi playwright Vijay Tendulkar incorporates the proverbs related to women and clearly indicates the glorification of women on one hand and subjugation on the other hand. Simone de Beauvoir's statement "One is not born, but rather becomes, woman." (330) is applicable to the play as proverbs in the play make the female characters alike under the guise of tradition.

In general sense, the term subaltern refers to a person or a group of persons who is inferior with regard to caste, class, gender, ethnicity, or religion. The term was coined by Antonio Gramsci in his article *Notes on Italian History*. According to Antonio, the term subaltern means any low position individual or group of individuals in a specific culture suffering under authoritative control of a dominating superior group that rejects the fundamental rights of contribution in the creation of history and culture of the nation actively. In nutshell, the term subaltern relates to the persons who are marginalized or oppressed. It was Gayatri Chakravorty Spivak who explained the term subaltern in an interview with Leon De Kock. She explains that, "everybody thinks the subaltern is just a classy word for oppressed, for Other, for somebody who's not getting a piece of the pie...., everything that has limited or no access to the cultural imperialism is subaltern – a space of difference" (45).

The term subaltern in this sense is applicable to the women characters in the play as they are considered culturally inferior in some of the proverbs in the play. The term subaltern is applicable to the central character Ms. Leela Benare as she is, even though in a mock court trial, socially excluded from being a free person. Ms. Leela Benare is verbally tortured by others and made to suffer psychologically. The use of proverbs in this context proves to be effective language tool for others to use against Ms. Leela Benare. Ms. Leena Benare in the words of Spivak cannot speak in the "situation of extreme poignancy" (44). She is in a very difficult situation where she can neither hide her condition and nor tell it to anyone. Thus, she is compelled to stay silent but at last she speaks and explains her situation.

Proverbs reveal culture as they are called sensible words of elders which are orally conveyed to next generation. These wisdom words, which lay down the foundations of social behaviour, have been formed by people in the society. While discussing the origin of proverbs, Mieder states that "Someone at some time and somewhere couches a general observation, behavior, or experience into a short complete sentence that subsequently is picked up by others who might well change the wording slightly resulting in a number of variants until a standard formulation results" (28). The persons forming proverbs for either glorifying women or dishonoring them might be the men. The present play includes proverbs which glorify as well as humiliate women. The present research article is a study of proverbs from the point of view of subjugation of women.

Vijay Tendulkar is a notable playwright of Marathi theatre famous for his dramas entitled *Shantata! Court ChaluAahe* (1967), *Ghashiram Kotwal* (1972), and *Sakharam Binder* (1972). Along with writing twenty-eight full length dramas, twenty-four one-act plays, and eleven plays for children, he is well-known for his political commentary, writings for television, translated works and social remarks. The sources of his many plays have been the real-life events or social disorders, which throw clear light on harsh realities. The present play *Silence! The Court is in Session* is a translation of Marathi play *Shantata! Court ChaluAahe*. Priya Adarkar apparently translated the play in precise manner and it is included in the book *Vijay Tendulkar: Five Plays* (1992).

In the beginning of the play, Ms. Leela Benare and Mr. Samant enter into a village community hall. There is a performance of drama for the villagers. One after another, all the actors come to the hall but professor Damale informs that he would be late as there is an important symposium he has to attend. It is also revealed that Mr. Ravate is sick and cannot attend the performance. Hence, there is a problem that they needed someone to replace Mr. Ravate. They decide to use Mr. Samant as replacement for Mr. Ravate. Mr. Samant is not a professional performer; so a performance of mock court is planned to make Mr. Samant aware of the procedure of court of law and they decide to have a different matter for the trial. They decide to change the convict as well. Everyone agrees with Mr. Sukhatme that Ms. Benare should be made the culprit and no one even asks her about it. A charge of infanticide is put on Ms. Benare. The case of infanticide is carried out against Ms. Benare in a mock court. Accordingly, the mock court is organized. Ms. Benare is placed in the criminal's wooden dock. She is put under mock trial where her personal life is exposed by others. The mock court becomes real court for Ms. Benare as every detail of her secret is opened. While making the arguments in the mock court, characters use proverbs pertaining to women to prove their point. These proverbs about women indicate glorification and subjugation of women in general and subjugation of Ms. Benare in particular.

Proverbs and Subjugation of Women in the Play

The play includes different proverbs which pertain to different themes. There are a few select proverbs which directly relate to women either glorifying or humiliating them. While analyzing the proverbs, the contextual background is taken into consideration to make commentary on the way women are portrayed in the proverbs.

The first instance of the proverb related to women appears to be glorifying them. Because Ms. Benare is charged of infanticide, every character in the court starts glorifying the role of a mother. Mr. Sukhatme who is performing the role of a counsel for prosecution makes his opening statement. He starts making grounds for his arguments by glorifying motherhood using a Sanskrit proverb "*Matrudevo Bhava*" (Tendulkar 37) in which a mother is given the status of a God. "Be thy mother as a God" (Tendulkar 30).

Ms. Benare is accused of infanticide. Mr. Sukhatme begins his opening statement with persuading quotes about mother and her role in order to form base for his arguments. He tries to glorify mother as holy and honorable to make his allegations firm. He uses the above mentioned proverb to glorify the mother and to prove that Ms. Benare has blotted the image of a mother by killing her own child in her womb. Traditionally, a woman is recognized as mother of all. Children are taught that mother is another form of God. He argues that in such a noble culture, there are some women who commit the crime of infanticide and this is shameful. He gives numerous examples in the praise of mother and accuses that Ms. Benare is not fit to be called a noble woman as she has committed a grave crime. Though this is a mock court trial, there was such incident in her life and she thinks that this is going against her. Later on in the play, she explains her position but everyone in the performance stick to their point that Ms. Benare is a bad woman and the arguments make her feel uneasy. She is tormented by the discussion of issues related to her private life. Thus, the above proverb is used to glorify mother on the one hand and to make grounds against Ms. Benare on the other hand.

While Mr. Sukhatme is presenting his arguments, he is interrupted by Mr. Kashikar who quotes another Sanskrit proverb "*Janani janmabhumis chasvargadapigariyasi*" (Tendulkar 30) which means that the mother and the nation are higher than the heaven. "Mother and the motherland both are even higher than heaven" (Tendulkar 30). Mr. Sukhatme is reminded that even heaven is not the holiest place than a mother. By using this proverb, Mr. Kashikar tries to support Mr. Sukhatme's argument that mother is the noblest of all human beings and Ms. Benare has spoiled the image of a mother by killing her child thus darkening the image of a mother. The proverb glorifies mother yet it is used to express contempt for another mother. In reality, the court case and the accusation is just a rehearsal but Ms. Benare takes a doubt that all others have come to know her secrets and they are intentionally harassing her by choosing the subject of infanticide.

The court proceedings go on very intensely and all of sudden Mr. Ponkshe asks Mr. Sukhatme to call him as the next witness because he is very eager to inform something about Ms. Benare. Mr. Ponkshe exposes that before some days, Ms. Benare insisted him to meet in a restaurant near her school. She asked him to marry her and she also told him that she was pregnant. This gives everyone a shock. Mrs. Kashikar becomes very impatient to know the details. Mr. Kashikar tells her to be patient as the truth will be revealed soon. Everyone becomes very impatient to know the name of father of Ms. Benare's child. Mrs. Kashikar cannot hold her eagerness and asks for the name of the child's father. Mr. Kashikar forces her to be quiet. She is made silent as he tells her, "The cat'll be out of the bag soon, anyway" (Tendulkar 60). Here, he makes her keep quiet as the reality is going to be revealed. Here, Mrs. Kashikar is also forced by her husband to keep quiet. She is suppressed many times by her husband in the play. The proverb also suggests that truth cannot be hidden for longer time. Soon, the name of the child's father is revealed and everyone becomes shocked. Thus, Ms. Benare's secret affair is revealed and she is tormented by further enquiries.

Mr. Kashikar also happens to be a man of social importance. He informs everyone about Ms. Benare's expulsion from her job as a teacher. He tells everyone that she will be relieved from her duty as a result of her illicit affair out of which she conceived a child. Mr. Kashikar adds this information about Ms. Benare as everyone in one or the other way giving bits of information about her. He informs that he is a friend of Mr. Nanasaheb Shinde who is the chairman of an educational institution. When Mr. Kashikar went to meet him to convey his best wishes on his birthday, he overhears that Mr. Shinde is telling someone to take strict action against such woman who has become pregnant before marriage. Thus, Mr. Sukhatme concludes that a person gets repaid the result of his/her deeds. Ms. Benare is going to be suspended from her job as a result of her mistake. Hence, he says, "Tit for tat. As you sow, so shall you reap" (Tendulkar 69). Ms. Benare has received punishment of her immoral deeds. This is actually a part of mock court trial but it starts to become a real test for Ms. Benare as information provided by others make her nervous and she knows that it is true. Intentionally or unintentionally, everyone is harassing Ms. Benare.

When everyone gives information about Ms. Benare, Mr. Sukhatme, who is performing the role of a lawyer, concludes that Ms. Benare's crime is very grave and it affects the society very badly. He questions whether women should be allowed to be free or not. Through the concluding remarks, Mr. Sukhatme requests the court to take serious action against Ms. Benare as she has committed a very severe offense. As a result of the freedom given to Ms. Benare, she has crossed the limits of womanhood. Culturally, she cannot conceive child before marriage as it is not allowed in Indian society. On this basis, he requests the court to declare her guilty of her crime as it would make a good example for the society. As a result of freedom, Ms. Benare crossed the cultural borders hence he concludes that" *Na striswatantryamarhati*" (Tendulkar 71) "Woman is not fit for independence" (Tendulkar 71). The proverb puts limits on women's freedom by making a generalization that freedom to women becomes reason for social disorder. It confines women to live as per the norms of the society. It is not claimed here that women should be given ultimate freedom but they should not be suppressed under the cause of social harmony.

In the end, Ms. Benare is given an opportunity to say something about the allegations against her. She tells that she has been quiet for many years but now she wants to express her thoughts. She begins to tell everyone about each and everything in her life. According to her, each and every moment in life should be enjoyed nevertheless; she complaints about life as "Life is not worthy of life" (Tendulkar 73). For Ms. Benare, enjoying the smallest everyday moment is life. In her soliloquy, she explains that things such as skies, birds, different noises, the flapping curtains, smell of different things are full of life. She blames people for wasting their time in futile things than enjoying life. She puts a bold question to all that when God has offered us a life to live, then why we do not live the life as per our wish. She further says that life is a treachery. It is a decomposing book, a venomous snake which bites itself. Life is something and something is nothing. She says, "*Na jeevanjeevanamarhati*" (Tendulkar 73) because we are unable to live life according to our desire. We have to keep our wishes aside and live life according to the norms of the society because we are bound by the socio-cultural ethics. Ms. Benare says that body is the only thing which is primary and emotions are secondary in the society. It is not worthy of living life, if we cannot live as per our desire. It is of no use to call life worthy of living if one lives life fearing what others will say. She expresses her contempt as she was told from her childhood to behave according to the social norms. She was even seduced by her uncle when she was young but she tolerated everything. She questions why women have to make adjustments every time. If it is so then life is not life at all.

Conclusion

It becomes clear from the above study that proverbs are used both to glorify and dishonor women. The central character Ms. Benare is at the core of subjugation as she is made a culprit of the crime. Though it is just a mock trial, many real incidents from her life are revealed by others. Every character including Mrs. Kashikar, who is also a woman, tries to harass her psychologically. Ms. Benare finally talks about the things happened in her life and asks what was wrong if she chose to live her life as per her convenience. Some of the proverbs used in the play superficially seem glorifying women but they are used to suppress the central character Ms. Benare. Some other proverbs specifically put limitations on women as it would result in the violation of social norms which are different for different genders. There is no proverb which accuses men for violating social norms. Even in the play, Ms. Benare is pregnant before marriage which is considered adultery but the person, who made her pregnant, has not been accused for violating the social norms. Hence, it becomes clear from the above study that proverbs related to woman in the play are used to subjugate Ms. Benare.

Works Cited

Beauvoir, Simonede. *The Second Sex*. Translated by Constance Borde and Sheila Malovany-Chevallier. New York: Vintage Books, 2009.

Gotthardt, Hrisztalina Hrisztova, and Melita Aleksa Varga, editors. *Introduction to Paremiology: A Comprehensive Guide to Proverb Studies.* Berlin: De Gruyter Open, 2014.

Kock, Leon De. "Interview with Gayatri Chakravorty Spivak: New Nation Writers Conference in South Africa." *Ariel: A Review of International English Literature.* vol. 23, no. 3, July, 1992, pp. 29-47.

Tendulkar, Vijay. *Silence! The Court is in Session.* Translated by Priya Adarkar, Oxford: Oxford UP, 1978.

Shantata! Court ChaluAahe. Pune: Nilkanth Prakashan, 1986.

Works Consulted

Das, Ratan Chandra. "Gender Discrimination, Sexism and Violence: A Study of Vijay Tendulkar's Selected Plays." *International Journal of Humanities & Social Science Studies,* vol. II, no. II, September, 2015, pp. 102-108.

Ganmote, Dipak P. "Cultural Implications in Proverbs& Sayings in Vijay Tendulkar's *Silence! The Court is in Session.*" *Asian Journal of English Studies,* vol. 7, no. 1, January, 2018, pp. 118-126.

Meider, Wolfgang, and Alan Dundes., editors. *The Wisdom of Many: Essays on the Proverb.*New York: Garland, 1995.

Mieder, Wolfgang. *Proverbs Are Never Out of Season: Popular Wisdom in the Modern Age.* New York: Oxford UP. 1993.

.... *Proverbs: A Handbook.* London. Greenwood P, 2004.

Misir, Prem. editor. *The Subaltern Indian Woman: Domination and Social Degradation.* Singapore: Palgrave Macmillan. 2018.

Spivak, GayatriChakravorty. "Can the Subaltern Speak?" *Marxism and the Interpretation of Culture,* edited by Cary Nelson, Lawrence Grossberg. Basingstoke: Macmillan. pp. 271–313.

Vibha. "Women in the Plays of Vijay Tendulkar." *International Journal of English Language, Literature and Humanities,* vol. III, no. VIII, October, 2015, pp. 111-115.

Author's Bio-Note

Dipak P. Ganmote is doing Ph. D. at Department of English, Sangamner College, Sangamner. He has done M. A., M. Phil. from Pune University and PGDTE from The EFL University Hyderabad. He has qualified both SET & NET in English. His areas of interest are Linguistics, Literature, Pragmatics and Paremiology.

Dr. Umesh S. Jagadale is an Associate Professor at Department of English, Sangamner College, Sangamner and a member of BOS in English SPPU, Pune. Besides, he is an author, poet, translator, editor, blogger and a freelance journalist having interest in Communication Studies, Films & Theatre.

18

Spatial Dynamics of Caste, Gender and Colonization in Ravindranath Tagore's Short Stories *Forbidden Entry, False Hope* and *Hungry Stones*

Manisha Patil

Abstract

Space is never neutral. It is always marked by caste, class, race, religion and gender of its users and non-users. It privileges a chosen few at the expense of forbidden many. By constructing walls and boundaries, space is not only enclosed but also encroached. Further, any trespassing is punished severely. Yet, human beings can hardly be restricted by such artificial limits; they do trespass the boundaries and, in the process, transform the identities as well. Ravindranath Tagore's two short stories viz. *Forbidden Entry* and *False Hope* narrate the tales of two such trespassing which challenge the pre-given notions of space and identity. His third story *Hungry Stones* constructs a spatial narrative of colonization.

Keywords: caste, gender, space, identity, colonization

Introduction

Space is never neutral. It is always marked by the caste, class, race, religion and gender of its users and non-users. It privileges a chosen, few at the expense of forbidden many. By constructing walls and boundaries, space is not only enclosed but also encroached. Further, any trespassing is punished severely. Yet, human beings can hardly be restricted by such artificial limits; they do trespass the boundaries and, in the process, transform the identities as well. Ravindranath Tagore's two short stories viz. *Forbidden Entry* and *False Hope* narrate the tales of two such trespassing which challenge the pre-given notions of space and identity. His third story *Hungry Stones* constructs a spatial narrative of colonization.

Forbidden Entry

If home is the metaphoric dwelling place of soul, a temple is the physical abode of the Gods on this earth. In India, every village, town and city has its own presiding deity such as Mumbadevi of Mumbai, Kali Mata of Calcutta, Lord Pandurang of Pandharpur, Lord Jagannath of Puri and Kashi Vishweshwar of Banaras to name a few. These *Teerth-Kshetras* are considered to be the most sacred, pure and holy places whose *Yatra* by the devotees earns them great spiritual merit i.e., *Punya* leading to the liberation of soul called *Moksha*. However, ironically entry to these temples was forbidden by tradition to certain so-called low caste people whose unholy, impure touch was considered to be powerful enough to pollute even the Gods.

The traditional Hindu society in India was (and is) subdivided into various castes. Just as people and their occupations were organized on the basis of caste, even the space in which they moved was also demarcated by caste. In a village, people belonging to same caste lived (and continue to live) in the same area, thereby creating smaller ghettoes. Normally at the heart of a village lies a temple considered to be the holiest place surrounded by the quarters of Brahmins, the priestly caste. Then according to the social status of the various castes, Kshatriyas, Vaishyas and Shudras were allotted their respective spatial zones. The lowest caste people called the untouchables or outcastes literally lived outside the village border. Undue emphasis on the so-called idea of purity and pollution – the concept of contamination of one's body and thereby violation of one's purity and faith by the touch of a lower caste person – pervaded (and still continues to pervade in some cases) the entire spatial dynamics of a village. As per the hierarchy of castes, lower caste people were not allowed within the high caste spaces and in turn high caste people avoided the low caste spaces. Even in those spaces like market where people of different castes mingle together, rigid caste distinctions were (and up to some extent are) followed.

Rooted in the unscientific idea of the purity of blood, the Hindu caste system insists upon a closed system of stratification (inherent, permanent, irreversible hierarchy of castes) determined by one's birth and perpetuated by compulsory hereditary occupation and strict adherence to the code of endogamy (marriage within the caste). According to Dr. B. R. Ambedkar, 'the superposition of endogamy on exogamy means the creation of caste'. In his landmark study titled *Castes in India: Their Mechanism, Genesis and Development,* he argues that to preserve its social privileges, the priestly class i.e., Brahmins converted themselves into a caste through the enforced endogamy. It was later imitated by the other groups as well due to the Brahmanical hegemony. The mechanism behind creation of caste through enforced endogamy consisted of managing surplus men (widowers) through girl marriage and disposing of surplus women (widows) by imposing compulsory widowhood and Sati system. Needless to say, sexism was both the handmaid and the mid-wife who delivered the casteism.

In this process of genesis and development of castes, the freedom of women was extremely curtailed. To prevent the pitfall of love, women were segregated from men and their spatial movements were restricted in all possible ways. First of all, women were excluded as far as possible from all the public spaces such as school, library, market, restaurant, hospital and even certain routes. Their access to the public space was governed by the utility principle whereby they could cross their threshold only when it was absolutely necessary and no other alternative was available. Then even the private space of home was dichotomously subdivided into male and female zones. In a traditional household, the front part of the house which was normally spacious, well-ventilated and well-arranged consisting of front balcony, living room, study and the room for the visitors was exclusively a male area. In turn, kitchen, store room, plus special maternity room for menstruating, pregnant and newly delivered women comprised the exclusive female zone at the back of the house. This part of the house used to be usually dark and smoky. The women in the house could breathe the fresh air only in the inner courtyard and the kitchen garden at the back of the house. Though bedroom was the contact zone between the sexes both literally and metaphorically, that contact was restricted to night only. Thus, even the private space of home was further squeezed for women.

In such a case, it was remarkable that the public space of a temple provided much wider access to women, though the do's and don'ts for women's movement in a holy place were even more complicated. There was (and is) a taboo regarding menstruation which was (and is) considered unclean, unholy and pollutant. As a result, menstruating women were (and are) not allowed inside the temple to preserve the purity of the holy shrine. Similarly, a widow was generally considered inauspicious and so was barred from all the holy places and occasions. However, she was supposed to spend most of her time in a temple worshipping the God so that evil (i.e. sexual) thoughts do not cross her mind. The implicit irony of these peculiar cases is a clear and direct reflection of double standard of sexual morality propagated by patriarchy whereby it valorizes motherhood but at the same time denounces female sexuality, the necessary pre-condition of that motherhood. Consequently, the lunatic concepts of purity and pollution of the Gods haunt the mental sanity of even the holiest of devotees and it requires a lot of courage and the true spiritual awakening to transcend the borders of dogma to reach the ultimate salvation.

Now against this lengthy discussion regarding the limited access to temples in India, let's analyze Tagore's terse story titled *Forbidden Entry.* The protagonist of this story is an elderly childless widow Jaykali Devi who is the guardian of the Sri Krishna temple. Her personality and her sacred role lend her authority over the entire village. Tagore writes,

> She kept close tabs on everything that happened in the village, good or bad. She effortlessly dominated all its affairs. Wherever she went she was in charge: neither she nor anyone doubted it... Her tall, strict presence hung over the village like the Judgment of God; no one loved her, yet no one dared to defy her. She knew everyone, yet no one was as isolated as she (Tagore 147).

Jaykali Devi is a pious and orthodox woman who rigorously follows and makes others follow the religious code of conduct regarding purity and pollution of the temple without any exception. With her iron rule she restores the sanctity of the temple by getting rid of the 'temple-maid' (*Devdasi,* a religious prostitute) and by debarring her brother-in-law from entering the temple as he consumes meat cooked by a Muslim. She even mercilessly beats her nephew for such a petty crime as a failed attempt to steal flowers from the *Madhabi* creeper in the temple yard. Tagore comments,

> The temple was Jaykali's most precious possession. She was never remiss in tending, dressing and bathing the deity. The two attendant Brahmins feared her far more than the god himself... The widow made sure that the courtyard of the temple stayed spotlessly clean... She could not bear the slightest invasion of the sanctity, cleanliness and orderliness of the temple (Tagore 147).

The reason for Jaykali Devi's extraordinary attachment to the temple and its stone deity lies in her socio-economic-political position in the village. Unlike other women in the village, she enjoys special privilege and unchallenged authority sanctioned by the religion. As an elderly rich Brahmin widow from a family endowed with the hereditary rights to supervise the affairs of the temple, she has both means and power to allow or not to allow people entry to the temple. Plus her masculine personality with the qualities such as physical strength, tough-mindedness, economic scrupulousness, independence, haughtiness, aversion to gossip, small talk and tears further reinforce her supremacy. However, its flip side is her inability to share her gentle emotions with an intimate friend. As a childless widow, she is emotionally starved of love. The orthodox religion that she devoutly follows does not allow her to remarry. Unlike a man who can marry as many times and as many women at any age, a woman is supposed to remain devoted to her dead husband till the last breath of her life. Thus her female sexuality and motherly instinct are both permanently impaired by the patriarchal religion which permits devotion to a non-living stone god as an only outlet for the pent up emotional turbulence of a living female devotee.

> To the image inside it she was mother, wife and slave: she treated it with watchfulness, tenderness, grace and humility. The stone temple with its stone image was the only thing that brought out her femininity. It was her husband and son: her entire world. (Tagore 148)

One day 'an extremely dirty and frightened pig' (Tagore 149) enters the temple premises to escape a group of people who intend to sacrifice it. In orthodox Hindu mindset, even animals are hierarchically arranged like the caste system with a cow being the holiest and a pig being the filthiest. In other words, a pig is like an untouchable whose unholy, impure presence in the temple can pollute the God himself. So naturally everybody expected Jaykali Devi to shoo away the pig. But to their utter surprise, she instead shoos away the pig chasers shouting "Don't you dare besmirch my temple." (Tagore 150) This behavior though seems weird from the perspective of the onlookers is perfectly comprehensible from Jaykali Devi's angle of perception. For her, in spite of her dogma, God symbolizes mercy (*daya*) and protects the vulnerable. Entry to his temple is forbidden to the sinners but not to those who are the victims of that sin. With this conviction, she emotionally identifies with the scared beast that is to be sacrificed literally as she has been metaphorically at the altar of crazy religion. By giving 'asylum to an unclean animal inside her Krishna temple' (Tagore 150), Jaykali Devi transcends the borders of dogma to reach the ultimate salvation. Tagore concludes the story with the laconic remark:

> The great god of all mortal creatures was delighted at this odd little episode, even if the petty god of mean and narrow social custom was mightily outraged. (Tagore 150)

False Hope

Set against the backdrop of the Revolt of 1857, *False Hope* foregrounds the crazy spatial dynamics of caste, religion, gender and nation in India through the imaginative space of a detached narrator. The story has a Chinese Box structure i.e. narrative within a narrative. In the frame story, the narrator meets an unknown elderly lady in distress on a deserted Calcutta Road in Darjeeling on a stormy night. She offers to tell him the sad story of her life which he agrees to listen with the hope of amusement. In the core story, the elderly lady reveals her life's journey from a young Muslim princess in *purdah* to 'a *sanyasini* sitting on the mountainside' (Tagore 217).

As per the story, the Muslim princess, daughter of Nawab of Badraon, at the age of sixteen falls in love with Keshar Lal, a Hindu Brahmin commander of her father's army fighting against the British. When he is fatally wounded in a battle, the narrator princess nurses him back to health with the hope of winning his heart. But instead he rejects her out rightly for defiling his religion saying, "Daughter of an arch-traitor! Heretic! You, a Muslim, have profaned my religion by giving me water at my time of death!" (Tagore 223) Later he resumes his doomed fight with the British using the technique of guerilla warfare well-known for its sudden and swift attack on the enemy followed by rapid movement and dispersal across terrain. Thus he keeps on chasing, fighting and retreating from the British army unless and until British score the decisive victory and to save his life Keshar Lal is forced to escape first to Nepal and then to Bhutan. In her equally fatal love for Keshar Lal, the narrator princess goes through a lifelong penance to convert herself into a devout Hindu Brahmin lady. She keeps wandering at various Hindu pilgrimage sites, learns Hindu scriptures and strictly follows the Brahmin code of conduct. She tells the narrator, 'I wandered through a thick forest, but I can't remember which path I took when.' (Tagore 225); 'I wandered from road to road, shrine to shrine, to ashrams and temples…'; 'I became a Brahmin inside out; in habit and behavior; in body, mind and speech.' (Tagore 226); 'I took great pains to avoid being touched by anything unclean.' (Tagore 227) For 38 long years, she chases the mirage of love with the hope that eventually she would win Keshar Lal's heart with her great devotion. But alas! When she finally spots old Keshar Lal in a Bhutanese village with his Bhutanese wife and grandchildren, she finds that he is a completely different man. She is greatly disillusioned with Keshar Lal's abandonment of his Brahmin code of conduct and regrets her own delusive love for him.

The story is remarkable for its demonstration of how space plays a pivotal role in the construction of one's identity. Like any other concept, concept of space is the product of mind. It is the mind that maps the actual physical space in which one moves and converts it into a mental picture so that it can be known, understood, interpreted, manipulated and utilized for one's purpose. Mapping helps the mind to arrange the infinity of space into finite measurable units such as a room, house, building, locality, village, district, state, country/nation, continent, earth, solar system, galaxy and the universe. By scaling down the space, mind attempts to compress the outside space inside it. Thus by reversing its relationship with space from the contained to the container, mind achieves a sense of contentment in mastering the outside space. The process of mapping involves drawing the boundaries which are more often artificial rather than natural. For instance, boundaries of nations are not fixed; they keep on changing when

a) One nation invades the other and snatches some of its land: China taking over Tibet
b) A single nation is partitioned into two or more nations: India's partition
c) When two or more nations merge together to form a united nation: Unification of East and West Germany

Similarly, spaces are not the watertight compartments; both naturally and through human intervention, they flow into each other or transform from one form to another. For instance, a river can change its current and direction due to geological and climatic factors such as earthquake and flood or due to construction of a dam; a forest can be converted into a farmland by humans or a desert can expand into a farmland by wind. One more factor that influences the creation of spaces is nothing but the language. Simply by changing the nomenclature of a place, its cultural connotation in one's mind space also changes. For instance, when Madras is renamed as Chennai its colonial legacy is replaced by its pride in its Dravidian roots. Language is also instrumental in the construction of one's identity. In fact, it is the language that links the space and identity by invoking shared cultural links between the two in one's mind. Thus similar to the construction, deconstruction and reconstruction of natural geographical terrain into social-economic-political spaces, the natural biological self too is constructed, deconstructed and reconstructed into the biographical identity. In plain words, as one moves across the space, one also shifts one's identity and vice versa.

In the story, when the Muslim princess steps out of her *zenana*, she willingly gives up her socio-political privileges. When Keshar Lal crosses the border and lands in a Buddhist country, he loses the religious significance of his Brahmin caste. In both the cases, transgression of boundaries transforms the identities. Just as the Muslim princess changes her identity to an orthodox Brahmin lady through her spatial adventure, the spatial escapade of Keshar Lal transforms him from an Indian to a Bhutanese. Similarly, identity of the narrator of the frame story too undergoes the spatial shift from an Anglicized *sahib* to an Indianized *babuji*. He leaves his hotel in Darjeeling dressed in 'heavy boots and a full-length mackintosh' as a *sahib*, yet as he walks 'along the deserted Calcutta Road' and meets the strange *sanyasini* 'sitting on a rock by the road', she addresses him, without hesitation as '*Babuji*'. (Tagore 216)

Apart from these physical spaces, Tagore also highlights the mind space as a significant factor in shaping one's identity. The narrator of the frame story comments,

> I shut my eyes for a while and let all she had described roll through my mind. I saw the young, sixteen-year-old Nawab's daughter sitting on a fine carpet in her room overlooking the Yamuna; I saw the statuesque figure of a *yogini* rapt in ecstatic devotion during evening worship in a place of pilgrimage; and then I saw also an image of heart-broken disillusionment in an older woman, shrouded in mist, on the edge of the Calcutta Road in Darjeeling, and the poignant music of beautiful, pure Urdu, formed by the clash of Brahmin and Muslim blood flowing through this woman in opposite ways, reverberating in my mind. (Tagore 228)

In the above passage, the spatial images of water/ *Jal* (Yamuna River), *Ghat* (a place of pilgrimage) and land/ *Sthal* (Calcutta Road in Darjeeling), showcase the gradual shift from idealism to realism accompanied with the eternal conflict between the two. Like 'the poignant music of beautiful, pure Urdu', idealism and realism clash and flow in opposite ways but in the process mingle and reverberate as well. In the absence of narrator's mind space, the whole story evaporates like the thin air as time has already wiped it out from the slate of physical space. Even the narrator suspended between the limbo of reality and imagination, cannot decide its factual accuracy. He just muses:

> ...in the bright light of this sunny world I could no longer believe in the stormy story I had heard. My imagination had made it up, out of mist mixed with ample tobacco-smoke. That Muslim-Brahmin woman, that Brahmin hero, that fort on the bank of Yamuna, had perhaps no truth in them at all. (Tagore 228)

Thus, Tagore obliquely demonstrates that all the physical spaces are indeed the manifestations of mind spaces (rather than vice versa) and when a person alters his/her mind space, s/he automatically changes the socio-cultural-political pattern of the society and gives rise to new spatial identities.

The Hungry Stones: A Spatial Narrative of Colonization

> Although there was not a soul but me in that palace with its hundreds of rooms and immense emptiness, where sound slept and only echoes were awake, I still walked in fear of waking someone. (Tagore 237)

The narrator of *The Hungry Stones* is a 'a Bengali Babu' dressed like 'a Muslim from Northern India' who with his authority over all subjects like 'God's personal adviser' and resultant 'supernatural aura'(Tagore 233) mesmerizes all his listeners with his remarkable stories. In a waiting room at a railway junction, to his fellow passengers he narrates the tale of his life experience at 'a white marble palace' situated at Barich, 'a most romantic place' (Tagore 234) where he was posted as a cotton tax collector by the Nizam of Hyderabad. This marble palace was constructed about 250 years ago by Shah Mahmud II as 'a private pleasure-dome'. (Tagore 234)

> Once upon a time the palace had been churned by insatiable lust, by flames of wild pleasure. Cursed by those passions, those vain desires, every stone now hungered and thirsted, strove like a vampire to consume every soul who came near. Of those who stayed for more than three nights in the palace, only Meher Ali had emerged, with his wits gone. No one else till now had escaped its grasp. (Tagore 242)

Since then, Meher Ali used to go around the town shouting, "Keep away, keep away. All is false! All is false!" Even the old clerk Karim Khan tells the narrator, "If you want, go there during the day, but don't ever spend a night." (Tagore 234) Yet the narrator feels 'a strange attraction' towards the marble palace and as soon as it was dusk, finds himself drawn to the palace. Carefully dressed like a prince, the narrator wanders from room to room at night. He even hallucinates the various invisible inhabitants of that palace – an Arab woman, 'whose marble-white hands emerged from voluminous sleeves hard and flawless hands' (Tagore 238); a Persian slave-girl, the protagonist of 'a stranger and sadder tale [which] was never heard' (Tagore 242); an African eunuch, 'a Negro like Hell's messenger but in Heaven's garb, standing with sword unsheathed' (Tagore 240) – all dead long ago. Still their presence is echoed in 'the music of the dead' (Tagore 236) symbolizing 'unlimited wealth, eternal imprisonment!' (Tagore 240) Thus he starts living a double life – one at day and the other at night.

> During the day I would go about my work in a state of exhaustion, cursing my nights with their empty delusions and dreams; but at night it was my work-bound existence that seemed trivial, false and ridiculous. After dark I lived in a trance, in a maze of intoxication. I took on a strange *alter ego,* hidden in an unwritten history of hundreds of years ago. (Tagore 238)

Finally, the narrator gets so overwhelmed by his own hallucinations that he scares himself out of his wit. Identifying himself with the mad Meher Ali, he wants to know, 'what is false?' (Tagore 242) Obviously, it is his hallucination which is false but it is not stated directly. Instead, there is a false start of a new story of the Persian slave-girl which is interrupted by the arrival of the train. Tagore further gives the finishing twist to this unfinished story by indicating two conflicting responses of the listeners – one accepting the story and the other rejecting it.

> ...the train arrived. A sleepy Englishman stuck his head out of a first-class compartment to read the name of the station. 'Hello', he shouted, recognizing our

> companion and let him into his carriage. We got into the second class. We never found out who the gentleman was, and we never heard the end of the story either.
>
> I said, 'The fellow took us for fools and was pulling our legs; he made the whole thing up.' My theosophist relative disagreed, and our dispute caused a rift which was never healed. (Tagore 242-3)

From a spatial perspective, there are two locations in the story – a waiting room at the railway junction and the marble palace at Barich – symbolizing reality and fantasy respectively. A waiting room, a perfect place to meet the strangers is juxtaposed with a pleasure-dome, an ideal space to dream of heart's intimate dwellers. Against the banal backdrop of a railway station is weaved a story of pseudo-romantic pleasure-dome. Against the noisy crowd of station is petted the empty silence of the marble palace. Ironically, structurally, a lot of space is devoted to the eloquent description of the emptiness of the palace while the crowded space of waiting room is relegated to the margins of narration hardly occupying a couple of lines at the beginning and the end as a frame story. This structure represents the mind space which as the name suggests, is not the actual physical space but rather the virtual space created inside the mind. The physical space and the mind space have the dialectical relation – the human mind first mirrors the physical space around through its sensory perceptions; then transforms it using imagination and at last reconstructs it according to one's own will. This dynamic process of converting physical space into mind space and vice versa revolves around the axis of interest. The mind is intrigued by the existing landscape and absorbs its colors until it is drained of all novelty. When the outside space becomes dull and boring, the mind willfully draws the colorful portrait of its own wish-fulfillment. Ultimately, the rising mental pressure of wish-fulfillment leads to inventions transforming the virtuality into reality. This is how the mind works and thus develops science and technology. Nonetheless, with the passing time, the wonders of science and technology themselves turn mundane and mechanical, thereby once again force the mind to seek refuge in the fantasy. This oscillation between fact and fantasy, in turn, becomes all the more exciting for the mind as it gives rise to the amusing swing of fiction. Tagore brilliantly captures this trajectory of mind space in his fiction. Through the use of frame story i.e. story within a story and their multiple narrators, he creates a heterotopia of illusion.

Michael Foucault coined the word heterotopia to "contrast with the 'no-space' of utopias, in other words, as an ambiguous status, possessing material actuality but also bringing complexity to location." (Seed 96) According to Foucault, heterotopias are the spaces (both actual and virtual) that function in non-hegemonic conditions. They are also the spaces of otherness which can either create a space of illusion that exposes every real space (like theatre) or a space of compensation, a real space that is other (like colonies). For Foucault, mirror image is a 'placeless place' (an unreal virtual place that allows one to see one's own visibility) which is at once absolutely real, relating with the real space surrounding it and absolutely unreal, creating a virtual image.

Tagore's illusory tale of marble palace as a pleasure-dome of romance paradoxically alludes to the horrors of lust and power turning it instead into a pleasure-tomb. It exposes both racism and sexism – the real forces of domination, colonization and exploitation – inherent in the fantasy of eternal pleasure. The Englishman, the Bengali Babu, the Nizam of Hyderabad, the Arab woman, the Persian slave-girl and the African eunuch – these are not just the identities derived from their place of origin but also the geographical markers of layers of colonization in India. The horizontal spatial movement of people across Indian terrain both influences and is influenced by their vertical socio-political status as well. When the colonizers like Englishman and Nizam migrate voluntarily from one place to another, their mobility, liberty and power is self-evident. Conversely, when the Persian slave-girl and the African eunuch are forcefully brought to India, it is an equally crystal-clear case of displacement which severed their roots, dislocated them from their homelands and pressurized them to assimilate as subalterns into an alien culture. Somewhere between these two extremes, lies the ambivalent journey of the narrator, the Bengali Babu. On the surface level, his affinity with the British and the Nawabs (of Junagar and Hyderabad) reflected in his language, manners, lifestyle, privileges and voluntary profitable expeditions across the country, testifies the success of his appropriation of the power of the colonizers. Yet, his fascination for the romantic, splendid but haunted white marble palace which 'echoed all the time with its own emptiness' (Tagore 236), threatens to turn him into a lunatic like Meher Ali who too is a subaltern like the Persian slave-girl and the African eunuch. This snare of white marble palace for the narrator is similar to that of white ivory for Kurtz in Joseph Conrad's *Heart of Darkness* and Ishmael's obsession for revenge of the white whale in Herman Melville's *Mobi-Dick.* All these three cases create the illusion of power based on racist and sexist implications of masculine pursuit of whiteness, potentially driving their protagonists crazy towards their own destruction. However, unlike Kurtz and Ishmael, Tagore's narrator is very much sane who evidently gives up the pleasure-dome and moves on with life returning from Barich to Calcutta by train.

Conclusion

Rabindranath Tagore in his works extensively explores the space – not merely physical but psychological and social as well – and places people in them – both literally and metaphorically. The most frequently used spatial images by him include home, temple, doors and walls, market, garden, sea, boats and voyages. By juxtaposing these various locales in diverse contexts, he tries to bring out their meanings in human life. He pits the divinity of nature against the vulgarity of manmade divisions such as caste, class, race, religion, gender etc. by using same spatial images to inspire awe and devotion for the Almighty on one hand and to critique socio-economic-and-political scenario of the country on the other. He strongly condemns the construction of walls, fences and borders and instead advocates transcendence of all the limits.

Works Cited

Ambedkar, B. R. *Castes in India: Their Mechanism, Genesis and Development.* Indian Antiquary. Vol. XLI. May 1917. Reprinted: *Dr. Babasaheb Ambedkar: Writings and Speeches (Vol. 1).* Bombay Education Department, Govt. of Maharashtra, 1979. P 3-22. www.columbia.edu/itc/mealac/pritchett/00ambedkar/txt_ambedkar_castes.html

(Retrieved on 2nd May 2019)

Bachelard, Gaston (1958). The Poetics of Space. Trans. Maria Jolas (1964). Boston: Beacon Press, 1994.

Conrad, Joseph. *Heart of Darkness.* Blackwood's Magazine. 1902.

Foucault, Michael. *Of Other Spaces.* Spring. 1986.

Melville, Herman. *Moby-Dick.* New York: Harper & Brothers. 1851.

Tagore, Ravindranath. *Selected Short Stories.* Trans. William Radice. Penguin Books India, 2000.

Seed, David. *Science Fiction: A Very Short Introduction.* Oxford University Press, 2011.

Tally, Robert. *Spatiality.* London: Routledge, 2013.

19

Queer, Sexuality & Gender in Jeet Thayil's *Narcopolis*: An Analysis

Dinesh A.

Abstract

The world is constantly pursuing with boundless alertness on finding the limitations of others, as they are very much confident in their perfectness and do visualise themselves as beyond any negative or drawback. Such people are constantly oblivious and insensitive to the feelings of their fellow beings. Even in the 21st century, people are not at all ready to accept the third gender – the LGBTQ (Lesbian, Gay, Bisexual, Transgender and Queer). The Queer theory or the voice of the marginalized, generally meant to upright or to represent the strange minority – the Lesbian, the Gay, the Transsexual, the Bisexual and the Queer. The glitches and hitches of this community were not at all entirely opened in front of the public through literature and other art forms until the 1990's. Jeet Thayil is daringly experimenting with this infrequent issue in his debut novel *Narcopolis*. Dimple in *Narcopolis* is not only the protagonist of the story, but she is the epitome or the representative of the whole LGBTQ, the third gender. She is essentially a specimen, who has endured havoc and harassment since early childhood. It is a well-known and well discussed topic now-a-days that the male centred society is not at all even prepared themselves to recognize the identity of the third sex along with the second sex. They perceive the world and its beings as merely made for his entertainment. Thayil presents Dimple as a victim of her own fate as well as a powerful yet conceding character as God has made her physique that is, as both male and female. This paper tries to focus on the identity as well as the identity crisis which is usually confronted by the third gender or the so called *hijras* in the light of Dimple in *Narcopolis*.

Keywords: LGBTQ (Lesbian, Gay, Bisexual, Transgender, Queer), Hijra, Third gender, etc.

Even in the 21st century, the social structure is not at all prepared to acknowledge the presence of the third gender as a part of the system or admit them at least as a gender or a living being. Everywhere they are being ridiculed by the attendance of the other two genders, particularly the first gender, as those are not at all kind enough to impart their benevolence upon the third gender or the so called LGBTQ. As their collective theory suggests that they are queers – the strange populace in front of the eyes of the mass. It is impossible for a human being to stay away or to be completely insentient regarding one's gender.

Emma Shepard aptly points out an instance from "A Study on Queer and Disabled Students," in which a participant distressfully encloses, "I don't feel comfortable expressing my gender identity or sharing it because people will either ask too many questions or be confused or would not respect it." This reveals the quest for identity and existence of the marginalized called LGBTQ. At the time of filling up an application form, in a queue, in wash rooms and at each and every place, there are only two commonly predictable inscriptions – 'male' or 'female.' From this instance itself it is understood that there is no existence for the non-binary or there is no room for the LGBTQ in this colossal world.

Jeet Thayil, in his debut and semi-autobiographical novel, *Narcopolis*, presents a strong and beautiful but wrecked heroine, Dimple, who is a transgender or belonged to the collection of the purged-out multitude. *Narcopolis* is also measured as a paradigm for drug literature, flourished during the 1970's and 1980's, as the heroine herself is an opium maker at Rashid's khana at Shuklaji Street. As most part of the novel takes place within Rashid's Chandukhana, an opium den at the Shuklaji Street, the writer has pertinently adopted the stream of conscious method of narration to impart the drowsy mumbness effect after the opium consumption to the readers also. The readers will be highly intoxicated with the narrative strategy of Jeet Thayil. It is a semi-autobiographical novel and the novelist has chanced and passed through by the same situation that of the hero narrator. He has been caught by the strong claws of drug, while working in Bombay. The title itself suggests the theme and tone of the novel – the literal meaning of the word 'narcopolis' means 'a cemetery, especially a large one belonging to an ancient city.' So the place is supposed to be a very sad, forlorn and mysterious place as the life of the forsaken heroine.

The life of Dimple can be surveyed as the epitome anguish of the whole transgender community. She is a mere representative of that particular LGBTQ. Her birth, childhood, puberty, youth and maturity, loneliness, maltreatment and everything are very much inclined to the affliction of the non-binary multitude. Like the second gender, the third gender is also financially dependent and insecure. Althuser Reid perfectly remarks on the economical status of these LGBTQ as:

> "The economic subject is an erotic subject, and economic theories deal with unique identities where sexual and racial componentsinterrelate with class and gender constructions, producing complex resuts in terms of oppression" (Reid 166).

They remained economically unprivileged as being demoted everywhere, even from the professional world utill the recent proclamation of the Supreme Court on recognizing the third gender. This verdict has broken the dual construction – 'man' and 'woman' construction of the society.

Dimple lives in a brothel with only transgeder sex workers, at the beginning of the story. She sees the hero narrator, at the den, who is a regular customer there. She shares some of her childhood memories with him. She is born as a Hindu eunuch and has been sold by her own parents and leads the life of a prostitute and a part time worker at the opium den. She has some vague ideas on her mother who hides her Gods of Christianity in a cupboard and Dimple must have had an intuition on Christianity in her early childhood. Her memories are always mixed up with the hardships she faced at the brothel and her immense drug consumption. The hero narrator comments on the non-existence and oblivious consciousness of Dimple as:

> "Had she stolen the memory? Perhaps she had no memories at all; perhaps she was stealing other people's because she had none of her own" (240).

During the course of living, she has to play different religious roles also which includes her life as a Hindu eunuch, a Muslim wife and a Christian priest. Through these inter religions, she has been undergoing a process of identification of the self or she is trying to aquire a space by herself where she is spiritually, sexually and socially free from all the barriers of a transgender. But all these come to null and void because she is after all a *hijra* or a transgender who belongs to none and to no religion and to no society.

The harassments which is confronted by Dimple confirms the societal hidden agenda on a transgender. She is a public possession, she is born to become a prostitute, to entertain the men folk. The illustration of her castration is truly dreadful as well as ruthless in which she has been moulded as a vigorous prostitute, who should be fit and perfect to gratify her customers. The castration has done when she was only nine and as a religious ritual. Dimple recounts the incident: "there was singing and dancing... the daima told me to chant the goddess' name" (65). As a part of this ritual, which is actually a 'she' is making out of a 'he,' in which her genital, both testes and penis are amputated. Hot oil has been smeared afterwards, as baptizing herself from the male to the female.

She is undergoing severe exploitation at the betrothel. In an instance she reveals the narrator that as prostitutes they, the *hijras* are highly demanded because they know the desires of men as they are also men between times. At an instance Rashid asks her, "What I want to know do you feel pleasure or not?" (124). To this Dimple replies: "not like you do and not the way a woman does.... I feel pleasure but not, what's the word? Relief?" (124). Eventhough she is meant to please the men folk, that same sexual fulfilment is denied to her. This shows the sexual disempowerment of the *hijras*.

Thayil gives instances of a female prostitute and a boy, named Salim who are also forced to conduct a sort of distressing existence by the male brutality and dominance on account of their economic and the gender imbalance. The unnamed female prostitute is being maltreated and abused by her Brahmin customer, Rumi, on expressing pleasure, at the middle of having sex with him. He considers her as only a commodity or substance that he has hired for a short period of time and a thing which is meant only to please and not to be pleased. Salim is a young man who is persistently raped by the local Muslim gangster, Lala and when it feels unbearable, he cuts the penis of his exploiter. In both these cases male oppression is intolerable as they belong to the higher strata of the society and the victims as always to the lower strata. So the social construction plays a vital role in suppressing the less privileged on socio-economic and on gender grounds too. Patriarchy here stresses on the oppression by the privileged on the less privileged on all grounds.

As Rashid's wife, as Zeenat, her life is smoother than that of her life at the brothel. She is free and Rashid cares for her problems. Yet Dimple feels a kind of insecurity and self-consciousness as she begins to live with Rashid, by the presence of his earlier wives. Rashid never displays any kind of dislike towards her and while, he always criticizes his other wives for their disregard and it is not due to her jealousy towards them, but she is absolutely conscious of the nonexistence of a womb inside her. She cannot procreate. So she is not at all socially legitimized as his wife. She lives as a virginal whore as her imaginary vagina – she assumes herself as feminine – is not at all penetrated, and at the same time she is a whore in the social eye.

Dress is a serious discourse which is always vital to one's identity. Dimple wears sari as a prostitute and she is comfortable in that dress. Rashid gives her a new name, Zeenat and a new dress – burka, which covers her whole body. It becomes easy for her to travel everywhere in the burka. She observes: "this was something very different. The tools were fewer." Her physical body parts are indicated by the word, 'the tools' and while wearing burka a few are visible, where sari discloses many more. According to Dimple, the men must have feared of their own cravings and as a result of this he must have designed such a dress to cover almost all body parts. Yet she opines that the body parts, which are observable after wearing the burka are hyper-sexualized and it can fascinate men than wearing sari. At this juncture, dress designates her distinctiveness. In sari, she is acknowledged as a Hindu eunuch; but in burka, she is accepted as a Muslim wife. At last, Soporo has to wear the attire of a Christian priest. In that outfit she is venerated and honoured. Dress exposes one's religion as well.

Spirituality is the next phase of her life, for which she chooses the locked down Gods of her mother – Jusus. When she was working at the brothel, even during the initial stage of her youth, the regulars at the opium den and the night visitors at the brothel, confessed their sins before Dimple. This spirit of consoling the needy and the suppressed is inherent in her and she is able to find her vision of life and satisfies it through the Christian priest. As the backdrop of the novel is North India, the author cannot skip himself from mentioning at least one communal riot between Hindus and Muslims. She desires to live away from all the religious confusions. At the time of insurgence, she arrives at a rehabilitation centre for the drug addicts and it turns her destiny. It is actually a period of revelation for her, where she has to play the role of the first gender as Father Soporo Onar, the manager, priest and confessor for the drug addicts. Now she has to adopt the attire of a priet to console and lead the deprived and the depressed, where her dress has a different colour – the colour of spirituality, in which, she is honoured and respected.

As a human being, she has passed through three different phases, along with the three different religions and attires. She has started her life as a Hindu eunuch, or *hijra*, where she wears sari. At this juncture, she wants to pull men towards her and in the best of her belief, sari is the paramount apparel for seduction. Her next phase is the phase of burka or as a Muslim wife where she lives with Rashid in his home. She feels security here as his wife and plays the role of a woman. Even then a feeling of insecurity still encompasses her on the absence of a fertile womb in her body. She knows it very well that she can satisfy Rashid with her body, but not with her progeny. Actually, it is a journey towards the third phase where she has to act the role of a Christian priest in the attire of a priest. There 'she' is a 'he,' Father Soporo Onar, the young Chinese Cristian priest, where she has to console and guide the wounded drug addicts to a better life.

Today, the transgender issue and marriage is a well discussed and arresting theme. The marriage between Surya and Ishan has revolutuonized the transgender concept in Kerala. Now they get the suffrage after a long struggle. Even though the society does not approve gay marriage and the lesbian marriage, some brave and educated gays and lesbians have started to live together. Recently, some of the Malayalam films like *Njan Marykutty* and *Aalorukkam* confer the same topic and it is positive to note that these are really accepted and well discussed films by the contemporary society. People began to recognize the fact that sex is not physical but it is psychological as well. It is definite that almost all LGBTQ must have undergone or confronted with the situations of identity crisis and sexual harassment as those are faced by Dimple in *Narcopolis*. Dimple is not mere an individual but she is the archetype for the entire transgender or the LGBTQ community, who are denied individuality by the universe. Through Dimple, Jeet Thayil is actualizing the transgender issue in the contemporary world.

Works Cited

Primarysource

Thayil, Jeet. *Narcoplois*. Faber and Faber. 2012.

Web resources

https://www.amazon.com>Narcoplis

http://www.publishersweekly.com

http://www.penguinrandomhouse.com

20

Family as an Oppressive Structure: A Study of Arundhati Roy's *The God of Small Things* and Kiran Desai's *The Inheritance of Loss*

Pawel Veliventi

Abstract

Women are often excluded from the dominant power structures. Their limited access to the structures of authority brings them under the umbrella term 'subaltern.' Family is used as a tool by the dominant sections to continue their hegemony. It plays an important role in the formation of values, beliefs and even an individual's identity. There have been debates into family studies in India for ages and there are diverse opinions on the role it plays in one's life. It received a great deal of prominence in Indian English novel as well. The present study focuses on two Booker Prize winning novels – Arundhati Roy's *The God of Small Things* (1997) and Kiran Desai's *The Inheritance of Loss* (2006). Family is meant to make its members feel secure. The members generally rely on it for encouragement, understanding, hope, comfort, advice, values, morals, ideals, and faith. But whether the Indian family meets the expectations of its members, especially of the women is a question of debate. Both the novels by creative Indian writers raise different aspects of this debate. Indian culture is largely gender stratified. Man is the controller of sexual, economic and political power. The two novels expose the vulnerability of women in the Indian family where the voices and desires of women are muted using both physical and psychological forces. The two novels shed light on how the household structure affects the autonomy of women in Indian society. They open a dialogue on the need for adoption of a system of values and beliefs that promote gender equality.

Keywords: Family, subaltern, oppression, subjugation, gender, patriarchy, resistance

Family is a universal institution. It is a unit working towards mutual need fulfillment and acts as a building block of social structure. Its role cannot be underestimated in nurturing and preserving our cultural and social values. Family plays an important role in the formation of values, beliefs and even an individual's identity. It also plays an important role in oppressing women. Women are often excluded from the dominant power structures. Their limited access to the structures of authority brings them under the umbrella term 'subaltern.' Family is used as a tool by the dominant sections to continue their hegemony. There have been debates into family studies in India for ages and there are diverse opinions on the role it plays in one's life. The family received a great deal of interest and importance in Indian English novel as well. Many works of fiction have discussed the changes in the Indian family structures and the strengths and weaknesses of the system of family in India. The present study focuses on two Booker Prize winning novels – Arundhati Roy's *The God of Small Things* (1997) and Kiran Desai's *The Inheritance of Loss* (2006).

Arundhati Roy and Kiran Desai are towering stars in the contemporary Indian English literature. Born in 1959 in Shillong, Arundhati Roy turned to fiction writing after a brief stint in the film industry. She shot into limelight with the warm and receptive criticism of her first novel *The God of Small Things* which won the prestigious Man Booker Prize in 1997. Gillian Beer, Chairman of the Booker Prize Committee praised *The God of Small Things* for "its linguistic inventiveness, its narrative power and its courage." Kiran Desai is the daughter of famous novelist Anita Desai. She was born on 3rd September, 1971. She graduated from Bennington College. She studied creative writing at Columbia University. Her second novel *The Inheritance of Loss*, published in early 2006, won that year's Man Booker Prize.

Both the Booker Prize-winning novels have beautiful methods of articulation. They have blazed a new trail for Indian English novelists. Both the novels have multi-pronged story lines and narrative technique of vacillation in time and space. There are undercurrents of power politics against the background of family in both the novels. Both the novels taken up for the study depict the plight of Indian women in family and society at large. Though both the novels are multilayered thematically, they narrate different tales of woe women face and the incessant exploitation they undergo. Family is meant to make its members feel secure. The members generally rely on it for encouragement, understanding, hope, comfort, advice, values, morals, ideals, and faith. This makes it an institution that has survived through ages. But whether the Indian family meets the expectations of its members, especially of the women is a question of debate.

Arundhati Roy's debut novel *The God of Small Things* is based in Southwestern Indian village Ayemenem of lush Kerala. The story line is not simple, but has multiple layers. Ammu, the female protagonist of the novel marries a man of her choice to escape from the suffocating family. Her dreams of having her individual family are soon shattered when she realizes that her husband is an alcoholic. He abuses her physically and sexually. She is forced to come back to her parental home. In Indian tradition the woman is expected to be totally faithful to man-father or uncles in the early days of her life and husband in the later stages. Ammu violates this norm again and again. She first does it by marrying against the will of her family. The family cannot tolerate when she violates the traditions again by coming away from her husband. Her situation becomes worse when she cannot resist loving Velutha, a Paravan (a victim of the class system). She loves Velutha for his fiery spirit of protest. Controlling the behavior of the fair sex of the homes is a way of exerting male dominance and Ammu cannot bear with such domination. She finds respite in an affair with Velutha. Moreover, he is admired by her children as well. The author very powerfully says that she 'loves by night the man her children love by day'. The family cannot tolerate that sexual liaison as sexual attraction to the socially subjugated male is considered a taboo. After a series of dramatic events culminating in Sophie Mol's death, Baby Kochamma sends Ammu from the house leading to her death at a young age of thirty one.

The power to control by authority or money is generally considered the prerogative of men. The author shows powerlessness as the central crisis of the novel. This powerlessness is generally experienced by the women in both the society and the family. Through the relation between Ammu and Velutha, she shows how private love relationships are actually socially and politically regulated. The gender dictates power relations. The family and the state reciprocate the enforcement of patriarchal norms and subjugation of women. The ideology of male domination is seeped into the minds of people like tea from a teabag. Unfortunately, women themselves propagate this ideology. Baby Kochamma takes revenge against Ammu and Velutha because of her unrequited love for the Irish catholic priest Father Mulligan. This act shows how a woman can become enemy of another woman. Women shall exhibit solidarity among themselves and fight against patriarchy in the family. But ironically women in the Indian family develop animosity against one another. Similarly, Mammachi is revengeful against Ammu because she sees the latter as a threat to her existence in the house.

Patriarchal attitudes, physical aggressions and exploitation of women are not the issues of today. They lay ingrained in the psyche of Indian women. One dominant aspect of the male dominance is demonizing women's sexual desires. The family expects women to subscribe to the logic and ethics of the male chauvinism. It cannot tolerate when women try to gratify their desires outside the tradition. There are unwritten love-laws. Baby Kochamma and Ammu in *The God of Small Things* defy the sexual norms prescribed by the family. Baby Kochamma is rescued and accepted by the family because she has converted to another religion but her virginity is intact. But her failed love makes her psychotic. She experiences emptiness and developes bitter spite towards others, especially the women. Her spite ultimately destroys the lives of Ammu, Velutha and the twins. The character of Kochamma is similar to Chhaya of Neel Mukherjee's *The Lives of Others*. Chayya behaves in a psychotic manner as she remains unmarried because of her dark complexion. She cannot bear to see the women of the house happy. She exposes the relation of her niece Baisakhi with her neighbor Sobhan. She enjoys humiliating her sister-in-law Purba who is a poor widow. Both the characters show how women falling prey to patriarchal ideology often fail to empathise with the other victims of the same gender. Ammu's fate is more pathetic as she is sexually exploited by husband and then by the state in the form of police. The atrocities of the police on the women are because of their institutional belief that women exist to provide sexual gratification to men. Moreover, the family condones the violence inflicted over the woman and it reinforces masculine norms over generations. The family cannot accept Ammu transgressing into the forbidden territories of love and developing physical intimacy with a man other than her husband, that too with a man from the subaltern community. This affair disrupts social politics and challenges the family that act as an agent of the state in enforcing social politics. Thus, Ammu's family in connivance with the state machinery brutally ends their relation.

Arundhati Roy powerfully exposes the double standards that operate in the family. The same family that even does not hesitate killing a person for violating the tradition overlooks the sexual liaisons of Chacko. Emma Goldman in her *The Traffic in Woman and Other Essays* observes, "Society considers the sex experiences of man as attributes of his general development, while similar experiences in the life of a woman are looked upon as a terrible calamity, a loss of honor and of all that is good and noble in a human being" (71). Sai's mother in *The Inheritance of Loss* also violates the social norms as she is engaged in an interethnic marriage. Prasanta Bhattacharyya points out, "Born of a Hindu mother and a Zoroastrian father she is the true inheritor of a hybrid identity whose secularity is put to the strains of personal tragedy and political vicissitudes in order, as if, to see its chances of survival" (226).

The Inheritance of Loss (2006) is the second novel of Kiran Desai who is a writer of second generation of diaspora. The book won National Book Critics Circle Award besides the Man Booker Prize. Though the main theme is the effects of migration, the novelist also focuses on how the family can make or break lives. The plot revolves around two families – those of the judge and the cook. While *The God of Small Things* revolves around the sense of powerlessness experienced by the women and the dalits, Kiran Desai focuses on the sense of loss experienced by the women and the people from the third world countries. The title itself indicates the inheritance of loss from generation to generation. Generally positive things like property are inherited from the parents by the offspring. But ironically in the family of the Judge the sense of loss is inherited. Superficially, it appears that the prime sufferer is the anglophile Judge because of his sense of alienation. But Kiran Desai indirectly shows the judge's wife as the worst sufferer. The power to control using authority, money and decision-making is generally seen as the prerogative of the men in Indian society. The women in both the novels are victims of this and they try in their own way to assert their identity. A woman is generally maimed and truncated by the institution of marriage. The fate of the Judge's wife Bela is a classic example. The Judge's treatment of his wife is brutal. He wrecks revenge on the poor woman for all the humiliations he has suffered in England.

The physical abuse she is subjected to reminds the readers of Pappachi trashing his wife with a brass vase. Both the Judge and Pappachi are the vestiges of imperial power. While the former served as the dispenser of justice during colonial rule, the latter is an imperial Entomologist at the Pusa Institute. Both were incurable MCPs. They work hard on their public profiles as sophisticated and modern men; with their wives they behave as monstrous and suspicious bullies. They cannot tolerate the individuality of their life partners. Mammachi rebels against her husband's supremacy by entering into the business of the pickle factory; while Bela cannot show such strength. But her participation in the rally is her form of rebellion against the total subordination. Of course, even Mammachi's involvement in the factory is stopped by her son Chacko who makes her just a sleeping partner in the business. Sai, the Judge's grand daughter too is a victim of male domination. She is mercilessly beaten and thrown into bushes by Gyan, her lover. The worst sufferer is Ammu who is brutally tortured by her husband whom she has loved and sacrificed her family for. This shows that the plight of the woman remains unchanged through generations. Ammu and Sai are educated, modern women while Bela is orthodox and uneducated. Their backgrounds also bring no change in their fate.

Both the authors show the degeneration of the family through the physical description of the houses they inhabit. Arundhati Roy begins the novel with these lines:

> May in Ayemenem is a hot, brooding month....But by early June the south-west monsoon breaks...It was raining when Rahel came back to Ayemenem....The old house on the hill wore its steep, gabbled roof pulled over its ears like a low hat. The walls, streaked with moss, had grown soft, and bulged a little with dampness that seeped up from the ground. The wild, overgrown garden was full of the whisper and scurry of small lives. In the undergrowth a rat snake rubbed itself against a glistening stone....The house itself looked empty. The doors and windows were locked. The front verandah bare. Unfurnished. (p.1-2)

The description of the physical milieu indicates the degeneration of the house and the traditional norms of the family. The house symbolizes the tragic loss of happiness of its inhabitants. Throughout the novel the author is preoccupied with investigating the reasons for this degeneration of the House and the lives associated with it. At various parts of the novel, the author utilizes the House, the Plymouth and the "Paradise Pickles & Preserves" factory to show the moral decay of the family. She says, "Filth had laid siege to the Ayemenem house like a medieval army advancing on an enemy castle. It clotted every crevice and clung to the windowpanes. Midges whizzed in teapots. Dead insects lay in empty vases." (p.88)

Ironically, the members of such a decaying house cannot allow a Paravan entering their family.

Interestingly, Kiran Desai too employs the technique of using the house as a symbol for moral degeneration. This coincidence may be due to the fact that both the authors as women have a lot of affinity towards homes which is the basic feminine quality. The description of the geographical location in the initial chapter of *The Inheritance of Loss* hints at the alienation in the family and its inhabitants. The Judge and Sai "sipped and ate, all of existence passed over by nonexistence, the gate leading nowhere, and they watched the tea spill copious ribbony curls of vapor, watched their breath join the mist slowly twisting and turning, twisting and turning" (4). The barrenness is made clearer when Desai describes, "Time might have died in the house that sat on the mountain ledge, its lines, grown distinct with moss, its roof loaded with ferns" (17).

Both the authors know that an unhappy family can destroy the life of the future generations as well. The plot of Rahel and Estha shows that the family can sometimes destroy lives of the children. The destructive elements of their childhood wrecks Estha's life completely. Similarly, the abandonment of Sai by the family for no fault of hers disturbs her life. Sai inherits the loss and depravation from her parents. At the age of six she is sent away from parents to a convent school in India. The abandoned feeing thus caused has created an awareness of solitude in Sai Mistry. Being cut off from the normal childhood, Sai has transformed into a tough child at the convent. As a student with an unconventional background, she cannot adapt to the rigid rules of her school. She reminds the readers of Rahel in Arundhati Roy's *The God of Small Things*. Rahel behaves in a very notorious manner in the convent where she is expelled thrice for decorating a knob of cow dung with flowers, for smoking and for setting fire to the headmistress's bun. Both Sai Mistry and Rahel are children away from their families and express their anger by exhibiting the tendency to dismantle authority. While Rahel and Estha are treated as outcasts as they are children of a woman who breaks love laws, Sai too faces the same predicament as her Hindu mother has violated the laws by marrying a Parsi. Her hybrid inter-ethnic descent makes her an alien. She cannot be accepted by her grandfather. The family tries to regulate the sexuality of women and when the women attempt to resist it, not only they suffer but also their next generations are punished.

Conclusion

Family is believed to give a sense of security to its inmates and thus it has a prominent place in Indian society. But does it give equal security to both men and women? This issue continues to be a debate in the fields of sociology and literature as well. Both the novels by creative Indian writers raise different aspects of this debate. Indian culture is largely gender stratified. Man is the controller of sexual, economic and political power. The two novels *The God of Small Things* and *The Inheritance of Loss* expose the vulnerability of women in the Indian family where the voices and desires of women are muted using both physical and psychological forces. Family exerts a constant influence on children. It is expected to provide an environment to maximize the development of a child's personality. Family bonds and kinships ties are extremely important for the healthy future of the children as the family is a source of emotional gratification. Women empowerment leads to better socio-economic outcomes for children. The lack of that disturbs the next generations as well. This is evident in the inheritance of loss to the next generations in both the families portrayed in the novels. The two novels shed light on how the household structure affects the women autonomy in Indian society. They open a dialogue on the need for adoption of a system of values and beliefs that promote gender equality.

Works Cited

Bhattacharyya, Prasanta. "Kiran Desai's The Inheritance of Loss: The Story of A Diverse Diaspora Called India". The Fiction of Kiran Desai, Tapan K Ghosh, 1st ed., Prestige Books, New Delhi, 2005, Accessed 10 Jan 2021.

Desai, Kiran. *The Inheritance of Loss*. Penguin Books, 2006.

Goldman, Emma, and Alix Kates Shulman. *The Traffic In Women And Other Essays On Feminism*. Times Change Press, 1990.

Roy, Arundhati. *The God of Small Things*. Indian Ink, 1997.

Author's Bio-note

Dr. Pawel Veliventi is working as Senior Assistant Professor in LBR College of Engineering, Mylavaram, Andhra Pradesh. He is qualified in both UGC NET and APSET. He is qualified as Master Trainer by British Council twice. Being a voracious reader, he is also interested in translation. He is also passionate about training teachers and conducting quiz competitions.

Contributors

1. **Aishwarya Banerjee**, M.A. in English, University of Calcutta, Email:aishwaryabanerjee12@gmail.com, Contact:7003229321
2. **Aneeshya V.,** Assistant Professor of English, NSS College Ottapalam, Palakkad, Kerala, Email: aneeshyanss@gmail.com
3. **Ashmita Bora**, Research Scholar, Indian Institute of Information Technology, Guwahati, Email: ashmitabora14@gmail.com, Contact: 8638048470
4. **Dibyajit Mukherjee**, Assistant Professor in English, Prabhat Kumar College, Contai, Email: dibyajitmukherjee@gmail.com, Contact: 9836380596
5. **Dinesh A.,** Asst. Professor in English, Majlis Arts and Science college, Puramannur, Valanchery, Kerala, Email: rineshpmna@gmail.com, Contact: 9496361980
6. **Dipak P. Ganmote**, Ph.D. Research Scholar, SN Arts, DJ Malpani Commerce and BN Sarda Science College (Autonomous), Sangamner, Dist-Ahmadnagar-422605, Email: dganmote09@gmail.com, Contact: 9890109672
7. **Dr. Beulah E**, Assistant Professor of English, Government Arts College (Autonomous) Kumbakonam, Email: beulah.ramesh@yahoo.co.in, Contact: 9865655684
8. **Dr. L. Sangeetha,** Head, P.G. Department of English, Government Arts and Science College, Kallakurichi (Tamilnadu) – 606202
9. **Dr. Mamta Mahendru**, Assistant Professor of English, Khalsa College Amritsar, Email: mamta.mahendru@yahoo.in, Contact 9417275435
10. **Dr. Manisha Patil**, Asst. Professor (English), Gurunanak College of Arts, Science and Commerce, GTB Nagar, Mumbai 400037, 8454929155, Email: manishadnpatil@rediffmail.com
11. **Dr. Manoj S. Madavi,** Assistant Professor in English, Annasaheb Gundewar College, Katol Road, Nagpur, Email: manojmadavi2015@gmail.com, Contact-9730925380

12. **Dr. Pawel Veliventi**, Sr. Assistant Professor, LBR College of Engineering, Mylavaram, AP

13. **Dr. Prafulla Kumar Panda,** Lecturer in English, Udala College, Udala, Mayurbhanj, Odisha, India, E-mail: prpanda1979@gmail.com

14. **Dr. Umesh Jagadale**, Associate Professor, SN Arts, DJ Malpani Commerce and BN Sarda Science College (Autonomous), Sangamner, Dist-Ahmadnagar-422605, Email: 71umesh@gmail.com, Contact: 9689299812

15. **Dr. Varsha Vaidya**, Research Supervisor & Associate Professor, Taywade College, Koradi, Email ID: drvarshavaidy1972@gmail.com, Mob. No. +91 9822703052

16. **Manik Mandal,** State Aided College Teacher, Department of English, Egra S. S. B. College, Vidyasagar University

17. **Meghalee Mitra**, M.A., English Literature, University of Calcutta, Email: meghaleemitra@gmail.com, Contact: 8017702117

18. **Natabar Jena,** Lecturer in English, T.S.D. College, B. D. Pur, Ganjam, Odisha, Email: jenanatabar99@gmail.com, Contact: 9937442616

19. **Prachi Bhongale,** Research Scholar, R.T.M. Nagpur University, Nagpur, Maharashtra, India. EmailID: prachibhongale@gmail.com, Mob. No. +91 8600243449

20. **Rajdeep Guha**, PhD Scholar, Department of English, Lovely Professional University, Punjab, E mail: rajdeepguha@ymail.com, Contact no.: 9958498574

21. **Rimpa Pal**, State Aided College Teacher, Tarakeswar Degree College, rimpapal1995@gmail.com, Contact: 9641184887

22. **Santi Ranjan Sing**, Independent Researcher, The University of Burdwan (W.B.), Email: santiranjansing800@gmail.com, Contact: 7407303441

Index